The Germ

German Linguistic and Cultural Studies

Editor: Peter Rolf Lutzeier

Volume 2

Peter Lang · Bern

Nicholas Railton

The German Evangelical Alliance and the Third Reich

An Analysis of the «Evangelisches Allianzblatt»

Peter Lang · Bern

Die Deutsche Bibliothek – CIP-Einheitsaufnahme

Railton, Nicholas:
The German Evangelical Alliance and the Third Reich : an analysis of the "Evangelisches Allianzblatt" / Nicholas Railton. – Bern : Lang, 1998
(German linguistic and cultural studies ; Vol. 2)

ISSN 1422-1454
ISBN 3-906757-67-6
US-ISBN 0-8204-3412-4

© Peter Lang AG, European Academic Publishers, Berne 1998

All rights reserved.
All parts of this publication are protected by copyright.
Any utilisation outside the strict limits of the copyright law, without the permission of the publisher, is forbidden and liable to prosecution. This applies in particular to reproductions, translations, microfilming, and storage and processing in electronic retrieval systems.

Printed in Germany

Table of Contents

Introduction — 7

Chapter 1
Historical Backround — 13

Chapter Two
Three Evangelical Leaders — 25

Chapter Three
Initial Responses to National Socialism — 53

Chapter Four
The German Christians and the Church Struggle — 77

Chapter Five
Evangelical Religious Concerns — 119

Chapter Six
Evangelical Social Concerns — 141

Chapter Seven
The Jewish Question — 171

Chapter Eight
Hitler's Foreign Policy — 191

Chapter Nine
Evangelical Christendom, the British Evangelical Alliance and National Socialism — 219

Chapter Ten
Post-War Trends — 239

List of Works — 257

Index of Names — 263

Introduction

This portrayal and discusion of the reactions of evangelicals to the regime of National Socialism and to the measures taken by Adolf Hitler's government does not pretend to be an exhaustive treatment of all evangelical parties in Germany during the period 1933-1945. Works by Erich G. Rüppel (1969), Andrea Strübind (1995), Herbert Strahm (1989) and Gerhard Jordy (1986) have shed new light on the stance taken by Lutheran and Calvinist evangelicals as well as Baptist, Methodist and Brethren evangelicals. Two short essays by Werner Beyer (1988) and Gerhard Ruhbach (1988) on evangelicalism within the provincial churches during this period are also worth studying. There are also chapters dealing with evangelicalism in the Third Reich in Friedrich Heitmüller (1950), Hans von Sauberzweig (1959), Walter Michaelis (1949), Ernst Christian Helmreich (1979) and Wilhelm Nitsch (1955). John S. Conroy's excellent work (1968) only contains fleeting references to evangelicals and Free Church denominations. Günter Balders (1984) has a section on the Baptists during the Third Reich. There is no study as yet of the evangelical press under National Socialism. Bernd Reiner Densky (1983) wrote his master's dissertation at the University of Marburg on the Baptist weekly *Der Wahrheitszeuge* and its portrayal of the Third Reich. Densky has unveiled a whole range of areas where evangelicals proved to be ardent supporters of National Socialism.

There are still, however, a number of evangelical groups such as the Pentecostals and the Free Evangelical Fellowships whose role in this momentous epoch has still not been researched in any depth. Studies in the English language have naturally tended to focus on the politics and manoeuvrings of the Roman Catholic, Lutheran and Calvinist churches, without, in the case of the latter two denominations, seeking to differentiate between the different theological traditions. The Oxford Conference in 1937 presents an example of how the National Socialist government was successfully able to exploit such differences between Protestant traditions in Germany.

An analysis of the *Evangelisches Allianzblatt* during these years fills a gap in historical research. This should be of especial interest to evangelicals in the English-speaking world for obvious reasons. In discussions on this period of history their attention has in the past been drawn to the life and work of the vehemently anti-evangelical Dietrich Bonhoeffer. This courageous man still functions, in evangelical publications, as a type of evangelical resistance fighter. In fact he was very atypical of mainstream Protestant theologians, let alone ordinary evangelicals. The President of the British Evangelical Alliance Frederick R. Catherwood (1976) has underlined that Bonhoeffer's activities were not the reaction of a Christian, as a Christian, to the German war effort and to Hitler's political leadership; Bonhoeffer's resistance was primarily that of the offended Prussian aristocrat. The following pages will not focus on the anomalies of German Protestantism. The author has not found a single mention of the theological work of Bonhoeffer in any specifically evangelical publication in Germany in the period 1933-1945. Such silence reflected the importance of Bonhoeffer and his circle for German evangelicals.

The importance of the *Allianzblatt* lies in the fact that it was the official voice of the Evangelical Alliance of theologically conservative (and to a large degree fundamantalist) Christians: those who take the Scriptures to be the inspired and infallible expression of God's will, which each and every believer in the Lord Jesus Christ has the privilege of knowing. 'Evangelicalism' signifies a body of doctrine regarded as the core teachings of that infallible book:salvation and justification through faith in the finished work of Christ on Calvary; no reliance on the efficacy of good works and sacraments to radically transform depraved human nature; the priesthood of all believers and the right of all to approach God in faith. Most evangelicals insist on the importance of an assurance of one's own personal salvation through repentance, denying the doctrine of baptismal regeneration, and the application of the finished work of Christ to the human heart by means of the Holy Spirit experienced in spiritual rebirth: this is generally termed today 'being born again'. Evangelicals can be found in all denominations, including the Roman Catholic Church, and they are generally identified with a movement to restore or revive the spirituality of their respective denominations. The evangelical tradition can be traced back to the seventeenth-century Leyden theologian Cocceius, the German pietists Spener, A.H. Francke (1663-1727) and J.A. Bengel (1687-1752). These men were devoted to Biblical studies, but were also very active in founding institutions to meet real economic needs. In England a number of clergymen sought to imitate the evangelistic zeal and methodical approach to Bible study as practiced by the Methodists. John Newton (1725-1807), William Wilberforce (1759-1833) and Charles Simeon (1759-1836) were influential evangelicals within the Church of England. Evangelicalism has a longer history within Nonconformity. The Presbyterian

Matthew Henry (1662-1714), the Baptist Charles Haddon Spurgeon (1834-1892) and the Scot Thomas Chalmers (1780-1847), who left the State Church to organise the Free Church of Scotland, all adhered to evangelical views on Scripture and the need for individual salvation from the consequences of sin.

In Germany evangelicalism was mediated through pietism and the Moravianism of the followers of Count Zinzendorf (1700-1760). The early eighteenth-century revival fostered a neo-pietism within the three dozen provincial churches. From the 1830s the traditional Free Churches – Baptists and Methodists – took root in Germany. From the 1870s the holiness movement originally associated with the name of the American factory owner Robert Pearsall Smith began to influence the provincial churches. These are the four sources of modern German evangelicalism.

The *Evangelische Kirche*, a product of the union in 1817 of Lutheran and Calvinist-Reformed churches, adopted a term used since the Reformation to apply to the Protestant churches which claimed to base their teaching solely on the Bible (*sola scriptura*). 'Evangelisch' has also been used in Germany to distinguish the Lutheran from the Calvinist (*reformiert*) branch of the Reformed tradition. Today the terms generally used are *evangelisch-lutherisch* and *evangelisch-reformiert*. These churches have, particularly since the development of a higher critical approach to the Scriptures in the nineteenth century, generally lost any evangelical character as understood in the English-speaking world. For example, these churches, as bodies, do not stress the need for personal conversion. Few ministers today hold the Bible to be authoritative in all areas of religion and history, let alone infallible. Rationalism and liberalism have undermined such doctrines. The Evangelical Alliance in Germany held to these views and can be seen as an inter-denominational attempt to preserve what is left of the evangelical character of the *Evangelische Kirche*.

There are a few studies of modern German evangelicalism which, however, focus mainly on the post-1945 period. Erich Geldbach (1984) places the evangelical movement in its international context, stresses its Anglo-American roots and notes that the term *evangelikal* is used in Germany to describe 'a conservative and even reactionary attitude which relates not only to theological matters but also to economic and social phenomena'. Geldbach seeks to distinguish the various groupings usually subsumed under this term and gives a helpful list of the various educational, missionary, press and umbrella organisations which operate in Germany. He notes that, apart from the press service of the German Evangelical Alliance, there were in the mid-

1980s 144 evangelical newspapers and magazines with a total circulation of over thirty-five million copies a year. The Evangelical Alliance is just one of the umbrella organisations listed by Geldbach. The Conference of Confessing Fellowships in the Protestant Churches of Germany, the Lausanne Committee and the Working Group for Evangelical Theology (part of the Fellowship of European Evangelical Theologians) also play key roles in impacting German society with evangelical viewpoints. Manfred Marquardt (1984) has analysed the structures of evangelical theology and piety. For our purposes it is simply useful to note Marquardt's observation that 'inner connections' exist between evangelical groups and right-wing politicians, not only in Germany but also, and most notably, in the United States. The most pronounced right-wing conservative grouping within the Conference of Confessing Fellowships is the *Notgemeinschaft evangelischer Deutscher*. Most recently Friedhelm Jung (1992) has published his doctoral dissertation on the German evangelical movement. The work covers the period 1965-1985 and details the historical development and theology of evangelical and pentecostal-charismatic groups. He too outlines the Anglo-American roots of German evangelicalism. Jung finds the first recorded use of the term *evangelikal* in the *Evangelisches Allianzblatt* in 1965. This fact alone suggests the international nature of the Evangelical Alliance and a greater closeness and openness to Anglo-American trends than is found elsewhere within the wider evangelical movement.

The Alliance encompassed conservative believers in all the main Protestant denominations in Germany, as it does today. There were in the 1930s about one million evangelicals in Germany; today they number about one and a half million. In certain parts of Germany, such as the Erzgebirge and parts of Baden-Württemberg and Hessen, they constitute a significant percentage of the population, equivalent to the Bible belts in the southern states of the USA and the area around Ballymena in the north of Ireland, though German evangelicals have rarely tried to flex their political muscles as believers have done in these latter two countries. Today a number of explicitly evangelical parties are seeking to channel evangelical anger and frustration with mainline political parties in the Federal Republic, including the two nominally Christian parties which have together ruled Germany for most of the post-war period. This development could be observed in the pre-1933 period. Disappointment with the Weimar democratic system led many, indeed most evangelicals to look for alternative, radical and quick solutions to social, economic and political problems in their country. The man who seemed to offer those solutions did not smoke or drink alcohol and lived a sexually abstinent life; he was also said to carry a well-read New Testament around with him.

Such anecdotes, apparently harmless, led many evangelicals to respond positively to Adolf Hitler's message. The following pages outline other areas where Christians felt they could offer their political support. In several ways the *Allianzblatt* became a vehicle for National Socialist propaganda. Its editorials and 'prophetic' explanations of contemporary events reflect the views of a number of nationally respected evangelicals at that time, but especially of the Chairman of the Evangelical Alliance itself. They will be of interest not only to those with an historical interest in Germany, but especially to those evangelicals who seek to apply what they perceive to be Biblical truth to the complex politico-economic world around them. An analysis of this publication reveals the national, cultural and class limits to such an undertaking.

No single work can possibly deal with all the issues that the history of the Third Reich raises. German Protestantism has been fractured in many ways for many years and no single treatment can do justice to all the facets of that total picture. An analysis of one particular periodical can only throw light on certain areas of the Church-State relationship. The fact that the *Allianzblatt* was the mouthpiece of the German Evangelical Alliance, edited by its Chairman, should interest those seeking to understand how and why theologically conservative believers reacted to National Socialism in the way they did. Evangelicals need to study and learn from their history. Coming to terms with one's own past – something Germans call *Vergangenheitsbewältigung* – should, in the author's view, be an ongoing process. It is something German evangelicals as well as the wider Protestant population in that country have been loth to do. This is certainly not a peculiarly German trait. The following pages should be seen as a step taken towards understanding the reasons for evangelical passivity in the face of National Socialism.

Chapter One

Historical Background

Modern German evangelicalism traces its roots back through the Reformers Luther and Calvin to primitive Christianity itself. The Reformation, in rediscovering the biblical doctrine of *sola gratia* and reaffirming the doctrine of *sola scriptura*, is the foundational historical event of its belief system. Within two generations, however, the reform movement had itself been throttled by the political control of German provincial princes and had dried up into a dead and dogmatic orthodoxy. A new generation of church critics arose, this time within the fold of Protestantism. The Rostock pietist, Theophil Großgebauer (1627-1661) criticised the Protestant churches' focus on religious forms. Gottfried Arnold (1666-1714) called for the destruction of the Lutheran Church, as it had, in his view, ceased to serve God. Of even greater influence was Philipp Jacob Spener (1635-1705). He was more diplomatic, insisting that there remained a core of true believers in Lutheranism. He encouraged them to defend the Lutheran creeds from being neglected and called on all Church members to lead a life of commitment to God.[1] Spener set up prayer and fellowship meetings known as *collegia pietatis*, to foster their life of faith. The first of these 'house groups' was set up in Frankfurt a.M. in 1670. Spener's critics mocked him and his efforts. His followers were dubbed 'Pietisten'; this term of abuse would later define what was a very significant revival movement within German Protestantism.

Other key representatives of the movement were Johann Arndt (1555-1621), J.A. Bengel (1687-1752), author of the well-known Bible commentary *Gnomon*, and August Hermann Francke (1663-1727), a professor at Halle whose orphanages, soup kitchens and employment schemes earned him worldwide respect.[2] Evangelicals in Germany stress the great contribution made by the Pietists to the restoration of biblical Christianity in the motherland of the Reformation.

One fruit of the pietist revival was the rebirth of the Moravian Church in the eighteenth century. The Moravian Brethren – who themselves had a major influence on John Wesley and ignited what would become the Methodist revival[3] – were given political asylum in 1722 by Nikolaus Ludwig Count Zinzendorf (1700-1760); they settled on his estate at Berthelsdorf in Saxony and their colony, named Herrnhut, became the base for travelling missionaries.

It was a community open to all denominations, opposed to narrow sectarian thinking and seeking always to recreate the close fellowship of the Early Church. Zinzendorf, before becoming a Moravian bishop, had been ordained a Lutheran minister. In a similar way, the Moravians were initially accepted as committed members of the Lutheran Church in Saxony – a church within a church, just as the early pietist gatherings had been seen as *ecclesiolae in ecclesia*.[4] The goal they set themselves, however, and worked towards in the wider church, remains up to the present day a *unitas fratrum*, a union of brethren.[5]

Pietism and Moravianism prepared the ground for the German equivalent of the evangelical revival at the end of the eighteenth and beginning of the nineteenth century: the *Erweckungsbewegung*.[6] Lay members of the Protestant churches played an all-important role in this third revival phase. Initial sparks were provided by the all-male Deutsche Christentumsgesellschaft organised by Johann August Urlsperger in Basle and the Nürnberger Kreis gathered around Johann Tobias Kießling.[7] Karl Friedrich Adolph Steinkopf, from 1801 pastor of the Lutheran Mariengemeinde in London, became heavily involved in tract and Bible societies and was the bridge between German and British evangelicalism. His trips throughout Germany and Switzerland as agent of the Tract Society contributed to the organisation of the Basle Bible Society. Bible depots were also set up in Frankfurt, Lübeck, Altona and Zürich. By 1820 over forty such Bible and Tract Societies were in operation in Germany.[8]

A Bible-based revival broke out in all parts of Germany. It was essentially a laymen's revival. In Berlin house meetings and conferences were organised by the Silesian landowner Baron Hans Ernst von Kottwitz (1757-1843) that particularly attracted aristocrats, top civil servants and members of the royal family.[9] Two other Pomeranian landowners, the brothers von Bülow, held revival meetings on their estates.[10] Adolf von Thadden (1792-1882) organised conferences from 1829 onwards for 'revived' pastors on his estate at Trieglaff that impacted the whole of northern Germany.[11] G.H. von Schubert (1780-1845) and Karl von Raumer (1783-1865) led the revival in Nuremberg. Wilhelm Löhe (1808-1872) helped to turn Neuendettelsau into what has been called the 'Herrnhut of the evangelical revival within Lutheranism'. Two other laymen, Heinrich Weißgerber and Tillmann Siebel, were the leaders of the revival in the Siegerland area.

In other parts of Germany, however, pastors played a role too. The Reformed minister, Gottfried Daniel Krummacher (1774-1837) was the key individual in the lower Rhine region. Another Reformed minister, Gottfried

Menken (1768-1831), was active in Bremen. Christian Krafft, a Reformed pastor and professor of theology, brought new life to Erlangen. In Württemberg Pastor Ludwig Hofacker (1798-1828) was the commanding influence.[12] In Halle another professor of theology, Frederick August Gottreu Tholuck (1799-1877), 'brought the movement back to science and to public life'[13] and influenced numerous pastors and professors in his generation.

An inter-denominational, Bible-based missionary movement came into being, embodied perhaps most clearly in the Evangelische Gesellschaft für Deutschland, which 53 pastors had set up in Barmen in 1848.[14] At the same time these evangelical groups were looking overseas for inspiration, support and world-wide fellowship. Dean Kniewel of Danzig, for example, travelled around Europe in 1842 proposing 'the foundation of a spiritual union amongst all those who in all lands are fighting for God's holy cause and for the pure gospel'.[15] Germans were, not surprisingly, also involved in the founding of the Evangelical Alliance: at least eight were active in the proceedings of the conference held at Freemasons' Hall in London from 19 August to 2 September 1846.[16] They were Dr Christian Barth (Calw), Pastor Jean Bonnet (Frankfurt a.M.), Dr Johann König (Mainz), Dr Karl Reinthaler (Erfurt), Professor August Tholuck (Halle), the Baptist pastor Johann Oncken (Hamburg), Dr Wilhelm Hoffmann of the Basle Missionary Society and Pastor Eduard Kuntze (Berlin). Some of the German contingent seem to have felt that they had been excluded from several of the committees set up in London but were grateful that the district organisations recommended by the conference – one for the north of Germany, another for the south of Germany plus German Switzerland – were to be 'separate' and 'independent' and able to express their own views and opinions.[17] The proceedings of this first-ever ecumenical organisation was given extensive coverage in German periodicals. The *Volksblatt* noted that 'the devout and zealous friends of evangelical piety have welcomed the movement with deep interest'.[18] German evangelicals had after all sought for over a century to put into practice the motto of the Alliance: *Unum corpus sumus in Christo* – we are one body in Christ.[19] Indeed, the *Geistliche Fama*, the magazine of the German revival in the first half of the eighteenth century had called in 1730 for a 'free, loose alliance' of all 'genuine children of God' irrespective of their denominational attachments to meet regularly for prayer and fellowship.[20]

The Chairman of the Evangelical Alliance in Britain, Sir Culling Eardley Smith, wrote to Johann Hinrich Wichern (1808-1881), the founder of the Home Mission in Germany, looking for cooperation between evangelicals in the two countries. Wichern was asked to prepare a report on Home Mission activities, which he was ready to do. Wichern, together with von Bethmann-Hollweg, the chairman of the German Kirchentag (Annual Church Conference), attended Alliance meetings in London in 1851. In return, six representatives of the British Alliance went to the Kirchentag held in Elberfeld in 1851 and to conferences held elsewhere in the following years.[21] Friendly relations were gradually established. By 1853 a North German branch of the Evangelical Alliance was founded in Berlin by Pastor Kuntze, who had been present in London in 1846, and the Baptist minister, Gottfried W. Lehmann, whose children had been baptised by Kuntze.[22] In 1853 there followed a branch in Hamburg.[23] It was not until 6 October 1880, however, that a West German branch of the Alliance was set up in Barmen, largely due to the efforts of Dr Friedrich Fabri, the director of a missionary society, and Professor Christlieb.[24] In 1898 a South German branch was established and in 1903 a Bavarian Alliance Committee came into being.[25] In numerous towns all over Germany Alliance groups sprang up. Unity was created, or rather supported, not by a central organisation but rather by decentralised prayer meetings, especially the Week of Prayer, held for the first time all over Germany in 1860.[26] A newspaper, the *Neue Evangelische Kirchenzeitung*, edited by Professor H. Meßner and appearing for the first time in 1859, was produced for the Alliance movement.[27]

The final phase of evangelical renewal within German Protestantism began with the conference of 68 pastors and theologians together with 74 laymen between 22 and 24 May 1888 in the small Herrnhut colony at Gnadau near Magdeburg.[28] The annual Whitsun Conferences that have taken place ever since have been a unifying forum to discuss issues such as sanctification, evangelism and church growth. The emphasis has always been practical. The conferences in turn led, in 1897, to the founding of the *Deutscher Verband für Gemeinschaftspflege und Evangelisation* (Gnadauer Verband), a loose organisation of evangelicals within the Lutheran, Reformed and United Churches geared to fostering inter-denominational fellowship on the basis of the Scriptures as well as to encouraging evangelism.[29]

Many of those men who were active in Alliance circles could be found on the platform and in the assembly halls of these conferences. One group of evangelicals who, at least after the Berlin Conference of September 1909, were, if not excluded, then made to feel most unwelcome, were the Pentecostals. Their forms of spirituality, in particular the gift of speaking in tongues, were deemed by the Berlin Declaration signed by fifty-six leading evangelical figures to be an expression of a 'spirit from hell'. Nevertheless, relations with Pentecostal groups were not completely severed: one recognised that they too were 'true children of God'.[30] E. von Eicken says that this Declaration, in warding off 'enthusiatic excesses', helped to heal the 'rift' in the evangelical movement that Pentecostalism had caused. It also marked, in his opinion, the end of 'the period of revival'.[31] Representatives of the Gnadau Association reiterated this stance towards what was generally termed 'the tongues movement' in 1924.[32]

The work of the Evangelical Alliance became really well known due to two features of its work: first, the Universal Week of Prayer in the first week of each new year (which was observed even during the Second World War) and, second, the annual Blankenburg Evangelical Alliance Conference, held generally in August in the Thuringian town of Bad Blankenburg. This second event began in 1886 when Anna von Weling invited a few Christians to spend some days together in prayer and Bible study. Her drawing-room soon became too small and a hall was built to hold 800 people but this, too, soon became too small for the numbers assembling. In 1906 a large Conference Hall was built to hold 2,200 people, which, even to the present day, is generally filled to overflowing.[33] At the official 50th Jubilee gathering in 1936 the mayor of Bad Blankenburg lent the Stadthalle to the Alliance because 5,000 had arrived to celebrate.[34]

It is not unimportant that aristocrats played the dominant role in the first decades of the Alliance in Germany. They undoubtedly shaped evangelical thinking on numerous issues; their own opinions on social and political matters, reflecting the dominant ideas of their class, became the ruling ideas within evangelicalism. Count Andreas von Bernstorff was for years President of the German Alliance and he was succeeded in 1908 by Carl de Neufville, a son of one of the oldest branches of French aristocracy. De Neufville remained in that office until 1921, becoming thereafter honorary President until his death.[35]

To support and publicise the work of the Alliance as well as to publish devotional articles and short Biblical studies, the *Evangelisches Allianzblatt* began to appear in 1890. The first editor of the weekly paper was Gustav Kaiser.[36] Its circulation grew to 4,000 under the editorial guidance of Bernhard Kühn up to 1914. Otto Dreibholz edited the paper during World War One before handing over the reins to G.F. Nagel. Nagel succeeded in expanding circulation to 5,000 copies weekly in the inter-war period. It fell, however, to 3,750 in 1941.

An Executive Committee was set up to manage the affairs of the Alliance. In October 1932 a new Committee was elected. Gustav Nagel remained chairman. His deputy was Pastor Michaelis (from Bethel). Other members of the leadership group were Dr Melle (Frankfurt a.M.), Pastor Jehle (Stuttgart), Herr Dick (Stuttgart) and Pastor Wilhelm Krause (Berlin).[37] The *Allianzblatt* of 30 October 1935 notes that the following brethren were present at the Committee meeting on 28 August 1935 which took place in the Alliance House in Bad Blankenburg:Nagel, Melle, Möller, Dreibholz, Rexroth, Kohnle, Jehle, Stritter, Mehl, Krause, Dick.

According to the results of the national census of 17 May 1939 there were 79.3 million residents in the Greater German Reich – an increase of 12 million since 1937. Fifty-four percent of the population (i.e. 42.6 million Germans) were members of a Protestant Provincial Church or a Free Church and forty percent (i.e. 31.9 million) were Roman Catholics.[38] Most evangelicals were members of a Provincial Church. The two largest non-Lutheran Free Churches were the Baptists (1936:70,000 members) and the Methodists (1936: 54,000 members), most of whose memberships could be classified at the time as evangelical.[39]

Personal links with the Evangelical Alliance were numerous. For example, Dr Otto Melle was at the time of his election to the Executive Committee the Director of the Methodist Pastoral Seminary in Frankfurt and had been editor of the evangelical paper *Christian Teetotaller* since 1923.[40] He was to become the bishop of the Methodist Church in the Third Reich. He was also Chairman of the Blankenburg Committee, which organised the Blankenburg Conference. Another member of the Executive Committee, Dr Walter Michaelis, was simultaneously Chairman of the *Gnadauer Verband*, an association comprising some 500,000 Bible-oriented Christians committed to fellowship and evangelisation within the Provincial Churches. Each organisation, of course, had its own press. Just as the Baptists had their *Wahrheitszeuge* (Witness to the Truth) and the Methodists their *Evangelist*, so there were a number of publications aimed at those evangelical Christians within the Provincial Churches. *Heilig dem Herrn* was edited by Ernst Modersohn (1870-1948) and had a circulation of 25,000 in 1933; Karl Möbius (1878-1962) edited *Auf der Warte*, which had a circulation that year of 1,875; Theophil Krawielitzki (1866-1942) edited the *Deutsches Gemeinschaftsblatt* (9,000 copies); Joseph Gauger (1866-1938) was editor of *Licht und Leben* (12,000 copies); and Walter Michaelis (1866-1953) edited the *Gnadauer Gemeinschaftsblatt* (3,600 copies).[41]

All these evangelical papers had sections in them devoted to analysing and interpreting social and political events, in which political opinions mingled with eschatological convictions were presented as binding truth. Wilhelm Göbel wrote for *Heilig dem Herrn*, Hans Pförtner for the *Reichsgottesarbeiter*, Joseph Gauger[42] for *Licht und Leben* and the editor of the *Wormser Zeitung*, Berhard Peters, for both the *Gemeinschaftsblatt* and the *Evangelisches Allianzblatt*. These commentators, in unison with their editors, determined the political line taken by the papers for decades. Judging from the letters pages, there was not much, if any criticism of these assessments of Germany's spiritual health and the remedies suggested. It seems fair to say that the opinions which ruled the evangelical world in Germany were the opinions of its intellectual-spiritual leaders and they were far from being politically neutral. The men were, to use a modern analogy, the Hal Lindseys of their age, end-times specialists whose articles, tracts and books were very influential in the period of the Weimar Republic and the Third Reich. Studying the prophetic scriptures to find clues about one's position in the divine timetable was popular not only with individual Christians and the hobby continued throughout the Third Reich. The *Allianzblatt* reported on 15 June 1939, for example, that meetings of the 'Friends of the Prophetic Word' were taking place regularly in the *Evangelisches Vereinshaus* in Barmen. Pastor Kuhlmann, the Deputy Chairman of the Evangelical Alliance at the time, was chairing the meetings.

The ideal of the Evangelical Alliance had gained many adherents in the inter-war period. Tens of thousands of people attended the Alliance Conferences held throughout Germany; over 100,000 took part in the Alliance Prayer Week each year. These were the people who would consume the ideas of their 'prophets' and look to them for leadership and guidance in the political turmoil of their times.

Before turning to look at the lives of three men who helped to shape German evangelicalism in the first half of the twentieth century, it is worth considering the society which shaped them and their thinking. They all grew up in the Second Reich, founded in 1871, under Emperor William I, coming to an end in 1918 with William II's abdication. The Chancellor of the Empire was Otto von Bismarck (1815-1898) who dominated German politics until his dismissal in 1890. He had led a coup d'etat of the ruling class in Prussia in 1862 which had done away with the few elements of parliamentary independence in a state characterised by an absolute monarchy and a three-class suffrage. Bismarck used 'blood and iron' to crush all liberalising tendencies. As a result, he waged war on the workers' movement, passing the infamous Socialist Laws in 1878, which remained in force until his dismissal, as well as on Catholics and the Catholic Centre Party, in spite of the fact that Catholics made up one third of the population of the Reich. This *Kulturkampf* was essentially an attack on the ideas of democracy, opposition and spiritual independence.

During the Second Empire an 'exaggerated admiration of force' (Richard von Kühlmann) expressed itself in the 'wholesale persecution of millions of German citizens if they happened to be socialists or Catholics'[43] at a time when, through industrialisation, Germany was becoming the major economic power in Europe. The Junker landowning nobility and the army (two-thirds of all Prussian officers in 1860 were of noble birth) called the tune in a society where an emergent middle class (politically organised in the Free Conservative and National Liberal parties) became a vocal supporter of imperialism. This alliance of middle classes with autocratic, aristocratic militarists made the former almost immune to the liberal and democratic ideas in the country; the ruling class guaranteed the influence and wealth of the bourgeoisie.

Prussia had militarily defeated Austria in 1866 and France in 1870. These victories were seen in Germany as victories of Protestantism over Catholicism. There was, in the Empire, a close alliance between throne and altar as well as between church and army, which underlined the centuries-old tradition of Protestant subservience to the state in Germany. Until 1918 – the Weimar Constitution separated Church and State for the first time in the homeland of the Reformation – the Landesherr, or provincial ruler, was also the supreme bishop of the Landeskirche, the provincial church. The principle of *Cuius regio, eius religio* laid down in the Religious Peace of Augsburg (1555) and reaffirmed in the Treaty of Westphalia (1648) had settled that; denominational boundaries had remained stable ever since, guaranteeing a virtual monopoly to the state churches. It is not surprising, therefore, to find that in the period up to and even after 1918 70-80 per cent of Protestant pastors in Germany were authoritarian, nationalistic, conservative and anti-democratic in character[44] and that they supported the rise of the National Socialist German Workers' Party to a decisive degree.

Apart from the political subservience and authoritarianism of German Protestantism, its anti-semitism, rooted in part in the writings of Martin Luther and in part in its reading of various New Testament passages, had been a perennial feature of its character.[45] Anti-semites were organised in a number of parties between 1887 and 1918 – the German Reform Party, the German Social Party, the German Social Reform Party and, after 1907, the Economic

Association – all of which were attempts to draw workers away from the labour movement (1914:2 million members) as well as from the Socialist Party (1912:34.8% of the vote making it the largest party in the Reichstag with 110 seats). The largest anti-semitic party in the Second Empire, the Christian Social Workers' Party, was founded in 1879 by the Lutheran minister at the imperial court, Adolf Stoecker (1835-1909). It was very conservative and monarchist, based on 'the Christian faith and love of King and Fatherland', and as such was at one time able to win 16 seats in the Reichstag. Like many conservative-minded Christians of that time, he resented and fought against what he perceived to be the economic dominance of Jews who he saw behind German capitalism. Equally, he railed against assimilated, areligious Jews who he blamed for the atheism and rationalism in society. He believed that the powerful Jewish influence on public opinion by means of the press was undermining the religious consciousness of the masses. Ironically, this was partially brought about by his own politics of envy and resentment, of nationalism and anti-semitism, something Nietzsche castigated as the 'German disease'.[46] The psychology of hatred inculcated by Stoecker's and similar parties did much to destroy moral restraints, but nothing to end the economic and social enslavement of the labouring masses.

This disease festered on throughout the period of the Weimar Republic (1918-33). Popular sovereignty had been achieved, but the real powers in Germany – the army, the Junkers, big business and the civil service – remained and resented the fact that Germany alone was being blamed for the First World War and Germany alone was being forced to disarm. Conservatives and Free Conservatives combined to form the German National People's Party (DNVP) – the party which attracted Protestant, including evangelical support throughout the 1920s.[47] It opposed democracy and social progress with a belief in monarchy and nationalism. In terms of religion, it called for the teaching of religion in schools and the 'penetration of our people with the powerful, living force of Christianity'. Before the 1920 election Pastor Gauger, a respected evangelical leader, recommended a vote for the DNVP as the 'lesser evil'. The German Democratic Party had too many adherents of a liberal theological bent while the Social Democratic and Communist Parties were materialistic and atheist expressions of a 'class selfishness' which was, in his view, even more detestable than the class spirit of the Prussian Junkers, who at least had 'noble goals'. He openly expressed his loathing for the democratic state which, he said, was characterised by an unprincipled corruption and was controlled by a 'Jewish spirit' (*Judengeist*).[48] The DNVP championed the ideas of pan-Germanism, anti-semitism and rearmament, and defended the ideas of private property and free enterprise, i.e. it supported the landed interests of the Junkers and the economic interests of industrialists. The party was personified by the businessman Alfred Hugenberg, who, as leader, allied the DNVP with the National Socialists in October 1931, paving the way for Hitler's rise to power. It was also the Nationalists' paramilitary organisation, the Stahlhelm (Steel Helmet), which kept alive the spirit and traditions of German militarism, circumventing the restrictions imposed by the Versailles Treaty. Its founder joined Hitler's first cabinet; the organisation itself, along with its parent organisation, merged with the Nazi movement in 1933. Along with them went all the patriotic Christian voters of the DNVP.

Only for a short period, between December 1929 and June 1933, when the Christlich-Sozialer Volksdienst (CSVD) existed as an independent party particularly attractive to evangelicals, did the recommendations given by pietist editors to vote for the extreme right-wing DNVP become less frequent. In the run-up to the 1930 election, Wilhelm Goebel recommended all the right-wing parties, including – for the first time in the evangelical press – the NSDAP. *Auf der Warte* and Friedrich Heitmüller's paper *In Jesu Dienst* and the Independent Evangelical *Der Gärtner* all initially expressed support, however, for the CSVD.[49] Paul Schmidt, the key Baptist figure during the 1930s, was for some years a CSVD member of the Reichstag. Dr F.H. Otto Melle, at that time director of the Methodist Seminary at Frankfurt a.M., was also very involved in the party. The CSVD won 14 seats in the election of September 1930, but this fell to 4 in March 1933. It voluntarily dissolved itself shortly after voting to give Hitler total, dictatorial powers in March 1933; its Reichstag representatives joined the ranks of the NSDAP as associates – a move symbolic of the drift of evangelicalism and, more generally, Protestantism towards welcoming the stability of dictatorship and a government which, for once, it was willing to call godly. Even those evangelical groups traditionally opposed to any involvement in the political realm, such as the Plymouth Brethren, were elated. *Die Tenne*, a Brethren periodical, talked of Hitler's government as a 'godsend', a government which 'recognises Him and, all in all, acts in accordance with His thoughts'. Hitler was 'the man God chose and equipped' to renew Germany.[50] Hans Pförtner, a writer for the *Reichsgottesarbeiter*, wrote in 1934, in a pamphlet produced for evangelistic purposes, that 'the German people united in the National Socialist movement has once again saved the cross and Christian civilisation in the West from the onslaught from the East'. One year of National Socialist rule had proved that the German nation, in his view, had remained true to its divine calling of being 'the saviour of the cross', even though not all 'the brown hosts of salvation (*braune Retterscharen*) who followed the call of the Führer were aware of the fact'.[51] Behind Hitler stood the Lord of History. Resistance to Hitler and his salvation army was tantamount to resisting the divine purposes for the German nation. This was the united testimony of the whole range of evangelical publications in 1933.

Notes

1. Gert Wendelborn (1979, 10-11).
2. G. Wendelborn (1979,15); Erich Beyreuther (1987); J. Hastings (1912, 602ff); Etymologisches Wörterbuch (1989) 1276-1277.
3. Archibald W. Harrison (1942, Chapter 5).
4. A.W. Harrison (1942, 33); G. Wendelborn (1979, 14-15).
5. Helmut Hickel (1967, 17,34). Just as there were slight differences between various strands of Pietism, there were also differences between Pietism and Moravianism. Indeed, the Pietists of Saxony accused Zinzendorf of not being truly converted, for he had not experienced struggle during the process of repentence.
6. The German word 'Erweckungsbewegung' literally means 'revival movement'.
7. Erich Beyreuther (1968, 91-93).
8. E. Beyreuther (1968, 95).
9. Hans-Jürgen Gabriel (1987, 154-155).
10. G. Wendelborn (1979, 63).
11. G. Wendelborn (1979, 64); E. Beyreuther (1968, 99-100).
12. E. Beyreuther (1968, 99).
13. J. Hastings (1912, 607).
14. E. Beyreuther (1968, 102).
15. Ruth Rouse/ Stephen C. Neill (1967, 318); J.W. Massie (1847, 84).
16. E. Beyreuther (1969, 13); J.W. Massie (1847, 392-395, 416-417).
17. J.W. Massie (1847, 339, 417).
18. J. W. Massie (1847, 417).
19. J. Hastings (1912, 601). See also John Wolffe (1986).
20. Jakob Schmitt (1954, 112-113). Interestingly, the call was also addressed to Roman Catholic brethren.
21. E. Beyreuther (1969, 14-15).
22. E. Beyreuther (1969, 19, 20-22).

23. E. Beyreuther (1969, 23).
24. E. Beyreuther (1969, 54); J. Schmitt (1954, 350).
25. E. Beyreuther (1969, 59, 77).
26. E. Beyreuther (1969, 47-48).
27. E. Beyreuther (1969, 46).
28. J. Schmitt (1954, 352-354); Dieter Lange (1988, 9-20); Walter Michaelis (1949, Chapter 12).
29. Dieter Lange (1988,13); W. Michaelis (1949, Chapter 13).
30. Dieter Lange (1988,14-18); W. Michaelis (1949,139-158); E. Beyreuther (1969, 83-84); W. Bühne (1994, 105-108); W. J. Hollenweger (1972, 221-228).
31. W. Hollenweger (1972, 231).
32. D. Lange (1988, 17).
33. *Evangelical Christendom* (hereafter EC), 1937,174.
34. EC, 1936, 195-6. A photograph of the members of the Blankenburg Committee at the Jubilee Conference can be found on p.195. The British equivalent of Blankenburg is the Keswick Conference.
35. EC, 1938, 94; EC, 1936, 109.
36. EA 30.01.1936 (Nr.2), 31.
37. EA 09.10.1932.
38. P. Matheson (1981, 99).
39. K. Zehrer (1986, 183).
40. EA 28.05.1933 (Nr 22), 348.
41. Figures according to E.G. Rüppel (1969, 45). According to K. Nowak (1988, 107) circulation of *Heilig dem Herrn* was 34,000 and *Licht und Leben* 18,000 in 1920.
42. Gauger also edited the *Gotthard-Briefe* which were devoted to interpreting historical events in the light of Biblical prophecy.
43. W. Ebenstein (1945, 29).
44. K.-W. Dahm (1965, 148).
45. H.A. Oberman (1985, 519-530); R.Hirsch/R.Schuder (1985, 355-423). The various New Testament passages and other anti-semitic writings of Church Fathers (Justin Martyr, Tertullian, Origen and especially Johan Chrysostomus) are analysed by J. Kahl (1968, 34-41).
46. W. Ebenstein (1945, 151).
47. K. Nowak (1988, 29).
48. T. Stammen (1987, 210).
49. Günther Rüther (1987, 281-285); G. Opitz (1969, 250f); K. Nowak (1988, 107-108).
50. G. Jordy (1986, 62,64); G. Opitz (1969, 254).
51. H. Pförtner (1934, 7-8).

Chapter Two

Three Evangelical Leaders

There are still no monographs dealing with the three key figures in the world of German evangelicalism in the 1930s. The three men portrayed in this chapter represented the three pillars of evangelicalism: Walter Michaelis was a pastor in the provincial church, Otto Melle was the first bishop of the united Episcopal Methodist Church in Germany and Gustav Nagel an Independent Evangelical pastor. The three men corresponded frequently with each other and many of the letters have survived. Michaelis was Nagel's deputy in the Evangelical Alliance until 1937; Melle was chairman of the Alliance's central conference, held in Bad Blankenburg each year. A familiarity with these figures is necessary if one is to fully comprehend the evangelical perspective on National Socialism. The following short treatment of these figures will show that only one, Michaelis, was able to extricate himself in part from the totalitarian temptation. This had less to do with differing attitudes to the Confessing Church (Michaelis was not a member) than with the fact that Free Church Christians in Germany had always, since their beginnings in the middle of the nineteenth century, had to fight against the alliance of throne and altar to preserve their independence. What the *Allianzblatt* referred to throughout the 1930s as the *Kirchenkrise* helped the smaller churches to gain ground in the country. The Third Reich brought all the Free Churches legal rights and a greater measure of freedom for what they considered the essential task of evangelism. In spite of the creation of a united *Deutsche Evangelische Kirche*, German Protestantism remained as divided as ever. The crisis, in the Free Church perspective, had little to do with National Socialism per se. Those newly won rights were not to be carelessly thrown to the winds for the sake of a Christian solidarity which they, the Free Churches, had themselves rarely experienced in the past century. There developed during the 1930s a split between the provincial church and Free Church brethren largely over the issues of the Confessing Church and German Christians. This split, however noticeable at conferences, did not, fortunately, lead to the end of the friendship between the three men.

Walter Michaelis (1866-1953)

As Chairman of the Gnadau Association to Promote Fellowship and Evangelisation, Michaelis, the brother of a former Reich Chancellor, had responsibility for 38 regional associations, 6,000 fellowships and nearly 500,000 members. His personal authority was so immense that he could not help but sway Christian voters towards his point of view. In an essay written prior to the elections in 1928, he wrote that he held the CSVD and the other newly formed Protestant parties – the Protestant Party of Germany, the German Reformation Party – to be politically insignificant and even harmful, because they threatened to split the Protestant vote. He told the readers of the *Gnadauer Gemeinschaftsblatt* to read party programmes to find out how much emphasis they placed on the moral and religious factors in politics. He welcomed the support given by the Social Democrats to the cause of the working class, but rejected their party because of its position on ethical issues and Christianity. The German Democratic Party and the German People's Party would not get his vote because 'their press was always to be found in the camp of liberal theology whenever questions of an ecclesiastical or theological nature came up'. He felt closest to the Centre Party because of its 'clear confession of faith in Christianity' and its 'worker-friendly social policies'; it was, however, not possible for a Protestant to vote for it because it sought to exploit any political advantage to 'ruthlessly promote the interests of the Roman Church'. Michaelis recommended that Christians vote for the DNVP in spite of the party's 'enslavement to the business class'. After all, it supported the idea of Protestant schools and had in its ranks 'socially minded and openly Christian figures who had come from the old Christian Social Party'.[1]

In fact, Michaelis, together with Gauger, Möbius and an evangelical member of the Reichstag, Veidt, tried unsuccessfully to persuade the DNVP Chairman to grant a number of safe seats to evangelical Christians. Voting for and even involvement in the DNVP was in accord with the widespread conviction which took for granted that Christians were right-wingers.[2] The alliance between German nationalists and National Socialists helped to draw evangelicals and the evangelical press into Hitler's camp. Pastor Möbius reckoned that most young evangelicals in the Gnadau Association supported the Nazis in 1930; by 1932 the large majority of all evangelicals, he believed, were voting for the National Socialists.[3] On 8 June 1933 *Licht und Leben* published the Gnadau Association's declaration explaining this stance:[4]

Liebe Brüder! Gottes hohe Hand hat durch den nationalen Aufbruch gewaltig in unser Volk eingegriffen. Durch den Sturmwind der nationalen Bewegung hat er es von den glaubens- und vaterlandslosen Strömungen losgerissen und zurückgeführt zu den gottgegebenen Grundlagen in Ehe, Familie, Volk und Staat. Darum sind wir dankbar, dass wie unser Reichspräsident Generalfeldmarschall von Hindenburg, so nun auch der erwählte Führer des deutschen Volkes, Reichskanzler Adolf Hitler, sich für ihre Person und das ganze deutsche Volk bekennen zum lebendigen Gott und seinen Segen erbitten.

Dear Brethren! God's hand has intervened mightily in our people's destiny through this national awakening. He has torn our people away from those who have no religious faith and love no fatherland and He has led us back to the God-given basics of marriage, family, nation and state. We are thankful that, just like our Reich President Field Marshal von Hindenburg, the elected leader of the German people, Chancellor Adolf Hitler, also publicly confesses his faith in the living God and asks for His blessing.

The pietists knew exactly how God had intervened and who His enemies were. They had been deeply impressed by Hitler's prayer at the opening of the Reichstag and were completely persuaded by his repeated use of religious vocabulary. And just as Hitler talked of *'God'*, *'the Lord'* and *'Providence'*, so now they began to talk of the *'Zeitenwende'*, the *'nationaler Aufbruch'* and *'Vorsehung'*. The language of the Third Reich was already becoming the language of German evangelicalism.

This can be seen in relation to three central issues at that time. Firstly, the attitude of many evangelicals towards Jews was impacted by the Nazi experience. In the May 1933 issue of *Gnadauer Gemeinschaftsblatt* Michaelis published an article on the relationship between the Church, the Jews and the German nation which revealed the traditional conservative anti-semitism of the Reformation Church. He talked about the Aryan Laws in the same way as the authors of a report on the subject produced by the Marburg Theological Faculty on 19 September 1933 and in the same way as conservative Lutherans like Walter Künneth: the Church of the Reformation could not accept or implement laws excluding Jews from their fellowship even though, in their view, the government certainly had a right to impose such laws on society as a whole. Michaelis saw such laws governing the life of the Church as standing in 'irreconcilable contradiction to the Bible' which reveals the importance of Israel in God's plan of salvation. Yet, on the basis of his reading of 1 Timothy 3,7, he would be willing to exclude Jews from positions of leadership in the Church as they no longer enjoyed a good reputation among non-Christians.

It was more important, in his view, that the Church remain free to preach the gospel and partake of the Lord's Supper. Anyway, it was clearly taught in the Bible that Israel's dispersion among the peoples of the earth was a divine curse on the Jews:'Giving Jews civic rights at the beginning of the nineteenth century was therefore a misunderstanding of the will of God'.5

Bible-based Christians, he believed, could have nothing against rolling back Jewish influence in society as long as it was done humanely. (On 1 April the Nazis had started a campaign of boycotting Jewish shops, doctors, lawyers, etc.) He saw the Jewish influence on the press, banking and the cultural life of the nation as corrupting and undermining its moral fibre (*zersetzendes Gärungsmitttel*). Although Gnadau fired no Jews or half-Jews, it offered encouragement to those who did.6

The second area of rapprochement with the Nazi system involved the Gnadau Associations and the German Christians. The Gnadau Association forged links with the Faith Movement of German Christians (GDC) at a meeting on 15/16 August 1933 (there were 13 'no' votes). The GDC was a union of various right-wing Protestant groups formed to rally Christians behind the banners of National Socialism. Many evangelicals joined in 1932/33 and the GDC swept to a landslide victory in the church synodal elections of 23 July 1933, capturing over 70% of the votes in parishes throughout Germany. Michaelis stepped down temporarily from his post after the link was made. Based in part on his belief that a Christian should not get too involved in the things of this world, he stated that he could not become a member of either the GDC or the NSDAP and he opposed mixing Christianity with ideas stemming from Germanic religion. He sensed danger in the 'enthusiasm' felt by many Christians for the 'National Socialist zest for life'.7

A reversal of policy was brought about by the end of the year, not least due to the impact of a speech given by Dr Krause, the leader of the GDC in Greater Berlin.8 At a meeting of the Gnadau Executive on 13 December 1933 in Bad Salzuflen all members of the Association who had joined the GDC were called upon to leave; the Executive itself broke off all contacts with the Faith Movement (on this occasion there was only one 'no' vote). The following year, on 13/15 November, the Executive repeated its call, asking all Gnadau regional associations to disassociate themselves from the GDC.

For the sake of the many believers who were members of the GDC, Michaelis explained his personal reasons for these decisions.9 He rejected the GDC's use of worldly power to achieve change as well as their claims to be entitled to lead the Church. He noted the divisions caused by the Movement among Christians and the 'unnatural alliances' brought about with non-Christians. The language of self-praise and the idealistic, self-righteous concepts permeating their publications were anathema to him. Most importantly, perhaps, they appeared to hold to the 'false doctrine' of equating the revelation of God's holy will in contemporary historical events, as interpreted by themselves, with the revelations of Holy Scripture.

Finally, there was the problematical relationship between Gnadau and the Confessing Church. By Christmas 1933 the Pastors' Emergency League, set up in September 1933 by Martin Niemöller, had gained 6,000 members, about one-third of all German Protestant pastors. These men, opposed to the regime of the German Christians, called for adherence to the Scriptures and the historical Confessions. 138 delegates from 18 of the 28 Provincial Churches met together between 29 and 31 May 1934 for the first Reich Confessing Church Synod in Barmen. A Second Reich Confessing Church Synod took place on 19/20 October 1934 in Dahlem.

On the spiritual and intellectual plane Gnadau members were torn into differing groups by these developments. Michaelis himself seems to have become critical of certain aspects of the totalitarian system, those, namely, which impinged upon his own freedom. Only the Confessing Church, he noted in a letter dated 25 January 1937, had fought to preserve the independence of the Church; the 'parties, the unions, the professors and teachers (with a few exceptions) and the rest of the Protestant Church had bowed their knee before the totalitarian state'.[10] The Church, he wrote to Pastor Liebchen, Magdeburg, on 19 October 1936, was on the way to becoming a state church, privileged by the National Socialists.[11] Michaelis was convinced that neutrality was not possible in this inner-church struggle and he resisted those Gnadau leaders, like the well-known evangelist Ernst Modersohn, Chairman of the Gnadau Association in Thuringia, who urged him to avoid any steps that might drag pietists into the *Kirchenkampf*. 'Should we be indifferent,' Michaelis wrote to Modersohn on 1 August 1934, 'to what happens in the Church to which we belong? Is it of no importance to us if an absolute führer system is introduced in the Church? For these reasons I accuse neutralists of a lack of insight and irresponsibility'.[12]

It is indeed noticeable that those pietists who called for neutrality frequently gave vocal expression to their 'unshakeable faith in the Führer' and his government's measures. For example, the editors of *Heilig dem Herrn* and the *Deutsches Gemeinschaftsblatt* found biblical justification for the killing of Ernst Röhm and others at the end of June 1934 and for the burning down of synagogues between 8 and 10 November 1938.[13] This does not mean, however, that those who supported the stance taken by the Confessing Church were opponents of Hitler's government. The evidence is overwhelming that Confessing Church pastors believed they were the better patriots.

A number of Michaelis' colleagues, and the Evangelical Alliance as an organisation, had 'good reasons' for keeping out of the *Kirchenkampf*.[14] The Confessing Church was not a uniform movement; there were many regional and theological differences. Some evangelicals were worried by the predominance of theological liberals in some regions; others were worried by theologically conservative Lutherans, who were, at best, reserved towards a lay movement like Gnadau. Nor could evangelicals forget the caustic criticisms levelled at them by one of the central figures in the Confessing Church, Karl Barth. His 'Commentary on the Letter to the Romans' equated the 'religious individualism' of pietism with the 'essence of this dark world' and claimed that pietism was 'apostasy'. He would, he said, rather be with a worldly church in hell than with pietists in heaven.[15] All evangelicals were, moreover, worried that a too close alliance with the Confessing Church would upset their good relations with the Third Reich and perhaps threaten their freedom to evangelise. To a large degree convinced National Socialists, they saw in the Confessing Church a 'weakening of the Third Reich and the community of Germans (*Volksgemeinschaft*).[16] Michaelis was eventually able to sway the Executive. He recommended working alongside the *Bekennende Kirche*, though not taking orders from its leaders nor becoming an organisational part of it. He was himself present on 25 October 1934 when an *Arbeitsgemeinschaft der missionarischen und diakonischen Werke und Verbände in der Deutschen Evangelischen Kirche*, led by a Council of Brethren and independent of the German Christian Church government, was founded. This grouping of missionary and nursing care organisations followed the lead given by the Confessing Church. By November 1934 all but four regional Gnadau associations had joined.[17] Moreover, the Executive allowed individual evangelicals to join a local Confessing Church group and granted to their local branches the power to allow their buildings to be used for Confessing Church meetings. Members were advised not to work with GDC groups if they were invited to do so. In some areas like the Rhineland or East Prussia Gnadau adherents were able to cooperate in local and regional Confessing Church Councils of Brethren. At Barmen, too, six Gnadau activists were present as synodalists at the *Bekenntnissynode*.[18]

The Executive Committee members remained divided on the question of whether they should publicly speak out on issues unrelated to fellowship and evangelisation.[19] They remained silent after the so-called Göring Decree of 1934 forbade all religious gatherings outside of churches or when, in 1938, their meeting places were requisitioned by the government so they could be used as granaries. On the other hand, in the context of his Deputy Chairmanship of the Evangelical Alliance, Michaelis repeatedly spoke out against attempts made by Alliance leaders to play down the difficulties in Hitler's Germany 'in order to avoid a struggle'. He felt the Alliance was not 'speaking the eternal gospel into our present situation'. On 3 April 1937 he stepped down from his post on the Executive Committee of the Evangelical Alliance. In a letter to the Chairman of the Blankenburg Committee, Bishop Melle, Michaelis lamented the state of God's church: 'many of God's children today [are] in a state of dangerous innocence, ignorance, often led astray by others, and also timid and anxious in the face of the *zeitgeist*'.[20]

Dr F.H. Otto Melle (1874-1947)

Otto Melle became bishop of the Methodist Church in 1936 and took upon himself the responsibility for 267 pastors and 53,773 (1936 figure) church members. He was known to evangelicals throughout the 1930s as Chairman of the Blankenburg Committee and a member of the Executive Committe of the Evangelical Alliance. In February 1932 Dr Melle held a speech in Atlanta, Georgia, which was reported in the *Evangelisches Allianzblatt*.[21] He spoke out against the 'injustice of the Versailles Treaty' and France's breach of the same by building up its armaments.[22] The reparations payments demanded under the treaty actually represented only about one-quarter of the cost of the war to the German people but many Germans blamed their economic hardships on the treaty nevertheless. The 1929 settlement organised by the American banker, Owen Young, enflamed nationalists and Melle was a nationalist. The vague implications of Germany's war guilt was hard to stomach. Melle dealt with the issue in Atlanta. Why should Germany stand idly by while all its neighbours 'were armed to the teeth'? Why was only Germany 'being forced to disarm'? Secondly, to achieve a 'true and lasting peace', the lie about Germany being solely responsible for the war – 'a judgement which we will never ever be able to accept' – had to be unmasked for what it was. 'All the most important historians in the world' had disproved it; the opposite, in fact, was true. 'Christians in Germany expect this reproach and talk about Germany's being alone guilty to be ended'. Germany's honour had to be saved and protected.

Melle's views were spread all over America and the *Allianzblatt* commented: 'Let us hope that God will richly bless the many testimonies given by our Seminary Director'. Not least due to Melle's diplomatic manoeuvrings, the General Conference of the Methodist Church meeting in Atlantic City between 2 and 25 May 1932 called for a revision of Article 231 of the Versailles Treaty:'Burdening Germany with all the blame for the World War can in all fairness not be defended'. The Conference called for multilateral disarmament and the ending of reparations.[23] The *Evangelisches Allianzblatt* was jubilant two weeks later when it could announce 'the end of German tribute payments'. From 1 July 1932 no reparations had to be paid any longer: 'The Young Plan is dead!' 'The lie about Germany's war guilt' could be buried.[24]

German resentment at the dictated peace was, however, just channelled in another direction. The middle classes, squeezed by the inflation of the 1920s and full of indignation at the social reforms pushed through by the left (eight-hour working day, unemployment insurance, collective labour agreements, housing improvements) blamed democracy and the republic for their flagging fortunes. As the extreme right-wing parties gained in strength, the *Evangelisches Allianzblatt* encouraged that process. This, the editor firmly believed, was the God-ordained way out of the democratic chaos.[25]

Although Melle had initially hoped that a spiritual revival would take place in 1933 to bring Germany back on to the straight and narrow path, he came to see Hitler's appointment as Chancellor as God's answer to his prayers: Hitler was the great leader, sent by God at a time the German people seemed heading for destruction.[26] Melle continued the policy of his predecessor, Bishop Nuelsen, who had urged his pastors in 1934 to stay neutral in the *Kirchenkampf* and the political debate. Melle, in 1938, claimed that this stance was necessary and he succeeded in enforcing it 'in spite of a lot of criticism and some opposition'.[27]

It was perhaps symbolic that the General Conference which elected Melle its new bishop (he received 53 of the 58 votes) was initially planned for the 9 to 13 September 1936 but was postponed for a week 'out of consideration for the Party Conference of the NSDAP'. The Gestapo, moreover, was very impressed by the 'unanimity' of the Conference delegates and their avoidance of 'critical comments about the government and the state of the country'.[28]

In his message to the Conference on the day prior to Melle's election, Nuelsen had claimed that the pastors and members of his Church 'faithfully supported the government' because it had neither hindered the Church's work nor put it under any kind of pressure.[29]

While still director of of the Preachers' Seminary of the Methodist Church, Melle, together with his bishop, and addressed an 'Appeal to Our Anglo-Saxon Sister Churches' (30 March 1933) in which they both protested against the public meetings and press reports in America and England centering on 'an alleged persecution of Jews and so-called attrocities being committed by the national movement in Germany'. They called on Methodists throughout the world to protest against such reporting which they interpreted as an attempt to rekindle the 'awful propaganda lies spread in the World War'. Law and order were not in danger in Germany, they claimed; the government had, moreover, punished those people, few in number, who had acted irresponsibly.[30]

While this letter documents political blindness, a later incident relating to the Jews lays bare the not uncommon experience of the moral senses of an educated German being dulled by a higher sense of duty to those in authority. In 1942 the Gestapo requested permission to read through the membership lists of a single Methodist Church in Hamburg. The Church initially refused, Bishop Melle explaining that this request seemed to imply that the State Security Police had some special reason to doubt the 'loyal attitude towards the government' and to keep it under surveillance 'although this doesn't appear necessary as regards other Churches'. The Reich Church Ministry thereupon reported to Bishop Melle the presence of a Jewess in one of his churches.

A Methodist pastor in Hamburg had told this woman, an active member, to withdraw from the church once he had found out (this was in January 1938) that she was Jewish. She returned to the church in the summer of 1939 after a new pastor had taken over. The new pastor visited the woman three times before the Gestapo made it known to him that her attendance at a Methodist chapel was not desirable. He stopped his visits and told the woman not to return to the church. The Gestapo, in 1942, had interrogated the woman who told them that other Jews were also members of this church. This was the reason the secret police wished to check the lists. The statement made by the Methodist Superintendent that he 'could make no distinction between Jews and non-Jews because of his faith' had increased the suspicions of the authorities. Melle requested a detailed report on the situation from this superintendent, Ernst Bräunlich. As it happened, no other Jewish names could be found among the members of this Methodist church. Melle passed on this report, in the original – although not requested to do so – to the Reich Church Ministry in January 1943 and considered the matter closed once the Gestapo were satisfied that no other Jews were hiding in the chapel.

No disciplinary action was ever taken against these 'pastors'; their actions were understood and accepted, as was the system of racial apartheid. Being 'loyal' in this situation did not mean, to Melle, being faithful to an active Jewish Methodist: it meant cooperating with the officials working at the Church Ministry and the Gestapo.[31] As Melle said at the Methodist Annual Conference in 1941: 'Methodists must be the most loyal members of the German community, people in whom the government can trust, willing to make sacrifices and always ready for action. Even if restrictive measures affect us badly, we must, precisely then, preserve our Christian faith and our loyalty and not give in to the temptation to moan and grumble. The biblical position is clearly mapped out for us: for conscience's sake we have to be faithful to the Führer and our nation'.[32]

One more example from the war period reveal his patriotic credentials. In 1944 Melle put propaganda material at the disposal of the Nazi regime. A report had been produced, originally only for internal church use, in which the damage done to Methodist buildings and injuries suffered by church members in bombing raids over Germany, were documented. It was entitled 'On the State of the Church in the Fifth Year of War'. Melle personally translated the report into English and passed it on to the Reich Church Ministry, which in turn passed it on to the government's Press Department, the Radio Section of the Propaganda Ministry, the Press Department of the NSDAP, the German Foreign Office and other Nazi organisations. Thorough use was made of Melle's report and he was asked repeatedly – but in vain – for a further report.[33]

Clearly, many evangelicals might not – even today – find fault with loyal and obedient and patriotic actions. One incident at the time did, however, send shock waves through German evangelicalism. It had to do with the World Conference for Practical Christianity, which was held in Oxford between 12 and 26 July 1937. Bishop Melle was sent as a delegate of the *Vereinigung Evangelischer Freikirchen* (VEF), the Association of Evangelical Free Churches, along with the Director of the German Baptist Federation, Paul Schmidt. At this Conference Melle conspicuously refused to vote for a resolution to send a message to the *Deutsche Evangelische Kirche*; Bishop Bell had refused Melle's request for a preamble to be attached to the message which would have pointed to the 'great achievements of the National Socialist Government in Germany'. After the resolution had been accepted Melle and Schmidt initially wanted to leave for Germany immediately out of protest at this decision. They took the German Embassy's advice and stayed.[34]

On 22 July 1937 Melle held a controversial speech.[35] He said that 'as a disciple of Jesus Christ' he and the churches in the VEF were 'thankful for the complete freedom to preach the gospel of Christ, to evangelise, to perform their pastoral duties and to build the Church'. The 'nationalist uprising' was seen in Germany as 'an act of divine Providence'. They prayed for those in authority and 'felt thankful that God in His Providence had sent a leader to ward off the danger of Bolshevism in Germany [and] to tear Germany back from the precipice, to replace its despair with a new faith in its mission and its future' – this, he said, was something the Churches had failed to do. The Free Churches desired to remain neutral in the conflict going on within the Provincial Protestant Churches. Christians themselves were to blame for that conflict. Church Minister, Hanns Kerrl, noted that Melle interpreted the so-called persecution of the Protestant Church as being 'solely a result of its involving itself in politics'.[36]

Neither the Conference of the British Methodist Church nor the Confessing Church in Germany had any criticism to make of Dr Melle's statements on Hitler's perceived role and religious freedom in Germany.[37] According to one historian of the German Evangelical Alliance, however, Melle's seven-minute speech caused a 'storm of indignation above all in Alliance circles,'[38] although he had not spoken in the name of the Alliance. Melle was, after all, one of the most prominent speakers at the Blankenburg Conference.

Pastor Zilz, who after 1945 was to take over as Chairman of the German Branch of the Alliance, wrote to the then chairman, Nagel, and spoke of the 'great displeasure' felt by evangelicals. The Honorary Chairman of the Alliance, Carl de Neufville, also wrote to Nagel and expressed his hope that Melle would explain his 'capitulation' in Oxford which had 'certainly done a lot of damage'. The Gnadau Association in Schleswig-Holstein claimed many friends of the Alliance had been embarrassed by the incident; the reputation of the Alliance, abroad and at home, had been quite considerably sullied. The Blankenburg Committee, meeting in Kassel, suddenly decided to change its rules and reelect its chairman annually – in order to avoid having to reelect Melle (Melle, who was still chairman, had not been invited to the meeting!). Two brethren, Dreibholz and Kröker, tried to persuade Melle in the meantime to resign, but unsuccessfully. Melle felt that the Protestant Church was persecuting him when the Stuttgart High Consistory temporarily ordered its pastors not to participate alongside Methodists at Alliance Conferences. The Bishop of Hamburg threatened to no longer permit the use of St. Michael's Church in the city for Alliance Conferences and to stop attending himself. The Methodists certainly pulled together as a result, thanking their bishop for his 'clear statement' in Oxford and expressing their 'sure confidence' that Melle would continue to 'contribute to bringing about peace in the whole situation in which the Church found itself'.[39] Not only the Methodists, all the Free Churches felt unable to honestly criticise or resist the German government,[40] as the preaching of the gospel had not, in their view, been prohibited at all.

Dr Melle was not alone in emphasising that Christians should not endanger this freedom to evangelise and felt that, should the large Churches start to crumble under the pressure of the state, then Christ's witnesses in the Free Churches could seize their opportunity and fill the vacuum. Melle was convinced that his was the only correct strategy to follow. Support among evangelicals for this position was not lacking. Theophil Krawielitzki, head of the *Deutscher Gemeinschafts-Diakonieverband* and a leading provincial church evangelical, identified himself completely and enthusiastically with the Hitler regime. There were also well-known evangelicals in Pommerania and Thuringia who were members of the NSDAP. The Alliance Conference in Bad Blankenburg had taken place under the swastika flag and evangelical leaders such as Friedrich Heitmüller, though not actually members of the NSDAP, had repeatedly expressed support not only for the government, but also for the German Christians. It is highly symbolic of the general sympathies of German evangelicalism that the traditionally politically abstinent Plymouth Brethren, who refused to join the Evangelical Alliance for biblical reasons, joined the Nazi organisations in large numbers. They were involved in the NSDAP as well as the SA and SS. The Brethren Assembly in Düsseldorf could count over fifty members of the Nazi Party. One Brethren leader, the vet Dr Otto Ohnesorg, was one of the very first members of the Party.[41]

The reputation of German evangelicalism had been particularly sullied by this incident in Oxford, even if one British paper carried the following headline after Melle's speech:'Wesley would certainly have been considered a National Socialist'.[42] There was no discussion of the incident, however, in *Evangelical Christendom*, or in the Executive Council of the British Branch of the Evangelical Alliance.

One side-effect of the speech should not pass unnoticed. Adolf Hitler personally granted the Methodist Church 10,000 Reichsmarks to buy a new organ for the church in Schneidemühl, which was officially consecrated in the presence of Bishop Melle in October 1938.[43] (The Baptists, for their part in the Oxford Conference, were granted permission to buy a building in Wilkau, Saxony). In a letter to the Chairman of the German Alliance, Melle had argued that it was his 'duty' to travel to Oxford because 'maybe the Lord will use us to render a service to the Church of Christ as well as to the our nation and Fatherland'.[44] Three years later he tried, unsuccessfully, to obtain a travel visa in order to take part in the Methodist General Conference in the USA. In his application he argued that his 'presence in America in the present world crisis would render not only the Church but also the Fatherland a good service'.[45] In war time Melle longed to be a good and faithful servant.

After the war had ended, in the summer of 1945, the German Methodist Annual Conference, meeting under Bishop Melle's chairmanship, sent a message to the United Methodist Church in the USA.[46] It expressed thanks to God for preserving Methodism in Germany and for the single-minded leadership of Dr Melle. Melle had always acted with 'a sense of his responsibility before God, history and the Mother Church of Methodism', it said. The American Methodists were willing to accept the statement as a step in the right direction, but rejected it as a confession of guilt and insisted on Melle's resignation. The American Council of Bishops called for a Central Conference of the German Branch of the Church to be held on 6 November 1946, under the chairmanship of Bishop R.J. Wade. Shortly before the Conference, Wade visited Melle, who was seriously ill in a Berlin hospital, and returned with a 'statement' from him in which he, Melle, requested permission to retire from his post. The German delegates in Frankfurt thanked Melle once again for his services, expressing their solidarity with him, and then proceeded to elect Dr I.W. Ernst Sommer as their new bishop. Melle died a few months later on 26 March 1947.[47]

Gustav Friedrich Nagel (1868-1944)

G.F. Nagel is the central figure in the work and life of the Evangelical Alliance between 1918 and 1944. Initially he was a preacher at the Freie Evangelische Gemeinde in Siegen (1929:12,000 members in the whole of Germany) but joined the Holstenwall Fellowship in Hamburg (3,200 members) in 1919.

Here he worked alongside Friedrich Heitmüller, another well-known speaker in evangelical circles.[48] Soon, however, Nagel recognised that his life-task would be within the Evangelical Alliance. A gifted preacher, he was a favourite at the annual Blankenburg Conferences. He continually visited fellowships open to the ideas of the Alliance and spread his views in the *Evangelisches Allianzblatt*. He took over as editor from Otto Dreibholz in 1918 (the latter had edited the paper during the war). In 1926, the year he became Chairman of the Evangelical Alliance (he had been Deputy Chairman since 1924), the *Allianzblatt* became the medium giving official expression to the views of the Alliance. As such, an analysis of its articles touching upon the socio-political changes in Germany in the 1930s – the bulk of the paper consisted of biblical interpretation and devotional studies – will reveal much about the views of Nagel and other ruling luminaries in the Alliance. Of especial importance are the commentaries of Bernhard Peters, writing from Worms, whose views and analysis were in complete agreement with those of his editor.[49]

Nagel believed that 'everyone should work with us and help us to interpret the Scriptures' and to discover how 'God rules and governs the world'.[50] He believed that Christ would soon return and that, before that event, the Antichrist would appear. 'The coming of the Antichrist can only happen once the powers that keep order have crumbled'. This partly explains Nagel's conviction that society needed a strong government, morally sound and replete with powers to delay the Coming of the Antichrist (Romans 13,2; 2 Thessalonians 2,6ff). The Weimar Republic seemed to Nagel to be an instrument geared to undermine morality. 'The world is being flooded with ideas about democracy', he wrote. 'We believe and are completely convinced' that this 'is preparing the way for the Antichrist'.[51] He bemoaned the collapse of the monarchical system in Germany, which, he believed, had been divinely sanctioned to bring strict discipline, law and order to the country. He could see nothing positive or constructive in the new democratic system, only chaos. Bismarck remained his hero and Bismarck's authoritarian, anti-democratic policies the ideal way of governing Germany. 'The creative forces of the gospel train one to be objective and strictly unbiased. A Christian trained in the Scriptures will not be a party man, either in the political or in the religious sense', wrote Nagel in 1925.[52] Why then did he publicise his view that the Catholic Centre Party and the Social Democratic Party were agents of Satan? Why did the *Allianzblatt*, long before 1933, provide a forum for polemical attacks on the League of Nations and call for 'the end to the shame of a small professional army'? 'God does not want to create organisations spanning the world', Nagel taught in 1920. On the contrary, he wanted to prevent their creation.[53]

Nagel believed in the idea of 'nation' and opposed international political organisations. He loved his own country and was very concerned about its future; his reading of the Bible clearly shaped his political choices. Of course, the *Allianzblatt* took a patriotic line long before Nagel became editor. He merely continued the tradition. During the First World War readers were treated to inflamed articles on 'Albion's mean and dirty tricks' and were told that 'it has pleased God to plunge Germany into a terrible war'. Evangelicals were surprised that, in spite of 'a Christian revival and interest in religion throughout the nation in the first weeks of the war', the war was lost and 'our dear, God-fearing, peace-loving Kaiser' had been dethroned.[54] Yet such events did not lead editors to encourage deep theological thinking on the concepts of nation and war.

The links between pietism and nationalism had been growing for centuries. Pietism initially provided nationalism with an enthusiastic, emotional impulse; its eschatological perspective formed a mentality into which a reactionary, nationalist ideology could neatly fit.[55] The Church liked to see itself as politically neutral; it always voted, however, for the nationalist option. The *Evangelisches Allianzblatt* gave vocal expression to a Christianised conservative, anti-democratic, bourgeois ideology. This ideology was held to be biblical Christianity and very few Germans, at least until 1945, could even begin to think otherwise. Hitler seemed to be the answer to Nagel's prayer for authoritarian, military-style leadership. Once Hitler had total power, the *Allianzblatt*, according to the historian of the German Evangelical Alliance, remained silent on the evils perpetrated before their very eyes to a degree far exceeding other Church newspapers.[56]

The war, which Nagel himself considered justified, put an end to the publication of the *Allianzblatt* in 1941 – a paper shortage was the official reason given for the prohibition of all Free Church newspapers the following year. Nagel died on 6 March 1944. Though nearly all his personal papers appear to have been lost, a number of books he wrote can still be found in German libraries. The contents of three are briefly summarised on the following pages. He also wrote a history of the German Evangelical Alliance called *Eine heilige christliche Kirche*, a work on the 'strong male aspects of Christianity' entitled *Über das Männlich-Starke im Christentum*, which was written for 'real men', and the self-explanatory *Revolution, Sozialismus und*

Bibel (1924). These works contain many references to the Scriptures, but also, perhaps surprisingly, many more quotes from secular works. Nagel clearly read a lot and was well-informed. Oliver Cromwell and Otto von Bismarck are the two statesmen he most respects and he quotes at length from their writings and speeches.

The two works published during the Third Reich are interesting not least because Nagel was encouraged by his Alliance colleagues to write them and to write them from the standpoint taken by the Evangelical Alliance. The works may be seen, then, as a collective attempt to 'throw light on a great subject [which] fitted in with the needs of the moment'.[57] It was apparently necessary to lay down official policy and it is perhaps this which lies behind the fact that many of the ideas which Nagel develops in his books are repeated *ad nauseam* in his numerous articles in the *Allianzblatt*. The earlier work tries to come to terms with socialism and a democratic state; the latter two with National Socialism and a totalitarian state.

Nagel wrote *Das biblische Urteil über die sozial-revolutionären Bewegungen der Gegenwart* (1920) because he believed the influence of Social Democracy in politics, the judicial system and the economy had become predominant: the 'whole moral and religious attitude of our nation is being largely determined by Social Democrats'.[58] He thus hopes to present 'the biblical view of present-day revolutionary movements'. In his first chapter ('Biblical Socialism'), Nagel claims that nothing in history compares with Christianity in bringing about fruitful social changes in spite of the fact that biblical Christianity rejects any violent change of social or economic relations (13). Slavery was gradually overcome through the influence of Christian forces because Christianity 'naturally sets its face against serfdom and human bondage, against tyranny and despotism of every kind' (11). God's grace had achieved this, not violent revolutions (10). In fact, rebellion against those in authority is rebellion against God's order and therefore sinful (15). Obedience, as long as one's conscience is not being violated, is the correct biblical attitude; the poor, therefore, should suffer ill-treatment, Nagel says, referring to 1 Peter 2,21 (15-6). The Bible teaches the impossibility of bringing about major improvements in people's lots through external changes (16). Nowhere does the Bible support the view that social or political revolutions can do away with injustice (17). The Bible doesn't tell believers to make suggestions on reforming society; rather, it calls on them to love God (7). This is all-important because 'the present world is moving towards catastrophes, the end of the process being world destruction (*Weltuntergang*), not world transfiguration (*Weltverklärung*) by means of social and cultural advancement' (17).

The next two chapters are devoted to analysing the revolutionary ideas of his time. He starts by looking at the idea of equality. Differences in social class, profession and wealth are part of God's order. There is nothing anti-Christian about them (19), but sin and selfishness abound and cause injustice. 'It is an injustice when someone uses favourable circumstances in order to accumulate an immense fortune, unconcerned about the bitter poverty around him. It is an injustice when a master turns his slave into a mere tool, when an employer treats his worker as a mere machine, when the strong use their advantage to oppress and exploit the weak' (20). The Bible calls for resistance to such phenomena with 'means which are holy and divine' (20). Nagel nowhere illustrates what he has in mind here. His solution remains abstract:sin can only be overcome, the 'noble goals of communism' can only be achieved, not by hatred and violence, but by 'the love of God and the love of man' (31). All other means are 'unholy' (20). Social Democracy, Communism and Bolshevism are rooted in the philosophical materialism that emanated from France in the eighteenth century (21). This, he believes, is more dangerous than the materialism which often parades itself 'under the cloak of piety and in the name of Christianity'. Every person is a born materialist (25), but the materialism of Social Democrats is a dark force, demonic and ruthless. Their 'ferocious hatred of God and Christ' is openly preached (24-8). No group of people is more awfully deceived by 'wild ideas and illusions' than socialists and communists (32). Evil will not cease once poverty is removed and people have houses to live in (32). In fact, poverty and hunger had often in German history proved to be a 'college of moral courage and excellency' (33). Of course, 'everything possible should be done to deal with certain social problems, like the housing shortages' (32), but wealth and prosperity have always been since the days of Rome a 'school of moral decay' (32). Christians should have nothing to do with a fairy-tale world of the future where all needs are met. Utopias deserve to be ridiculed (33). Then Nagel deals with the government's policies in Germany. Since 1918 censorship had been done away with, unleashing a 'flood of destruction'. 'Filth and licentiousness' had polluted the theatre, the cinema and publications as never before in German history (34). One of the first acts of the new government was to release numerous prisoners (36). He quotes Houston Stewart Chamberlain[59] at length to blame the Republic for 'lies, adultery, theft, assassinations, corruption, deception and laziness' (36-7):

> To give freedom to people who want to bury our Germanic ideals and freedoms would mean committing suicide. It would be better to live in a state where nothing, rather than everything was allowed. We should not idolise 'freedom' for that would mean granting legal protection to any act.

Nagel is willing to apportion a lot of the blame for the social revolutions of the time to 'the sins of capitalism and mammonism'(39). In fact, he calls capitalism the 'ultimate cause' of rebellion and interprets revolutions as a 'rod in the hand of God to remind society of its sins and to call it to repentence' (39). Social Democrats were only taking the practical godlessness of the ruling class seriously. 'The sins of the ruling classes' had brought social democracy into being. A care-free, selfish, ruthless, dishonest, profiteering ruling class was 'chiefly to blame' for what was happening in the world: they were reaping what they had sown (38).

He takes issue with those Christians who claimed one could, from a biblical point of view, support the social programmes introduced by socialists and communists in Europe, putting aside religious differences one may have with these groups. Yes, Nagel said, it was biblical and Christian for a government to do something to ease the burdens of the working class and to fight a ruthless plutocracy. Adam Smith's recommendation of *laissez faire, laissez aller* did not express the biblical view of the state's role in promoting good and fighting injustice. He quotes Luther who said that a tight rein should be kept on employers. The state could 'control and regulate wage problems' and protect workers from exploitation – all this, Nagel believes, could be biblically justified. But a communist 'controlled economy' infringes upon the rights of individuals, in spite of claims that people must be protected from injustice. Ironically, Nagel introduces Bismarck's social legislation into his argument as an exemplary approach to the social problem (40). Bismarck, however, treated welfare programmes 'like any other instrument of state power' and saw them merely as tools to preserve his own authoritarian power; he worried little about such matters as natural rights, freedoms of association and contract, or the due process of law. He brought in these progressive measures to appease the workers and, more importantly, to take revenge on his former allies, the Liberals.[60]

Nagel concludes that Christians 'do not approve of the way [the Weimar government] came to power. We do not approve of their methods of government, whose sad fruits are seen by all. We criticise it, but in all this we recognise it as placed in authority over us' (43). Christians had a duty to obey, 'whatever we may feel' about those in authority. The revolutionary movement, however, threatened to produce an even worse socialist state, for Scripture taught him that, in the future, a very centralised state (*Einheitsstaat*), an embodiment of anti-Christianity, would 'coerce and bind all its citizens with chains of iron' (41). Nagel could only perceive the political left as fulfilling that prophecy. When socialists moderated their criticisms of Christianity, this was seen to be only tactical (47). Nor does Nagel accept that the party programme of the SPD, which stated that religion was a private matter for socialists to decide for themselves, had abandoned atheism as an article of faith (48). All 'faithful and concerned friends of the German nation and Fatherland'(50), which had been 'robbed of true and genuine leadership'(50), should be alarmed, not least because 'there are many people, including even Christians' who do not clearly perceive the spirit behind the large social-democratic movements was Satan (54). Some Christians had begun to 'use language not far removed from that found in communist newspapers'; others even took part in communist demonstrations (55-7). Faithful believers were 'joining in the chorus of the deceived masses' and being 'led astray by calls for freedom, equality and brotherhood'. Genuine Christians were 'singing praises to the revolution' just because it had brought the eight-hour working day. Even Christian women were calling for the same rights as men.

Yet it is clear that the socialist ideals still attracted Nagel. If only German Social Democrats could be like their British comrades, he cries, many of whom were Christians and all of whom were patriotic, opening their meetings with a hymn and a prayer (51-2). Nagel at least felt the British Labour Party did owe more to Methodism than Marxism. Nagel detested a lack of patriotism in people, which he felt was a 'fruit of godlessness' (52). There were relations to one's ancestral people and fatherland which God wanted His people to foster. 'It isn't a sign of ethical progress when people in groups infiltrated by Jewish socialists throw away their loyalty to their own people in favour of an internationalist dream' (53). He refers here to the Socialists and Communists who were almost alone in the Weimar Republic in welcoming Jews into their ranks, as did the Russian revolutionary movements. Many Jews became prominent figures in the struggle for equality and international brotherhood. As a Bible-believing Christian, Nagel recognises he has a problem accepting parties which were internationalist in outlook. At the same time he cannot fully accept nationalism as a Christian ideal. 'We have warned often enough about exaggerating the idea of Fatherland'(53). 'Christianity is, after all, supranational and is not the Body of Christ a timeless, ultramundane organism, whose members are taken from all nations, whose members have equal value?' Nevertheless, 'a lack of patriotism should be equated with godlessness' (53). The *Volksgemeinschaft* had to be honoured and revered.

A second historical work on the the Biblical ideas on government *Der Staatsgedanke, biblisch und geschichtlich beleuchtet* (1934) was written to deal with 'questions and concerns'(5) that had arisen following the thorough transformation of the German state in 1933. A revolution had taken place, albeit a counter-revolution. Bolshevism finds only fleeting mention (19-20) perhaps because, as Nagel knew, all the Bolshevists were either in concentration camps or had emigrated. Nagel's focus is now on National Socialism rather than international socialism. The book also contains surveys of the 'heathen state of antiquity' (Chapter 3), the 'Religious State in its Fight against Dangerous Godlessness' (Chapter 5), and the systems set up by Roman Catholicism (Chapter 6). Nagel hoped to educate Christian readers for 'there were in Christian circles many who held that even studying subjects such as government or race was dangerous'(5). As in his earlier work on social revolutionaries, Nagel rejects the legacy of the French Revolution(19): the demand made by the Revolution for equality violated the God-given right to individuality.[61] This led on the one hand to an 'enslavement of the soul' and, on the other, to a 'tyranny which trod upon inalienable human rights' (20). According to the Bible, he says, it is wrong for a prince to declare '*l'état, c'est moi*' (as Louis XIV did) and it is equally wrong for a people to see itself as sovereign (6). His reservations towards the Weimar Republic are now spelled out. French thought and a liberal state had left behind 'nothing but a heap of ruins' (12). The 'authorities had in the post-war years allowed the moral bases of the state and nation to be undermined' and Christians had comforted themselves with the thought that 'the struggle had to be fought with spiritual weapons' (12). The root problem was a belief in the goodness of man (36). 'Our whole foreign policy in and after the war and, above all, our domestic and welfare policies were shaped by this illusory view of *man*: man is good and the nations are good'.

Looking back, Nagel sees Bismarck as a classic Christian statesman (40): limiting freedom whenever in the interests of the state (39), putting the state apparatus on a religious foundation (41), willing to use the sword (41), using his powers to outlaw blasphemy and godlessness (45) and to defend the state against the encroachment of Roman Catholicism (58). Nagel yearned for the good old days when everyone knew his place in the static hierarchy of an authoritarian, Protestant state able and willing to flex its muscles on the international stage. He wanted a monist state embodying one truth – something like the Body of Christ in armour.

A democracy with competing truths, tolerating different life-styles, remained anathema to him. 'In the biblical view of the state there is no talk of referenda and parliaments, of elections, parliamentary groups and parties. One cannot say that all these things, wherever they may be found, contradict Scripture. The Scriptures do not provide detailed instructions on the form of government permissible. But that these things are not indispensable elements of a biblical concept of government can be emphasised' (6). So he interprets Romans 13,1-7 as being a call for an absolute security state (*Ordnungs- und Machtstaat*) (6), even a 'total state' (10), to which 'not only the bodies, but also the souls and spirits' of people are submitted (11-12). Such a state cannot be content with just outward obedience, it has to command the soul's obedience: people's attitudes and opinions have to be brought into line too (15). Such a state would radically put an end to the 'false doctrines' of the French Revolution (19).

Let us turn to his treatment of Adolf Hitler's state. Nagel quotes at length from *Mein Kampf*, usually commenting that Hitler 'is right'. Hitler had 'good reasons' to emphasise that the Weimar form of government was a 'monstrosity' (6). The Chancellor had spoken 'splendidly' against the idea of a state disengaging itself from the people as a whole (9). On the other hand, a people cannot declare itself sovereign; its role is to solve the tasks assigned to it by Scripture (9). Christians in particular have to 'willingly and heartily accept the authorities given to them by God' and to intercede in prayer for them (12). Thanks are, in fact, now due to God for the 'complete freedom to preach and defend the gospel' which the new state had protected (17). Hitler's ideas of government were 'salutary' (19) and he had 'declared again and again that he wanted to build a nation on healthy and permanent foundations' (18). Moreover, Hitler had 'emphatically called for respect for the value of personality'; he had said that 'all means would be employed to encourage respect for the individual' because an individual person was 'irreplaceable' (25).

The Nazi call for a 'positive Christianity' was also welcome, Nagel explains, as long as this meant plumbing the depths of maleness, strength and triumphant pugnacity (26) – and at this point recommends to readers his own work on '*das Männlich-Starke im Christentum*'. Muscular Christianity would be a major influence in the new state even if, quite rightly, religion and government were carefully kept apart (32). Hitler, for example, used the name of God reverently and submitted himself to the Lord (32). In reconstructing Germany, he was acting 'from a deep sense of responsibility before God' (32). Hitler repeats again and again in his book phrases like 'I am responsible to God', 'I am fighting for the work of the Lord', 'This movement is a gift from God' (32); the chairman of the Evangelical Alliance, who knew *Mein Kampf* exceedingly well, clearly enjoys relating this to his readership. Nagel believes in Hitler's own personal faith in Christ the Saviour and in his integrity. Here was a statesman who even impressed on German believers, whatever their denomination, their duty 'not merely to talk about God's will, but to actually fulfil God's will and not let His Word be disgraced' (32).

Hitler warned of the danger of irreligion (35) and saw the fact that millions of Germans had been estranged from religion as a 'sign of decline' (36). The attacks on the dogmatic bases of the churches, like attacks on the legal foundation of the state, are deplored by the new Chancellor for they could lead, Hitler says, to anarchy and religious nihilism (36). The new German state required the values of Christianity. Nagel quotes the government's proclamation to the German people on 1 February 1933 in which the National Socialists publicly promised to protect and defend Christianity 'as the basis of all our morality' (35).

The reader of the constitution of the NSDAP, especially its 24th paragraph, which deals with Christianity, 'must be filled with surprise and joy', Nagel writes, 'to see that the National Socialist Programme at its core is identical with the gospel message'(13). Separation of the two kingdoms, church and state, respect for the Christian religion, protection and support of the Christian churches, in a word 'doing what the founder of the Christian religion advised: Give to Caesar what is due to Caesar, and to God what is due to God' (13). Nor do evangelicals disregard the 'concern to preserve those prime racial features which have cultural significance'. 'We do not deny the educational value of keeping one's race pure' even though this will not conquer the 'swine' (Hitler) in the heart of each man (62). The Nazi Programme was full of Christian realism, devoid of the deceptive lies and illusions (63) that had characterised the Weimar Republic. The fellowships of Christians were fighting the 'same kind of struggle' against evil, with different weapons, but with the 'same goal' (64) as National Socialism. 'Paul and Luther, Prince Bismarck and Adolf Hitler stand shoulder to shoulder'[62] in this struggle to bring 'salvation to the German people, the State and Christendom' (64).

In his book *Deutschland vor der Christusfrage* (1935), Nagel returns to the 'unbiblical' doctrines of political liberalism and Marxism which, he said, 'denied the importance of nation and Fatherland' and were the essential causes of the 'enormous tragedy of the German collapse' in 1918 (10). A new danger had now appeared, threatening Germany's spiritual substance: the neo-paganism of Germanic religion (11) which denied the sinfulness of man's nature (13). The newspaper of the German Faith Movement, *Reichswart*, was calling for a Germany free from the influence of Christianity (16). Attacks were being made on the Gospels which, it was claimed, had been 'spoiled and poisoned by Jews' (23).

People passionately opposed to Christianity were saying that Jesus, as an Aryan, had struggled against Jewry (23). Nagel responds by emphasising the Jewishness of Jesus and warning that destruction, not well-being, would result from elevating the concepts of *race* and *nation* to the status of articles of faith in society: 'an exaggerated consciousness of one's race and pride in one's nation do not protect society from decadence, but prepare the way for it' (24). He turns the argument of the Faith Movement around by claiming it was actually 'opening the door to the Jewish spirit' rather than combatting it, for the spirit of Jewry was essentially 'a spirit of legalism, pride in ancestry and fleshly security'. The spirit of the Faith Movement rejects Christ as the heaven-sent saviour of the world. 'Behind the racial theory in its naturalistic form there is the same materialistic Jewish spirit which, during the era of Marxism, led our people to the edge of destruction'(25). The racial enthusiasts did not realise they were the tools of Jewry. Nagel nowhere sees a link between the proponents of a new religion of race and the NSDAP. Alfred Rosenberg (in his *The Myth of the Twentieth Century*) and the whole German Faith Movement follow goals, Nagel writes, which are diametrically opposed to those set by the Führer and his National Socialist Party. Party members, as party members, were not allowed to spread the propaganda of a particular religion or church; nor does the government have a religious role to play in bringing about reforms, even if the government and the Church shared common interests (44-51). Once again, he thanks God for such a God-fearing head of state (46) and quotes from Hitler's prayer on National Work Day: 'Lord, we will not leave you! Please bless our struggle for freedom and bless the German nation and our Fatherland'.

In *Mein Kampf* Hitler, Nagel continues, had clearly warned about 'religious arguments' and saw the proponents of a Germanic religion as 'worse enemies than the most internationally minded communist' (51). Nagel hopes

Church and State will continue to be kept apart, for a Germanic Church in the Rosenberg sense would only divide the German people. He quotes Hitler's deputy, Rudolf Hess, who had on 15 May 1935 emphasised that the National Socialist government would remain religiously neutral (57). Only neutrality would ensure the continuing success and growing strength of Germany at home and abroad (50). He and his fellow journalists were 'thankful for all the success' achieved so far by the new government. It had done much to save a nation which had been, in their thinking, close to destruction. Hitler was certainly pointing Germany in the right direction and 'one could fill many pages' with the wonderfully relevant moral advice offered by Hitler in *Mein Kampf* (79). According to the leader of the Alliance, Hitler lived out what he preached: he ate no meat, drank no alcohol, smoked no tabacco and was no fornicator. Rumours like the one about Hitler always carrying a well-read New Testament around with him spread like wild-fire in evangelical circles. Here was the man to lead Germany forward. Nagel expresses these hopes by quoting Thomas Carlyle's avowed faith in Germany's future. 'From ancient times Germany has been the most peace-loving, the most pious, and the strongest of nations', Carlyle is quoted as saying. Germany was 'the nation commanding most respect'. 'Germany should be President of Europe and will, to all appearances, be entrusted in the future with that office for five hundred years' (79).

To summarise Nagel's thought: he was in every sense a reactionary, reacting like many bourgeois Germans to the defeat in the war, to the new 'un-German' system of parliamentary government, to mass unemployment and the increasingly radical stance of working-class people. The abyss of a country run by Communists drove him into the arms of a man whose work, *Mein Kampf*, suggested a deep trust in the Providence of Almighty God. Hitler's own disciplined life seemed a model to all young people. Hitler's desire for a clearer separation of Church and State accorded well with Nagel's independent evangelical viewpoint. Hitler's anti-semitism was shared by Nagel and the left-wing political parties were seen as corrupted by the Jewish spirit. Germania had to throw off the malignant French spirit too and seek to be true to her real self. Nagel had looked forward to the appearance of a mighty leader who would put an end to the moral corruption and irreligion that seemed to characterise the free capitalistic system. A radical overhaul had been needed in the affairs of state. Germany had been shown disrespect for far too long. Hitler was the fulfilment of his dreams and the embodiment of all his hopes. The *Allianzblatt* was used to persuade the evangelical community that Hitler meant freedom from Communism, peace through strength at home and abroad, a new moral beginning. For evangelicals, particularly in the Free Church tradition, National Socialist Germany did not entail a precarious belonging, but rather a state where they found security and refound a sense of pride in their nation. God's amazing grace had placed their feet on what they thought was solid rock. The fruits of economic, political and social freedom had proved too bitter to their taste. Nagel was willing to give the Catholic corporal an opportunity to cut back the powers of political Catholicism. He hoped the uniformed politician would teach the country discipline. He sensed that the Braunau bachelor would have no truck with the promiscuity that, in his view, undermined the Weimar system. In this, and in other areas, Nagel's optimism proved correct. Hitler did seem to be the man to take evangelical concerns seriously.

Notes

1. E.G. Rüppel (1969, 40-43).
2. E.G. Rüppel (1969, 27, 42).
3. G. Opitz (1969, 251-252).
4. E.G. Rüppel (1969, 76ff); Günther van Norden (1979, 72-73). Also in EA 16.07.1933 (Nr.29), 458.
5. E.G. Rüppel (1969, 121).
6. Du, Herr, hast uns gerufen (1988, 40).
7. E.G. Rüppel (1969, 120ff).
8. E.G. Rüppel (1969, 148ff).
9. *Allgemeine Evangelisch-lutherische Kirchenzeitung*, Nr.51, 22.12.1933, 1198-1199.
10. E.G. Rüppel (1969, 223f).
11. E.G. Rüppel (1969, 224).
12. E.G. Rüppel (1969, 213).
13. E.G. Rüppel (1969, 218-219).
14. Erich Beyreuther (1969, 94).
15. Du, Herr (1988, 33-34).
16. Du, Herr (1988, 33-34).
17. E.G. Rüppel (1969, 200ff).
18. E.G. Rüppel (1969, 202-204).
19. E.G. Rüppel (1969, 230-233).
20. E. Beyreuther (1969, 98).

21. EA 14.02.1932 (Nr 7), 110f.
22. On the nationalist *ressentiments* felt in Germany as a result of the Treaty, see K. Nowak (1988, 55-63,108-125,193-205). One tenth of the German population and one thirteenth of its territory had been taken away from Germany as a result of the treaty, W. Ebenstein (1945, 227).
23. EA 10.07.1932 (Nr 28), 441-442.
24. EA 24.07.1932 (Nr 30), 477-479.
25. EA 07.05.1933 (Nr 19), 299-300.
26. Karl Zehrer (1986, 91).
27. K. Zehrer (1986, 33).
28. K. Zehrer (1986, 41).
29. K. Zehrer (1986, 41)
30. K. Zehrer (1986, 109-110).
31. K. Zehrer (1986, 70).
32. K. Zehrer (1986, 67, 168). Zehrer notes that 67% of all Methodist pastors served as soldiers in the Wehrmacht.
33. K. Zehrer (1986, 74).
34. K. Zehrer (1986, 47).
35. K. Zehrer (1986, 140-141).
36. K. Zehrer (1986, 160).
37. K. Zehrer (1986, 49-50).
38. E. Beyreuther (1969, 99-106).
39. K. Zehrer (1986, 50-51).
40. E. Beyreuther (1969, 104).
41. G. Jordy (1986, 94,281); *Der Gärtner*, Nr 35, 27 August 1933; *Der Gärtner*, Nr 40, 1 October 1933.
42. K. Zehrer (1986, 49).
43. K. Zehrer (1986, 53).
44. E. Beyreuther (1969, 99).
45. K. Zehrer (1986, 64).
46. K. Zehrer (1986, 167-169).
47. K. Zehrer (1986, 77).
48. Heitmüller reacted in a typically evangelical manner to the National Socialist movement. His booklet *Um die Spitze des Entschlusses* (1932) contained criticisms of the Nazi racial theories, but tracts he wrote in 1933 (*Das deutsche Volk vor Gott* and *Die nationalsozialistische Revolution und ihre Vollendung*) show a change of mind and, above all, his belief that God had raised up Adolf Hitler to lead Germany back to Himself and to the basics of morality. Later, in April 1934, he took his *Verein für Gemeinschaftspflege und*

Evangelisation im Gebiet Unterelbe, part of the Gnadau network, out of the Reich Protestant Church and away from the GDC, after the new national Church had adopted a unified, hierarchical and very centralised structure together with the Aryan paragraphs. While rejecting such a structure for the Church, he nevertheless 'welcomed heartily the totalitarian powers of the state'. After the war he quite wrongly claimed in his autobiography, *Aus Vierzig Jahren Dienst am Evangelium* (1950), that he had been a persecuted victim of National Socialism. E. Beyreuther (1969, 97-98,107); E.G. Rüppel (1969, 39,167,170); K. Zehrer (1986, 99).

49. E. Beyreuther (1969, 89). I have been unable to find out anything about the fate of Peters. He was a prolific writer, a forerunner of the present-day German evangelical specialising in the prophecies surrounding the end-times, Klaus Gerth. Peters' books include *Germanenglaube. Wohin des Weges, Germane?*; *Das Schicksal Deutschlands. Ein Blick in die Gegenwart und Zukunft der Völkerpolitik*; *Die Völker am Scheideweg. Blicke in die Gegenwart und Zukunft Europas*; *Wir fordern Arbeit und Brot! Ein Warnruf an die Völker und ihre Führer*; *Arier und Jude. Ein Beitrag zur Judenfrage und ihrer Lösung*; *Deutschlandwende!Europawende!Weltwende! Durchblick durch die Völkerwelt der Gegenwart*. All the above were published by the Verlag Missions-Buchhandlung, Worms a.Rh. in the period 1930-1934. The Karl Bäuerle Verlagsbuchhandlung, Karlsruhe i.Br. published Peters' *Im Umbruch der Zeit. Ein Blick in die Völkerpolitik* in 1934. Many of the ideas contained in these books were also spread through the pages of the *Allianzblatt*.

50. E. Beyreuther (1969, 88).
51. E. Beyreuther (1969, 89).
52. EA, 1920, 18, quoted by E. Beyreuther (1969, 91).
53. E. Beyreuther (1969, 92).
54. E. Beyreuther (1969, 86).
55. H. Lehmann (1982); K.S. Pinson (1934).
57. G. Nagel (1934, 51); G. Nagel (1935, 49).
58. It was true that Socialists had achieved a position of power. Friedrich Ebert, a socialist, was President at the time Nagel wrote his book. But the Socialists' share of the vote declined enormously during the Weimar Republic, from 46% in 1919 to 20.4% in the free election in November 1932.
59. On H.S. Chamberlain (1855-1927) see David Thomson (1968, 437). In EA 13.08.1933 (Nr 33), 524, Nagel discusses the influence of Thomas Carlyle on German events.
60. W. Ebenstein (1945, 59). In the economic field, too, Bismarck foreshadowed Hitler. The measures introduced between 1881 and 1889 were in accord with Bismarck's ideal of a 'patriarchal and omnipresent state'. He asked the Reichstag to 'heal social evils by means of legislation based on the moral foundation of Christianity'. See S.H. Steinberg (1944,

235). Bismarck referred to himself as *God's soldier,* which, in Nagel's opinion, was the calling of a statesman. G. Nagel (1934,41-2).
61. One should not forget that the emancipation of Jews, peasants and the middle class in Germany was wrought by Napoleon after his army had defeated the 360 German states and weakened the position of German feudalism.
62. Nagel frequently compares Bismarck and Hitler, in particular in their Christian beliefs, their respect for religious institutions, their 'struggle against Marxism' and their declaration of a state of emergency requiring special laws. G. Nagel (1935, 7,14,43-4). On G.F. Nagel's discussion of Cromwell's leadership and Cromwell's statement that 'England is *the* nation blessed by God' (his italics), G. Nagel (1935, 68-77). Nagel recommends to all Christians a deep study of the Protector's life and work because 'Cromwell is the first who made the relationship between Christianity and the nation's life the foundation of his political activities and so donated to the peoples of the world a permanent blessing' (1935,73). The EA 02.07.1933, 430 noted that 'God and Nation are correlatives, they are interrelated. We have learnt that from Oliver Cromwell, with whom Adolf Hitler has been compared'.

Chapter Three

Initial Responses to National Socialism

The foundations of the Third Reich were laid in the period 1933-35. Most of what followed was the natural, inevitable consequence of decisions taken in the early period of the national revolution. This is true, too, of the Evangelical Alliance. The fundamental strategic decisions taken by the leaders of the Alliance in the formative years of Hitler's movement and especially in 1933 remained vitally important, valid and 'official' policy throughout the decade.

In the twenty-first issue of 1933, the forty-third year of the newspaper's existence, the editor, G.F. Nagel, explained that there was a 'need to shine a biblical light on contemporary events', though, he added, it would be deplorable if the Christian press would shift its emphasis from discussing eternal matters to analysing current afffairs.[1] The editor's goal, as 'one who by the Lord's mercy is trustworthy', was to portray political, social and economic events as God saw them, *sub specie aeternitatis*.[2]

The treatment of political subjects in the column entitled *Contemporary Issues* become relatively infrequent after 1936. Bernhard Peters, who contributed regularly in the early 1930s, faced a prohibition on discussing political issues and current affairs in Christian weeklies after 1936. The *Allianzblatt* announced the ban to its readers on 30 August 1935, 30 November 1935 and 15 April 1936. The government justified the regulations with a need to keep politics out of the domain of the Church. Nagel justified the ban with a reference to Romans 8,28, saying that Christian papers had all too frequently become infatuated with temporal issues that their columns had become closed to eternal matters. He lamented the fact that for many readers the sections in the Christian press dealing with social and political matters had become all-absorbing. Not a few readers, he said, would have been willing to forego the exegesis but not the 'politicising essays'. Christians should be grateful, he added, that the government was calling the Christian press back to its original and essential task of providing spiritual, upbuilding articles on Biblical matters.

One of the interesting features of the *Allianzblatt* was this cross-denominational fertilising process; the organ of the Confessing Church as well as the papers of the German Christians and Germanic faith sects all found a place in the Alliance's paper. The ban on discussing politics, moreover, like the repeated attempts to ban discussions of the Church struggle in ecclesiastical periodicals, was not always adhered to. The *Allianzblatt* began to concentrate solely on inspirational, biblical studies once the Second World War had broken out. Its work was drastically curtailed between 1939 and 1941 due to the impact of the war. On 15 October 1939 (number 19/20) it informed readers that 'necessary measures' had forced the paper to cease publication; it was able to reapear on 1 January 1940, before finally succumbing to a paper shortage in war-torn Germany.

In the 1932 debate on National Socialism within the pages of the *Allianzblatt*, Nagel overtly strove to remain supra-partisan, above the party conflict, strictly objective, but as he was wont to say: 'this non-partisan stance does not mean staying neutral in the face of anti-God and anti-Christ doctrines and activities'.[3] Letters from readers were received which expressed their thanks to him for voicing strong patriotic sentiments.[4] The 'Marxist poison' in the body politic had led in the 1920s to nationalist opinions being despised, Nagel wrote, adding that his views at that time had 'aroused suspicions that he was a right-winger'. Clearly he was, and in 1932 the right was sensing victory. Nagel was particularly annoyed that there were still members of Christian fellowships who voted for socialist and communist parties.[5] He quotes Pastor Albert Schmidt, who took offence at a report in which a CSVD official had denied that real Christians could either vote for or join the National Socialist party. The pastor insisted that 'people who seriously want to live as Christians can be found in all parties'. Nagel responded that this was generally true. He refused to accept, however, that 'those parties which called upon people to abandon God and their Fatherland' could possibly command the support of evangelicals.[6] Nagel certainly believed that genuine Christians could be found in the various nationalist parties.[7] He also accepted that the individual Christian should be left to decide for himself or herself[8] which party to vote for. The *Allianzblatt* refused to make recommendations to avoid politicising the fellowships.[9] It avoided taking an unequivocal position on whether Christians should vote for the National Socialists or not. Readers were apparently divided on the issue. Even those standing firmly in the faith, people who loved God and their Fatherland, who stood up for morality, law and order, were unsure. The Brethren weekly, *Die Tenne*, for example noted in its tenth issue in 1932 that political differences were creating tensions within its assemblies. It felt, however, that most of the younger members and many of the older members were turning to the NSDAP.[10]

For evangelicals in 1932 the choice seemed to be between the CSVD and the National Socialists. The discussion in the *Allianzblatt*, started by an article written in January by Nagel on 'National Socialism and Christian Faith', lasted throughout the year.[11] National Socialism was fighting against forces which boded ill for German culture, the German nation and the country itself. 'Every Christian in Germany should rejoice that National Socialism wants to keep law and order'. Its healthy nationalism was preferable to a 'godless internationalism'. Only people who wore blinkers would be unable to see that this was something to be glad about. He did not know, he said, what could be said *against* the forces of law and order embodied in the National Socialist movement. Its position on religion was central to any evangelical judgement and Nagel quotes Article 24 of the Party Programme of 1920 (which was declared unalterable by Hitler in 1926). How could Christians not be pleased with the NSDAP's commitment to freedom for all religious confessions in the state

> soweit sie nicht dessen Bestand gefährden oder gegen das Sittlichkeits- oder Moralgefühl der germanischen Rasse verstossen. Die Partei als solche vertritt den Standpunkt eines positiven Christentums, ohne sich konfessionell an ein bestimmtes Bekenntnis zu binden. Sie bekämpft den jüdisch-materialistischen Geist in uns und ausser uns und ist überzeugt, dass eine dauernde Genesung unseres Volkes nur erfolgen kann von innen heraus auf der Grundlage: 'Gemeinnutz vor Eigennutz'.

> provided they do not endanger its existence or offend the German race's sense of decency and morality. The Party as such stands for a positive Christianity, without binding itself denominationally to a particular confession. It fights against the Jewish-materialistic spirit in us and outside us and is convinced that any lasting recovery of our people must be based on the principle: the welfare of the community comes before that of the individual.

Nagel wonders if theologians or even perhaps Bible-believing Christians had helped to write the programme, for it sounded perfect. He quotes from *Mein Kampf* Hitler's passionate wish to help his people to 'fulfil the mission that the Creator of the universe had given to it'. Professor Strathmann, an official of the CSVD, is also quoted as saying that some things the National Socialists wanted to achieve were 'thoroughly acceptable'. It was also noble that 'lies are more detestable and shameful to them than prison'. Nagel notes that Germany needed people like them, standing up for 'truth, discipline and purity' and combatting 'filth and shameful deeds'. All were welcome who were willing to fight to 'purify the German atmosphere of all poisonous gases'.

Nevertheless, Nagel still had 'very serious concerns' about the 'hope-filled movement, in which good and evil are both fomenting'.[12] What, for example, did 'the moral feelings of the German race' mean? All patriots welcomed the 'strong moral aspects' of the movement, but why did it 'have to clothe itself with a new ideology?' Pastor Bruns of the CSVD applauded the willingness of the Nazis to make sacrifices and their emphasis on the God-given characteristics of the German people, but he felt they talked too little about human sin and guilt and were in danger of idolising their race and its physical features and of just 'using God as a means to an end'.[13] Other CSVD officials denied that National Socialists had a right to call themselves Christians.[14] Pastor Veidt felt 'voting for Hitler would mean in every respect a leap into the dark, because neither the National Socialists nor their German Workers Party nor their leaders have as yet shown that they are capable of governing'.[15] Professor Dr Karl Müller argued that there were enormous elements of truth in National Socialism. At heart, it contained basically sound ideas that had brought about its success. But their 'hybris and hatred' were characteristics which he found too intense.[16]

The *Allianzblatt* welcomed the fact that the Nazis had engaged the masses in a national struggle to renew the German state. This was seen to be a wonderful achievement, not a catastrophe. The dictatorial features of the movement were not, to use the words of the paper, 'the end of the world'.[17] In July the editors of the *Allianzblatt* felt it necessary to give credence to their assertion that their paper strove to be politically neutral. An article entitled 'Gaffes' was, they said, an example of 'being unbiased in the treatment of holy and unholy incidents'.[18] It was basically a criticism of an obituary notice which had appeared in the National Socialist paper, *Völkischer Beobachter*. A Nazi was said to have died 'a strong believer in Adolf Hitler and Germany's resurrection'. This obituary seemed to confirm critics' observations that such language betrayed an unforgiveable lack of tact and religious propriety. Paradoxically, the *Allianzblatt* called on all pastors who 'profess faith in National Socialism' to offer the stiffest resistance to such a distortion of Christian customs and to press the relevant Party organisations to put an end to such these blunders. The Nazi Party, which was portrayed by the paper as 'admirably organised' and full of 'character', needed to show a greater discipline and respect for religious traditions.

These are probably the strongest words the editorial staff of the *Allianzblatt* found before 1933 for the National Socialist German Workers Party. After 1933, much of the religious verbiage used by Hitler to describe his mission in Germany, which here causes offence, is in fact adopted by the *Allianzblatt*. This is probably due not least to the profound knowledge Nagel had of *Mein Kampf* and Hitler's speeches. On the other hand, any 'blunders' made after Hitler had been given absolute power by freely elected parliamentarians were explained away as incidents Hitler would never have sanctioned or even tolerated *if* he had known about them (one assumed he did not). Almost invariably 'youth' or 'indiscipline' on the part of 'over-enthusiastic' National Socialists are given the blame for gaffes. The leaders of evangelicalism had unbounded faith in the validity of statements made in *Mein Kampf*, public pronouncements made by Hitler and his deputy, and the constitution of the NSDAP.

On top of this, one made frequent reference to a pamphlet written by Professor J. Stark, 'National Socialism and the Catholic Church', which Hitler had personally checked three times and sanctioned as an authoritative statement of his government's policy on religious affairs. Professor Stark himself wrote to Christians on behalf of Hitler to calm those worried by statements attacking their religion. Christians, especially those who 'are adherents of the [National Socialist] movement', contacted Party headquarters about such incidents. August Grünweller, head of an evangelical organisation, wrote to Hitler personally and told him that 'true Christians' were concerned about pronouncements made by 'notable representatives of the National Socialist movement attacking biblical Christianity and biblical revelation'. How could this be in a Party proud of its iron discipline, unity and obedience to the will of its leader? Professor Stark replied to the letter, saying that the statements in question had been made without the consent of the Party leadership. The real situation was as Grünweller 'wished it to be'. The 'exaggerations' and 'stupidities' of a relatively young political movement should not be taken too seriously.[19] Nagel called for more clarity in NSDAP pronouncements. 'Unnecessary differences of opinion' which only 'confused' people and strengthened 'the forces hostile to God and the Fatherland' needed to be put behind them. The success of the Party surely depended on 'whether it wants to remain exclusively a patriotic movement or whether it wants to become in some way a church as well'.[20] Such a transformation of what was perceived to be a 'decent' party would have been insupportable. Initially, however, the editors could point to factors which did win their support.

At the beginning of 1932 Nagel emphasised that the question of who should be 'Führer' was of decisive importance for Germany – not whether the country needed a dictator, but who should be that man. The great spectre of a Bolshevik take-over of central Europe haunted the pages of the *Allianzblatt*. Brüning seemed to be too weak to respond effectively to the threat of national dissolution and class war. They recognised that Hitler's 'electrifying force' and his excellent organisational talents had captured the minds of many Germans. The middle classes were gaining confidence in him. There could be no doubt that Hitler was, in their view, a 'supremely important factor' in German politics. Yet Hitler seemed to be a passing symptom of the stressful times in which they lived. They did not believe that National Socialism could take firm root in German soil as fascism had done in Italy, for the last two years had produced stiff resistance to Hitler from the 'international Jewish finance capitalists'.[21]

Nor was Pastor Lüdecke (Finkenwalde) of the Gnadau Association sure that the movement would last and achieve its goals. He was, however, thankful for the fact that National Socialism had made a breach in the 'Marxist and materialistic' working masses.[22] Another was grateful that the NSDAP had 'raised up a dam against the approaching Communist-Bolshevist flood and had preserved Germany from conditions like those in Russia'.[23] The unexpected and sudden growth of the National Socialist movement inspired hope that Germany could, after all, 'pull itself out of its present deep economic and moral plight'.[24]

The numerous political murders were due, in the eyes of the *Allianzblatt*, almost exclusively to 'Bolshevist attacks on Christian culture' at a time when the strong arm of government was sorely missing. In three weeks in June 1932 82 people were murdered in Prussia alone; in the first two weeks of July another 76 had been killed in street battles. And on 17 July 11,000 SA men who had been brought in from all over the region marched, under the protection of a police escort, into the working-class citadel of Altona, and unleashed the Altona Bloody Sunday massacre, in which 19 people were killed and 285 seriously injured. According to the *Allianzblatt* this had been an 'attack on the state' organised and carried out by Communists. 'Communists opened fire on the police and National Socialists'.[25] The paper calculated that beween 1 June and 20 July 1932 322 political street fights had taken place; in only 75 cases, according to its calculations, had National Socialists started the fighting. It quoted an official declaration on the reasons for this wave of violence and murder which said it was 'being incited on the one hand by Communism, on the other by a number of young SA men who are not obeying their leaders'.[26] An evangelical double standard was developing, as it had been in May when the paper criticised Brüning's government for banning the SA. This move, it said, was irrational and would only increase tensions in the country. It was obvious that the government had 'given in to the pressure of the Social Democrats and the Catholic Centre Party'. These '400,000 young Germans' were preventing the 'slide of German culture into anti-Christianity'. The *Allianzblatt* believed the government was duty-bound to handle the nationalist military organisations with care, especially in view of the 'chains' the Versailles Treaty had placed on Germany. These groups kept the spirit of active service and camaraderie alive and should not be forced into a position of opposition to the government.[27] The paper rejoiced when the ban on the SA was lifted. It was particularly grateful that the mere sight of Storm Troopers marching through the streets again, in uniform, had put Communists to flight and seemed to vouchsafe not only an end to the 'murderous struggle' against the German nation[28] but also further electoral victories for the NSDAP.[29] The Altona blood-bath increased the fears of the middle class and their need for security, which was, of course, what the Nazis had intended. The call for a 'strong man' to put an end to the fighting became even louder in the *Allianzblatt*. When the Reich Chancellor proclaimed a state of emergency in Berlin and Brandenburg and had Social Democratic civil servants as well as the SPD Interior Minister arrested (even though he had been democratically elected and chosen by his party) on the grounds that he had shown favour to the Communists, this move was greeted with a sigh of relief as being 'long overdue'. No government should include officials or employ civil servants, the paper opined, who openly supported the Godless Movement[30] and tolerated attacks on confirmation celebrations. Nor could criticism of the behaviour of the German Army in the World War be tolerated. Those 'unworthy civil servants' deserved to be removed from their posts.[31]

When the Godless Movement (that is, the International Proletarian Freethinkers' Association) was forced by the Reich President to close all its offices in Germany in May 1932, Bernhard Peters commented in the *Allianzblatt*: 'About time too!'[32] In his opinion freedom did *not* mean freedom to think differently, as Rosa Luxemburg had suggested. Much like their President, Hindenburg, whom they greatly admired and saw as their brother in Christ, the editors of the *Allianzblatt* were inveterately opposed to a republic granting freedoms to unthinking masses of people who were led by 'blind instincts and slogans', in fact 'incapable of rational thought'.[33] Such was the anti-working class bigotry of evangelical spokesmen. Those teeming masses needed, in their view, the protection and guidance of strong Christian men. After the NSDAP lost two million votes in the September 1932 elections (their share of the vote dropped from 37% to 33%) the *Allianzblatt* worriedly spoke of the 'urgent necessity' of forming an 'authoritarian government'. Hindenburg, Chancellor Papen and Hitler all 'stood out head and shoulders above the average person in terms of having a dignified, worthy character and in their great love for the German people'. The hand of the Lord, an act of Providence, was seen in their timely presence. A new form of Reich was called for. They appealed to God to provide them with the 'gracious gift' of an 'authoritarian' government'[34] and a 'strong omnipotent state'.[35]

In May 1933 the *Allianzblatt* looked back over the tumultuous events of the previous six months in an article written by Bernhard Peters entitled 'Where do we stand'.[36] He recalled all the failed attempts of 'multi-party coalition governments' to implement get-tough policies. They had, in fact, prevented a solution being found for Germany's ills and intensified the 'fragmentation and dissipation of the nation's powers'. He also reminded readers how the *Allianzblatt* had, years previously, emphasised that salvation would only come from 'a great leader whom God would send' at the right time. There had seemed no hope of escaping the danger of Bolshevism. Wide sections of the middle classes had become despondent and the victims of cultural Bolshevism. Within the Catholic Centre Party more and more people had talked of the superiority of Eastern European collectivism over Western European capitalism. In 1932 a state of 'latent civil war' had developed. Parliamentary government was proving incapable of quenching fears and closing the fissures in the German party system, just as capitalism was not creating the necessary jobs. The Weimar system had created a widespread feeling of weariness and indifference throughout the Reich. The new year, 1933, however, had brought a change of great moment. When Adolf Hitler was entrusted with the office of Reich Chancellor on 30 January, an epoch of German decline finally came to an end, he wrote, and a period of national unity began. Hitler was 'the man whom God gave to the German people' to unite them. To withstand the spiritual forces controlling the West and the East Peters believed, however, that there remained only the choice between falling prey to Bolshevism or marching with Hitler towards national socialism. The German nation had to return to its real character. Foreign infiltration and influence in Germany would make Europe ripe for the final anti-Christian world empire; Hitler's resistance to this development meant delaying that final epoch in European history. Hitler had been called by God. He would herald a new age for those suffering under Communist rule and he would show those peoples where peace, work and bread were to be found. He had 'wonderfully' dealt with Bolshevism. Adolf Hitler's appearance in German history was 'simply wondrous', his rise to power 'mysterious', the first victory in the Reichstag election of 1930 'incredible'.[37] His success proved his divine calling. Hitler had 'broken the curse' which lay on Germany, he had banished foreign influences and ignited a new German idealism. Germany had once again become conscious of its mission among the peoples of this world. Faith in their rising fortunes was inspiring people. Germany might once again be strong and mighty, a bastion of peace in the centre of Europe. He had removed 'Marxism' from power in Prussia and Catholicism from power in the south. He alone could unite the country in a new Reich, in which his will would be the law. The union of the Protestant north and the Catholic south of Germany were also seen in an eschatological light as the divine plan to 'hold back the forces of destruction' and roll back the powers of the final Roman Empire, the ten-state European confederacy that would truly signify the end of history. It was indeed a 'period of grace'. Almighty God had heard the prayers of His children and had shown mercy to them.

Thus ended an attempt to understand religious, social and economic conflicts plaguing Germany in the 1920s and early 1930s. The *Allianzblatt* saw in all these struggles an eschatological conflict of vaste proportions. Hitler seemed to be a second King David, almost a Christ-like figure, a genius who alone seemed able to forge the competing groups in society into one harmonious whole. His movement was seen as the guarantor of peace on the streets of Germany and a source of strength in the face of what was perceived to be the evil empire of Soviet Communism. Books on the persecution of Christians in the Soviet Union, advertised in the *Allianzblatt*, were for decades part of the staple diet of evangelicals in Germany and indeed throughout the world. Their concerns about the activities of the Freethinkers Association and socio-cultural developments during the Weimar Republic have to be seen against this backdrop. Real fears of where freedoms could lead the nation led many to cling to a movement exuding confidence in their own strength and ability to swing the ship of state back to its traditional moorings.

By May 1933 the Nazi government had implemented policies close to the heart of evangelicals of all denominational loyalties: they began to count the blessings from heaven. One prime issue was the resurgent faith in Germany's ability to deal thoroughly and efficiently with social problems. Bernhard Peters wrote in June 1933 on 'Germany's Divine Mission'.[38] Starting from the premise that God had made all the nations, Peters referred his readers to the 'special task' and *'glorious vocation' of the German nation. Germany* was called to teach the world the 'great thoughts of God'. That special anointing had left the nation and a 'strange spirit' had taken control during the period of infidelity that now seemed over. Now had arrived a time of inner renewal to coincide with the great national uprising of 1933. That 'strange spirit' had been banished and the new Chancellor, Hitler, had called on the German people to 'renew itself by the spirit of Christ'. Hitler, Peters noted, had been called a 'man of prayer'. Such a man was required at such a crossroads in the nation's history. For only action rooted in prayer would be of any lasting benefit.

Peters picked up the same theme again in an article in March 1934 on 'Rosenberg on Ideology and Church'. The *Allianzblatt* repeatedly took issue with Alfred Rosenberg's religious views (as opposed to his politics) throughout the period. He was generally perceived to be a maverick within the National Socialist leadership. Peters, too, believed that the attempt to do away with racial categories was a Marxist plot. Races and nations were divine creations, each called to make a specific contribution to human development. The German race, too, had to live up to its calling to be a channel of blessing to the peoples of the world. He agreed with Rosenberg that all religious quarrels were counter-productive. Germany needed religious peace together with a revival of 'the pious element of the German soul'. Unbelief and impiety were declared to be alien to true German ways, an import from 'Latin countries'. Germany had a religious vocation to guard piety and the Christian faith, and it had a worldly vocation to help preserve peace among the nations. 'May this time of national renewal', Peters concluded, 'be a period of which later generations will say: Faith, fidelity and justice were reborn at that time and God blessed the German people and set it as a blessing on earth'.[39]

In a book he wrote in 1933 Peters went one step further. He claimed that God would use Germany to bring about peace and justice among all nations, for 'only the German people is still capable of being the bearer of blessings in one final period of grace'.[40] These blessings included the new socio-political system. He wrote on 28 February 1934 that Germany had the job of convincing the nations that its new political and economic structures best accorded with the welfare of the peoples. It had to show the world that a higher form of justice (*die bessere Gerechtigkeit*) was to be found in the social institutions and national community which had been freed from parliaments and parties. He believed the new Reich would exert a mighty attractive pull over nations.[41] Thus would Germany be a light to the world, a model to be imitated. The homeland of the Reformation would once again lead the way out of a world of darkness, political chaos and corruption. The hope of Thomas Carlyle would become a reality.

Evangelical interpretation of biblical prophecies seemed to suggest that the end was nigh. 'The anti-Christian epoch which began with the French Revolution' had temporarily come to a close.[42] Nationalism and fascism were interpreted as a return to the rule of Biblical law.[43] Paradoxically, it was also a period of grace, brought in by a leader who could inspire them with 'the saving idea'.[44] Nothing else could prevent the nations from falling prey to Bolshevism and eventually to the 'ten-state federation [prophesied] for the end-times'.[45] This eschatological idea had been discussed by Bible-believing Christians for centuries and the issue was topical in the inter-war period. 'Revelation tells us that the Roman Empire is to reappear', the paper stated.[46] The rise of the fascists in Italy was a clear sign from above, not least because one believed, even before Hitler's ascension to power, that 'links with Germany would be tightened again'. In December 1932 the *Allianzblatt* referred readers to the fact that according to the prophetic Word, at least the south and west of Germany would belong to the 'leg' of the future Roman Empire and, in its view, it was probable that fascism would be victorious in Western Europe.[47] The rape and annexation of Abyssinia by the Italian army and Mussolini's proclamations of a new Roman Empire on 9 May 1936 were interpreted in the light of Daniel's prophecies (Daniel 2,32-33).[48] As events brought about by God they were not to be criticised. Anecdotes typical of millenarian tracts were recited on the pages of the *Allianzblatt*. The paper claimed that Mussolini knew all the prophecies about the restoration of the old Roman Empire and saw his own calling in the light of Biblical prophecy. It even alerted readers to the fact that Mussolini had set up a brass plaque in Rome which showed the outlines of the old Roman Empire.[49]

Hitler was seen as a bulwark against what was considered to be a Russian-dominated northern confederacy (Gog of Magog, to which Gomer, i.e. Germany, or at least the parts north of the Rhine, would belong one day) and against the resurrected Roman Empire, which would perhaps be under Mussolini's leadership and to which, according to Scripture, parts of Germany would also belong.[50] Although trans-Atlantic evangelical thinking on the details of the last days was confused by events in Germany, they evidently felt safe as long as all parts of the country were united and allied with Rome. Hitler's Catholic background was never, even in the discussions of National Socialism prior to 1933, considered worthy of note. For only Hitler stood between them and the Bolshevist Antichrist.

Evangelicals, like other sections of the population, were simply overwhelmed that a turn-about in the fortunes of the German nation had seemingly been achieved. An article written by Nagel in the 7 May 1933 issue of the *Allianzblatt* discussed the reasons why Christians should be grateful and even get involved in the 'uprising'. In the distressing post-war years Christians too had suffered as they saw how governments which had 'never really been concerned about the true welfare of the German people' had come to power and exercised influence. The military 'collapse' was, in Nagel's opinion, not even perceived by the post-war government as a misfortune and disgrace; in fact it had been part of their overall plan. They had celebrated the military defeat as 'a total victory' for the German people. Now German militarism would be banished for ever, the politicians had said at the end of the war. They had talked of eternal peace and a republic guaranteeing everyone work and bread. Nagel could not stomach their assertion that Germany was guilty of starting the war and had militarily lost it. This assertion had in turn provided the basis for the system of 'reparations' which for Nagel had caused Germany's economic misery. The behaviour and attitude of the victor nations had been repellent. The 'curse of the dictated peace treaty' had to be broken. Quoting from the memoirs of Prince Bülow, Nagel says no defeated nation had ever been treated in so criminal a fashion as the German people after 1918. He rejoiced that 'accounts had been settled' with those who had negotiated such an iniquitous deal. He specifically refers to the Social Democrats who had deserved the punishment the Nazi government had meted out to them, for they had always sought not merely to 'revolutionise the state' but to 'do away with the whole idea of government with all its legal, religious and moral foundations'. The National Socialist government promised to put an end to the systematic duplicity practiced by post-war politicians. Lies had hung like 'a cloud of poisonous gas over the affairs of state'. In particular, the lie about Germany's war-guilt had to be seen for what it was. The National Socialists had responded valiantly to this challenge.

What we have here is a classic statement from a man unable or unwilling to draw the 'correct' lessons from history. Bound by the prejudices of his class, garnished and protected by what he and his generation considered to be biblical Christianity, he had between 1914 and 1918 given unflinching support to the irresponsible imperialism exhibited by the ruling class. The military defeat did not lead to a period of self-examination, a period of mourning for the sins of the past, but to a search for scape-goats. Respect for those in uniform, respect for military discipline and hierarchy – for militarism as a way of life – had eaten deep into his mind. The *Dolchstosslegende*, the legend of an undefeated army being stabbed in the back by unpatriotic politicians back home, was the way in which Germany tried to accept the past. The generals (and Prince Bülow) who had blundered their way into the war and to defeat passed the buck on to the Social Democrats who had opposed the annexionist war aims and advocated a negotiated peace based on mutual understanding.

This solution, as the election results showed, was not unpopular. As S.H. Steinberg argued, neither the bogey of Bolshevism nor the agitation against the 'dictated peace' seized the whole nation; it was only the middle classes which found in them a convenient outlet for their habitual inferiority complex.[51] Nor did these classes repent at the end of the war; their actions and beliefs were not even recognised as wrong. A spiritual change failed to materialise. A political revolution did not take place either, contrary to what Nagel believed. In fact, perhaps the very fact that a revolution did not take place in 1918 can be seen as a cause of the rise of the National Socialist movement; the military leaders and the ruling class of businessmen and financial magnates all lived on to fight another day.

Nor did Nagel have any right to talk of attacks on religion and morality:the Weimar Republic fully safeguarded the freedom to believe – or not to believe. Precisely this latter point was an issue he could never psychologically accept. Nagel's editorial policy of using catchwords – 'Fight against Bolshevism', 'The International Godless Movement' – fed on the dissatisfaction of his readers and were geared to stirring up emotions and channelling protest against the new constitution.

For the two million German casualties and further millions of maimed men Nagel found no words. His paper had after all poured out, between 1914 and 1918, patriotic sentimentalities for a war effort which sought to annex territories or occupy them permanently so that German companies could exploit their natural resources ('natural resources for the next war', to quote Hindenburg[52]). The military defeat festered in his soul and produced a fifteen-year lament about the injustices of the Versailles Treaty and the religious neutrality of the Weimar Constitution.

The attacks on the new constitution can be seen as basically a reaction to and an attack on modernity, a fundamentalist reaction to a modern, urban society. This is underlined by the theological approach to recent world history as expressed in a number of articles in the *Allianzblatt* in the 1930s. Gregor

Strasser was praised as a man who had contributed to and largely helped to shape the thinking and historical developments of the time. Of National Socialism Strasser said: 'We are the reaction to the French Revolution'. Nagel perceived the National Socialist experiment as a necessary 'historical correction of errors' that had, since 1789, brought ruin and disorder into the world. It was an attempt to hold on to 'the image of God' in humanity. An ill-treated, ill-fed nation had risen up to declare its resistance to the 'sick' and 'deadly' doctrines that had undermined states and all political morality. The National Socialist government had accepted the 'massive task' of turning the clock back to a day of divine order and harmony.[53] What these 'doctrines' were has already been noted in the analysis of Nagel's works: liberty, equality and brotherhood, the ideas at the root of all modern society.

The 'French spirit' had seduced and intoxicated all nations. Nagel explains how this spirit had permeated the nations. The rethinking process caused by the French Revolution meant first of all replacing Christianity with a faith in reason. God was dethroned and human reason took His place. Since then French rationalism had victoriously permeated the thinking of all peoples. From this grew individualism, the party system, 'democratism', the rule of the many in a parliament. From these grew Marxism, the 'atheistic economic system of socialism' which had impressed most peoples. The French Revolution had brought Jewish emancipation, the extinguishing of racial pride, 'Europeanisation' and the pan-European ideal. All these ideas were operative in the 150-year-long 'French' epoch of human history.[54]

Hitler was welcomed not least because he set to work to 'destroy everything the French Revolution brought'. It was necessary to do away with the 'Western type of formal democracy' for it had 'only created divisions, laming the cultural, political and economic forces' in the German body politic.[55] Social Democracy was declared to be 'the genuine heir of French democratism and rationalism'. Communism, with its admixture of 'Russian-Asiatic demonism', was an outgrowth of the same. Liberalism's faith in reason had separated people from the divine. Capitalism, socialism and the 'Jewish control over all the areas of culture' were all seen to be products of the 'French spirit' in the life of the German people.[56] The National Socialist accession to power had provided the long hoped-for 'breakthrough'. In particular, the Jews had been dethroned. This had 'enfuriated' world Jewry because Jewish freedoms had come from the French Revolution, and there was 'nothing Jews would like more than a powerful, strong France in Europe'.[57]

Germany's resistance to this French *zeitgeist* was praised as 'resistance to all attempts to introduce the final anti-Christian empire'.58 This 'work of salvation' (sic) had been wrought, Paul Burkhardt (Wuppertal-Barman) said, by a man who 'found strength in his belief in a divine mission, just as Cyrus was encouraged by the words of the prophet Isaiah'. It was 'like a dream, like a miracle'.59 In Burkhardt's view, the national uprising seemed to have been brought about by God to delay the victory of the spirit of Antichrist. He called on believers to stand in prayer for the new government, to pray for its unity and quick victories over Bolshevism. He hoped that Hitler would now lead the German people out of its terrible misery and inner strife 'to salvation and concord'.60

If, as many evangelicals believed, 'God has sent Hitler to us,'61 and if 'his national pride, his integrity and his sincerity' impressed the whole world, as they believed these character traits did, if he was indeed 'the saviour of the peace in Europe,'62 then it would obviously have been stupid and presumptuous to deny him the opportunities to put his government's policies into practice. To overcome 'hostile forces' in Germany as well as the 'Asiatic anti-culture' abroad, Hitler needed immense powers. At the time anything seemed preferable to the discredited party system. For these reasons the *Allianzblatt* was calling for an 'enabling Act', granting Hitler absolute power, as early as February 1933,63 in the first full report on Hitler's admission to the seat of power. So worried were the editors about a Communist general strike and a 'wave of socialist resistance' to the new Chancellor, that they called on him to destroy the last vestiges of Western democracy. Their willingness to take this step was eased by their belief that Hitler was 'calling on the Almighty to help him do what has to be done if Germany is not to sink into chaos and misery'.64 How could a Christian not want such a man to have a 'free hand'? In May 1932 the *Allianzblatt* had criticised the government for taking so long to ban the Freethinkers Association.65 In June 1932 it called for tougher measures to deal with the 'murderous demonism' of Bolshevism, reminding the government that neighbouring countries, having the law of God on their side, punished people for just being members of Communist parties. Elsewhere, Communist 'rabble-rousers' were arrested on the spot.66 While the *Allianzblatt* never once suggested banning the NSDAP (it had in fact criticised the earlier ban on the Storm Troopers), it called for the criminalisation of the Communist Party of Germany in July 1932: the 'divine law' as well as common sense supported taking such measures to prevent 'revolution and upheaval, incendiarism and murder'.67

When on 27 February 1933 the Reichstag building conveniently caught fire and a demented Dutchman was conveniently caught inside, Hermann Göring, who had probably planned everything, declared that it was further proof of a Communist conspiracy. In the same night Goebbels had thousands of Communist functionaries and even members of the Reichstag arrested. The following day two emergency decrees were passed, all constitutional rights were suspended 'till further notice' and, over the following weeks, all areas of the country's life were steadily brought into line and coordinated under NSDAP auspices. The *Allianzblatt* was not the only paper to follow the government line that emergency measures were required to protect the country against communism. The Brethren *Die Tenne* also gave credence to the Nazi interpretation of the Reichstag fire and the need to trust Hitler's judgement.

In the middle of the turmoil elections were held (5 March) which gave the NSDAP 288 seats and an extra ten percent of the vote, bringing its total to 43.9%. 7.2 million Germans still voted for the SPD (119 seats) and 4.8 million for the KPD (81 seats) – a large opposition force. Hitler's show of religion and respect for Prussian traditions on the ceremonious opening of the new Reichstag seems to have impressed conservatives to the point where they were willing to grant him absolute power. On 23 March nearly all the parties including the Catholic Centre Party and the predominantly evangelical CSVD voted for the enabling law, the *Ermächtigungsgesetz*. Only the Social Democrats voted against it. The 81 Communist Reichstag members, who had simply been dispossessed of their mandates, and 29 Socialist members were either in prison, abroad or in hiding.

In an article entitled 'Germany on a New Course', the *Allianzblatt* reported on the turn of events which, in the editor's opinion, seemed to even have significance for Russian Christians.[68] Moscow, he argued, had done everything in its power to prevent the victory of Hitler. It had sent its agitators to Germany and found a man to set fire to the Reichstag building in Berlin. But the flames which had destroyed the 'house of the German people', had not become, as intended, a signal for Bolshevism to rise up in Germany; on the contrary, the fire had become a beacon shining into the hinterland, calling to the whole nation to arise from its sleep and face 'the Asiatic Devil'. Following the Nazi Party line, Nagel argued that the 'Dutch Communist' had wanted to set Germany aflame and drag the country into the Soviet sphere of influence. The flames, however, were 'now consuming him'. Nagel pointed out that the police had occupied the Liebknecht House in Berlin, the

Communist headquarters, and found secret corridors and 'a lot of incriminating evidence' which revealed that a revolution had been planned. Everywhere the search for weapons and explosives was underway. The trade unions' buildings and Communist Party offices had been searched. Ammunition had been found in the homes of Communist sympathisers. Nagel said the government's call for plenary powers for a period of four years would allow it to do its work.[69] He prayed down God's blessing on the government and expressed his hope that the Enabling Act would allow it 'to give work and bread to a needy people'.[70] Yet he feared 'tragic consequences' would result from the struggle against Bolshevism. To be sure, he openly expressed his opinion that the government had the right to declare the Communist Party an unconstitutional party. Such a step was seen to be right and in line with 'the interests of national policy'. Christians believed the government had a divine right to carry the sword against all who stockpile weapons in preparation for a civil war. Such should not enjoy governmental protection. One just had to 'look at Russia to see what happens when that accursed party has power'. God had almost certainly protected Germans from terrible things.[71] The National Socialist government had earned the support of Christians by saving the country from 'the abyss of Bolshevism'. 'Who doubts', Nagel asked, 'that banning all Bolshevist activities in Germany is one of the godly duties of those in authority?' A government should not show mercy, he continued, to people who aimed to 'corrupt a nation and ruin a state'. The new government needed Christian support, too, to rebuild the country and fuse a new discipline into the populace. The spiritual power of prayer offered up by the Church was indispensable in conquering the 'anarchic forces' still at work.[72]

The attack on the German Communist Party, the KPD, was the first step on the slippery slope called *Gleichschaltung* (literally, putting into the same gear), an innocuous-sounding term which did not conjure up in the minds of people the human cost and pain involved in abolishing all political parties and unions outside the control of the NSDAP and removing all 'undesirables' and 'enemies of the state' (the latter, a Bismarckian term for people who disagreed with him) from public and professional life. The language employed by the *Alllianzblatt* was still characterised by the flowery, rhetorical excesses of the Wilhelmine Empire, but it had long since begun to employ the euphemisms and adjectives associated with National Socialism.[73] The *Gleichschaltung* law and the appointment of Reich Governors in the German provinces were seen to guarantee the uniformity of Reich policy in a way unknown since the Middle Ages as well as to resuscitate the Bismarckian struggle against all opposition. Hitler's regime had practically overcome the age-old contradiction between a unitary state and federalism. Unity had been brought about 'without the slightest resistance' and 'solely through the people's free choice'. The *Allianzblatt* regarded this as an historical achievement.

The economic, cultural and professional organisations had nearly all accepted the appointment of National Socialist commissars to conduct the change-over. Similar changes in trade and industry as well as agriculture boded well for the future. 'It won't be long before the trades unions are similarly realigned'. The paper looked forward to the time when May Day, which till then had resounded with 'the class war demagoguery of the Red International', would be turned into a National Day of Work when all citizens, farmers and workers, could 'clasp hands together' to celebrate their unswerving solidarity with one another. The changes, the editor believed, would restore to Germans pride in their country and have repercussions in the field of foreign policy. These should be welcomed by evangelicals, Nagel argued. A strong Reich would 'make conquests' and 'fight for its place at the heart of Europe'. This, no doubt, would not happen without bitter struggles. It was even possible that the hostility to the new German government in Eastern Europe and the Balkan region would 'explode' at some point. Most important, however, was the fact that the new Germany had 'regained faith in herself' and it was confident that victory would be hers. If this new Germany made a covenant with God, Nagel said, then this confidence, this faith would be justified and the Third Reich would become what Germany had once been: a tool in the hand of the Supreme Sovereign of the World to pull Europe away from destruction.[74]

As Nagel had hoped, the trade unions were indeed brought into line. On 2 May 1933 all the offices of the Free Unions were occupied to 'prevent Marxism finding a new area of activity after it has been eliminated from the political arena'. The government had forced the unions to sever all their links with socialist parties. The *Allianzblatt* reported how the leaders of the Free Unions had been removed from their posts, while the leaders of the Christian and Hirsch-Dunker Unions had been persuaded to leave voluntarily. Christian trade unionist leaders had freely submitted to the leadership of the Action Committee to Protect the Nation's Work. 'Who would have thought just six months ago that such a thing were possible!' the editor mused. He particularly welcomed the government's policy to smash the link between the Social Democratic Party and the trade unions. He noted how an initial audit of the union books had showed how the workers' money was being used for Party causes. The government, on discovering this, had 'quite correctly' confiscated all the assets of the Social Democratic Party and its military organisation, the Reich Banner[75], in order to ascertain to what extent workers' money, which was meant to improve workers' welfare, had been used for the Party's international work.[76]

Nagel, too, was suspicious of internationalism. His graphic description of the destruction of free trade unionism exudes admiration for the speed and efficiency of the whole operation. An enemy of the middle class had been finally dealt with. One door to the red peril had been closed. Nagel's article does not question the legality or propriety of these actions. Offices had been wrecked, furniture broken, files burnt, unionists (for example, in Duisburg) murdered. Eight million unionists lost their organisations and their independence and autonomy to determine wages in consultation with employers. As for the Christian Unions, the *Allianzblatt* report is substantially correct. Nationalist and anti-Semitic views had roots among the membership of these unions; for some time there had been little love here for the May Day celebrations. Christian unionists accomodated to the new system because their nationalism was in fact stronger than the ideals of internationalism and class solidarity. So they offered their 'honest and joyful cooperation in the new state'.[77]

One can recognise from such reports – the other evangelical papers contained the same articles written in essentially the same style – how little evangelicals were angered or worried about this seizure of power over all parts of the state's machinery. From a report on Alliance meetings in Lübeck between 11 and 14 May 1933 one can see how such events impinged on their very perception of worship services and evangelistic crusades. The editor specifically called for 'a *Gleichschaltung* everywhere in the Church of the Lord'. One should not be worried, the article said, when parties, political organisations 'of the old type', provinces and even churches in their previous forms were being swallowed up 'as if by a mysterious force'. Souls and spirits had been 'fitted together' (*gleichgeschaltet*) into one fellowship that would survive into eternity. Nagel hoped the current events would become a mirror image of holy things. The Lord desired 'a *Gleichschaltung* of all those born again' in a much deeper, more spiritual and more thorough sense than any earthly power could ever bring about. The Baptist *Wahrheitszeuge* published a similar article on 26 March 1933 supporting the *Gleichschaltung* process and calling on Baptists to allow themselves to be *gleichgeschaltet* with the

Spirit of Christ. This was not to be a legalistic re-ordering of things, but a change wrought by the loving power of Christ. At the same time Baptist leaders suddenly came to realise, contrary to all historical evidence, that their church had never been democratic. From 1933 to 1936 the Church actually adopted the *Führerprinzip* of church government.[78]

Submission to the will of the Führer became an expression of one's willingness to submit to God. Just as God's will controlled all events in His kingdom, so the will of the Führer could be trusted in earthly affairs. The German *Untertan* had his heyday. The *Allianzblatt* welcomed the end of the party system of government just as evangelicals longed for the end of the party spirit within Christendom. It gave its support to Hitler's view that thirty different political parties would never be able to achieve 'the liberation of Germany' from its enemies. The dissolution of the 'semi-Communist' and 'atheistic' Social Democratic Party in particular was welcomed. The only German opposition to the new government now seemed to be the 'Marxist centres' in France and Czechoslovakia. It was reported that these groups were receiving the backing of the 'Golden International' of wealthy Jews. The paper welcomed the admission of nationalist MPs into the ranks of the Nazi Party following the dissolution of the right-wing German National People's Party. It rejoiced that 'time is up for the Catholic parties too'. It recorded how action was taken against the Bavarian People's Party, whose leaders were arrested because there was 'strong suspicion, later substantiated', that Bavarian Catholicism had contacts with the Dollfuss government in Austria. In the Catholic south of Germany National Socialism now had unlimited power. In evangelical eyes, the Centre Party was politically incriminated because it had 'sought to satify its thirst for power in league with Marxism'. In spite of Dr Brüning's hesitation, whole sections of the Centre Party had already decided to leave and join the NSDAP. The Catholic Associations in league with the Centre were all dissolved. The *Allianzblatt* applauded. Nagel expressed his surprise that Catholicism 'announced its retreat from the political arena with a loud fanfare in the press'. Such a move squared with evangelical views on what Luther called the 'two kingdoms'. The separation of state and church and the belief that Christians were called to preach a politically neutral gospel was at the heart of Free Church thought. German evangelicals welcomed the Concordat's insistence on Catholic organizations preserving a purely religious character: 'The Catholic Church's field of work is once again exclusively the religious area'. They welcomed the announcement that the Vatican had declared itself willing to forbid any form of political activity on the part of its priests. This meant, in evangelical eyes, a massive retreat by Catholicism, a victory for the German state and a victory too for the Protestant view of the relationship between Church and State. It sensed, however, a degree of opportunism and hypocrisy on the part of the Catholic Church which had 'for a long time strongly rejected Hitler'. The Church had performed 'an amazing *volte face*' and was now 'hurrying to prove the genuineness of its own National Socialist credentials'. The *Allianzblatt* believed this turn-around signalled 'a new age'. Catholicism was 'now incorporated into National Socialism' and one could expect it to 'try to give National Socialism a Catholic stamp'. This was, in itself, felt to be somewhat worrying, even though German evangelicalism, unlike its British and American counterparts, has not been known for any virulent anti-Catholicism.

The editorial reminded readers that 'those of us who have fought against the Weimar State with all its parties for move than a decade will not cry and bewail the irretrievable loss of all those political parties'.[79] The 'party state' had disappeared without leaving many traces. The *Allianzblatt* sensed no danger or at least betrayed no fear when it noted on 6 August 1933 that the consequences of the counter-revolution were that 'nothing can now happen or be done against the will of the Führer'. On 15 March 1934 it even emphasised that 'we were in the fortunate position of being able, on the basis of Holy Scripture, to welcome a total state (*totaler Staat*) even before it was there'. When a special law proclaimed that any attempt to found a party again would be treated as high treason and punished accordingly they accepted the inevitable. The times of parliamentary strife were over. The ongoing 'French Revolution' had been stopped in its tracks. 'Real' German values like *Zucht, Ordnung, Disziplin* could once again resurface. Evangelicals opposed to the very concept of an organisation like the Alliance such as the Brethren accepted that the rejuvenation of old German values was a cause of thanksgiving for the new governmment. Ernst and Wilhelm Brockhaus, cousins and both leaders of the Closed Brethren, wrote a pre-election report in October 1933, reminding their fellows that their 'revered' Chancellor had done much to place these values along with 'a more serious Christian view of life' at the heart of his policies for the country. Like the Brethren, the *Allianzblatt* had, during the First World War, lifted aloft these values of discipline and order, as well as the willingness to sacrifice and suffer for a noble goal. It was not surprising that evangelicals were grateful when the era of individualism and free expression came to an end.[80] They remained grateful when the Second World War was well underway. Indeed, new reasons were found why National

Socialism could profit from evangelicalism. The *Allianzblatt* underlined on 1-15 April 1940 the importance of Christianity's 'pugnacious values' (*Kampfeswerte*) for the 'struggle to preserve Germany's existence'. The believer's 'inner strength and joy' (*glaubensfreudige Seelenhärte*), iron in the soul, was necessary for victory. Mollycoddled believers could not serve their government well, the paper stated, and evangelicals wanted to serve to the best of their ability and to the glory of God.

Notes

1. EA 21.05.1933 (Nr 21), 330.
2. 1 Corinthians 7, 25.
3. EA 25.09.1932 (Nr 39), 635.
4. EA 05.06.1932 (Nr 23), 363-365.
5. EA ibid; EA 06.11.1932 (Nr 45), 734f.
6. EA 14.08.1932 (Nr 33), 527. It was Bismarck who first drew a distinction between 'national' and 'unpatriotic' parties, S.H. Steinberg (1944, 269).
7. EA 24.04.1932 (Nr 17), 266-7.
8. The Republic which Nagel so detested had given women the right to vote in 1918. The NSDAP had officially decided in 1921 not to allow women into leadership posts.
9. EA 27.03.1932 (Nr 13), 204.
10. EA 08.05.1932 (Nr 19), 299-303; Friedhelm Menk (1986, 37).
11. EA 31.01.1932 (Nr 5), 78-80. Reader reactions to the article can be found in EA 27.03.1932, 08.05.1932, 15.05.1932, 14.08.1932, 20.11.1932.
12. EA 14.08.1932 (Nr 33), 525-527.
13. EA 23.10.1932 (Nr 43), 702-4.
14. EA 14.08.1932 (Nr 33), 527.
15. EA 08.05.1932 (Nr 19), 301.
16. EA 06.11.1932 (Nr 45), 734f.
17. EA 25.09.1932 (Nr 39), 635f.
18. EA 10.07.1932 (Nr 28), 442-3.
19. EA 05.02.1933 (Nr 6), 95f; EA 05.03.1933 (Nr l0), 159.
20. Ibid.
21. EA 10.01.1932 (Nr 2), 29-31.
22. Ibid.
23. EA 23.10.1932 (Nr 43), 703.
24. Ibid.

25. EA 07.08.1932 (Nr 32); EA 21.08.1932 (Nr 34).
26. EA 21.08.1932 (Nr 34), 542f.
27. EA 01.05.1932 (Nr 18), 284-7.
28. EA 10.07.1932 (Nr 28).
29. Ibid.
30. This was one of the prime bogey-men in the EA throughout the the period up to 1933:EA 26.03.1933 (Nr 13), 205; EA 26.06.1932 (Nr 26), 412; EA 07.02.1932 (Nr 6), 84-91, according to which there were '900,000 godless people' organised in Freethinkers Associations in Germany.
31. EA 07.08.1932 (Nr 32).
32. EA 14.08.1932 (Nr 33), 523; EA 29.05.1932 (Nr 22), 351.
33. EA 06.11.1932 (Nr 45), 734f.
34. EA 27.11.1932 (Nr 48), 782f.
35. EA 21.05.1933 (Nr 21), 335.
36. EA 21.05.1933 (Nr 21), 331-335. B. Peters (1933, 22-23, 105) insists that 'if God is to give the world a period of grace, then He will use Germany to bring it about' for 'only the German people, which is now returning to God, is capable of blessing the world in this last period of grace'. The success of the German revolution' of January 1933 'signifies the beginning of a last period of grace'. On the eschatological significance of German unity, B. Peters, Im Umbruch der Zeit (1934, 30-7).
37. The NSDAP received 6.4 million votes, 18.3% of the total, and so gained 107 seats, in the September 1930 elections. From being the twelfth strongest, it became over night the second strongest party, after the Social Democrats, in the Reichstag.
38. EA 11.06.1933 (Nr 24), 384.
39. EA 30.03.1934 (Nr 6), 100-104.
40. B. Peters (1933, 23).
41. EA 28.02.1934 (Nr 4), 71.
42. EA 30.06.1936 (Nr 14), 221.
43. EA 18.06.1933 (Nr 25), 397.
44. EA 30.06.1936 (Nr 14), 222.
45. Ibid.
46. In September 1933 B.Peters said 'the ten-state federation of the United States of Europe is not yet visible', EA 24.09.1933 (Nr 39), 640; L. Sale-Harrison, The Resurrection of the Old Roman Empire, the League of Nations and the Future of Europe (Harrisburg, Pa. 1934); L. Sale-Harrison, The Coming Great Northern Confederacy or the Future of Russia and Germany (London 1939); T.P. Weber (1987). The works by Peters all contain sections on the idea of a ten-state Europe at the end of time.
47. EA 11.12.1932 (Nr 50), 816.

48. EA 15.06.1936 (Nr 11), 174-176; EA 15.02.1937 (Nr 3), 16.
49. EA 15.06.1936 (Nr 11), 175.
50. Ezekiel Chapters 38 and 39.
51. S.H. Steinberg (1944, 269).
52. Bernt Engelmann (1988, 301).
53. EA 13.08.1933 (Nr 33), 526.
54. EA 11.06.1933 (Nr 24), 381.
55. EA 11.06.1933 (Nr 24), 382.
56. EA 11.06.1933 (Nr 24), 382.
57. EA 11.06.1933 (Nr 24), 382.
58. EA 11.06.1933 (Nr 24), 382.
59. EA 18.06.1933 (Nr 25), 396.
60. EA 18.06.1933 (Nr 25), 396,399.
61. EA 15.01.1934 (Nr 1), 16.
62. EA 15.01.1934 (Nr 1), 16.
63. EA 26.02.1933 (Nr 9), 143.
64. EA 26.02.1933 (Nr9), 143.
65. EA 29.05.1932 (Nr 22), 351.
66. EA 19.06.1932 (Nr 25), 399f.
67. EA 31.07.1932 (Nr 31).
68. EA 26.03.1933 (Nr 3), 206-207.
69. The Centre Party provided the two-thirds majority necessary to change the constitution – under the watchful eye of the SA men who filled the lobbies – and free Hitler from every constitutional restriction on his exercise of power. That was the 'end of the Weimar epoch' of German history (to use the EA phrase).
70. EA 26.03.1933 (Nr 13), 206-207.
71. EA 16.04.1933 (Nr 16), 254-255.
72. EA 09.04.1933 (Nr 15), 239-240.
73. The standard work on the language of the Third Reich is Victor Klemperer (1982).
74. EA 30.04.1933 (Nr 18), 286.
75. In 1928 the Reich Banner 'Black-Red-Gold' organisation consisted of almost 3 million workers and employees.
76. EA 28.05.1933 (Nr 22), 349-350. On the Free Unions and Christian Trades Unions in Germany in 1933, see M. Scharrer (1984).
77. M. Scharrer (1984, 197-209).
78. EA 11.06.1933 (Nr 24), 380.
79. EA 23.07.1933 (Nr 30), 477-479.
80. EA 06.08.1933 (Nr 32), 510-511.

Chapter Four

The German Christians and the Church Struggle

If we are to believe Kurt Lüdecke, a 'Nazi who escaped the Blood Purge', Hitler once claimed he was 'a heathen to the core'.[1] He was a strange heathen, for he never ceased to pay his church tax. Hitler and many of the NSDAP leadership found the Wotan cult and the resuscitated Germanic religion of the Faith Movement ridiculous and repudiated it.[2] Once, only once, Hitler did identify himself with the German Christians – shortly before the Church elections in July 1933. This cannot, however, be interpreted as an anti-Christian bias, because the Movement was basically a right-wing Christian pressure group using the verbiage typical of that era. A third of the German pastorate (including some evangelicals) became German Christians.[3]

If we are to believe Hermann Rauschning, a conservative who eventually turned his back on National Socialism, Hitler would have eventually turned on the churches. This does not necessarily mean he intended to persecute Christians one day. Both Lüdecke and Rauschning, who both had axes to grind, agree that Hitler avoided an open conflict with the Churches, not least because he was convinced that 'the Churches had lost all life and would wither away' and be replaced with the mass enthusiasm of nationalism.[4] He also believed that scepticism and higher criticism of the biblical foundations of Christianity had brought about a disintegration of Protestantism. Rauschning claims Hitler said on one occasion: 'Do you think these liberal priests, who no longer have a belief, only an office, will refuse to preach our God in their Churches? I can guarantee that, just as they have made Häckel and Darwin, Goethe and Stefan Georg the prophets of their Christianity, so they will replace the Cross with our Swastika'.[5] Hitler saw the religious needs of his contemporaries and he sought to use and exploit that need for his own purposes, not destroy or even weaken it.[6] He was perhaps typical of that modern creature, the 'Christian atheist', accepting the religious traditions and 'having a form of godliness but denying the substance and power' (2 Timothy 3,5).

Whatever Hitler may or may not have planned for the churches after the war, the Protestant Church itself had no objection to raising the swastika flag over its buildings and hanging it up within its buildings. It never sought to topple or obstruct Hitler's government. For such actions there simply was no tradition or precedent in the country. Anyway, it was neither politically desired nor organisationally possible, given the splits and rivalries between Lutheran, Reformed and United Churches, between liberals and evangelicals. Protestantism was, as we have seen, extremely conservative in political outlook. A number of leading figures in the Confessing Church movement had been (till 1933) members of the arch-reactionary German National People's Party (DNVP): Pastor Karl Koch sat as a DNVP representative in the Prussian Landtag and Bishop Theophil Wurm represented the party in the Württemberg Landtag. On the other hand, there were not a few Confessing Church adherents who were members of the NSDAP. Some of those signatories of the Theological Declaration of the first Confessional Synod at Wuppertal-Barmen (29-31 May 1934) were NSDAP members. One was Eduard Putz, who joined the Nazi party in 1923, winning the highest party decorations.[7] In all, about 10 per cent of Protestant pastors joined the NSDAP and they could be found in both the Confessing Church and the German Faith Movement.[8] Two thirds of all German Protestant pastors remained neutral throughout the period, though some of these were NSDAP members. Complicity with the Nazi regime was not the preserve of one particular grouping. For this reason the number of pastors who were categorised as 'guilty' under the terms of the Law to Free Germany from National Socialism and Militarism (March 1946) does not give a full picture of the degree of support among clerics for the National Socialst regime. Yet those figures are themselves startling. In Hesse 226 out of 645 Protestant ministers, in Bremen 51 out of 55 pastors, in Württemberg 333 out of 1,197 pastors and in Bavaria 302 out of 1,100 pastors were deemed to have been morally guilty of supporting the dictatorship in some fashion.[9]

Neither the German Christian Faith Movement nor the Confessing Church were monolithic, uniform movements. From their inception they were riven by divisions of a theological or political nature. Although German Christian support fell after 1933, the Pastors' Emergency League, set up in September 1933 by Martin Niemöller to protect the Church's constitution, also lost members (from 7,036 in 1933 to 3,933 in 1938, the latter figure representing 20.9 per cent of all active pastors).[10] The Confessing Church was, moreover, continually struggling to declare its loyalty to the National Socialist government and its Führer. Niemöller, who had voted ever since 1924 for the NSDAP, in an audience with Hitler on 25 January 1934, emphasised that the Emergency League was loyal to the Chancellor and stressed that its struggle for the maintenance of the Church's character was 'not directed against the Third Reich' but 'for the sake of this Reich'. Dietrich Bonhoeffer, in a letter to his Swiss friend, Erwin Sutz, called Niemöller one of those 'naive people and dreamers who still believe they are the true National Socialists'. It was not forgotten that Niemöller had welcomed the new government in 1933.[11] Years later, on 7 September 1939, Niemöller asked to be let out of his concentration camp so that he could serve his country by returning to his old job as a U-boat commander. Niemöller's co-pastor in the wealthy parish of Berlin-Dahlem, Friedrich Müller, who was a leading member of the Second Provisional Administration of the Confessing Church, also volunteered for military service in September 1939 and died in the 'struggle against Bolshevism' on 20 September 1942. Such patriotism, even in Hitler's Germany, was not felt to be in any way unspiritual. When Niemöller's autobiography appeared in Germany in 1934 (*Vom U-Boot zur Kanzel*) the reviewer in the *Allianzblatt*, Otto Dreibholz, did not take exception to Niemöller's impeccable patriotic and nationalist credentials but rather to the fact that 'a clearer testimony to sin and grace' could not be found in it. Niemöller was far from being evangelical in his theological views.[12]

Numerous declarations of support for political measures taken by the government were printed in *Junge Kirche*, the official paper of the Confessing Church which never suffered a government ban. The Saar referendum and the incorporation of the province into Germany, the reunification of Austria and Germany, the decision to take Germany out of the League of Nations – on all these issues the Confessing Church stood behind Hitler. It also sent telegrams of congratulation every year on Hitler's birthday and on the anniversary of his accession to power. They thanked God for protecting his life from assassination attempts and consciously refused to even put Dietrich Bonhoeffer's name on its prayer list for they did not want to be associated with political resistance to the regime. On 2 September 1939 the Confessing Church called on its adherents to support the German war effort and it remained patriotic throughout the war.

The Confessing Church struggled to maintain the purity of the Church's message: it felt itself bound only by Scriptural and Reformational teachings and opposed state interference in ecclesiastical affairs. Thus, they opposed Aryan paragraphs in church laws, though nearly all favoured such laws in the Civil Code. The Magna Carta of this struggle is the 'Theological Declaration on the Present State of the German Protestant Church' (Barmen, 31 May 1934) which was not intended to be a political manifesto of any kind. Nor did it refer to any concrete political issue. The reports and results of the Conference could, moreover, be printed, distributed and sold throughout Germany without let or hindrance.13 The 138 representatives of German Protestantism meeting in Barmen did not want to 'found a rival church to that of the German Christians, but to gather together the one true Church of Christ in Germany, on the basis of the July 1933 Constitution'.14 By breaching its own Constitution, the Declaration said, the Reich Church Government 'has forfeited its right to be the legitimate leadership of the German Protestant Church'.15

The Confessing Church's struggle to prevent Christian teachings being mingled with National Socialist ideas (Paragraph 3, Barmen Declaration) and to remind the government of the particular, God-ordained remit for the state and its insistence on a clear separation of Church and State (Paragraph 5) were solely geared to self-preservation, to preserving the purity of the Gospel message.

The Evangelical Alliance was loth to getting involved in a struggle which was not fought within its ranks with the same ardour as was typical of the provincial churches. The Alliance worked at all times to resolve conflict and bring brethren together who held differing views on this central issue. The *Allianzblatt* took note of the suspensions, reappointments and sackings, without, however, taking sides on the question of church organisation. The Barmen synod was reported on objectively. It was noted that Lutheran, Reformed and United pastors were present. The reference on 15 July 1934 to the multiplicity of 'associations emphasising the biblical and reformed creed' suggested that the editor recognised the doctrinal issue at stake and supported the stance of the Confessing grouping. More importantly for him, however, was the discussion that Barmen had unleashed within the wider community on the nature of the New Testament church. For Nagel the struggle seemed essentially to be the old conflict of whether a free church or a national *Volkskirche* was the more biblical. This conflict had been rehearsed so many times in evangelical circles that a new discussion did not seem to offer any fruitful outcome. Nagel was probably relieved that the Interior Minister suddenly announced in July 1934 that any public discussion in the press or in tracts of the *Kirchenstreit* and the 'bitter' *Kirchenkampf* was prohibited in the interests of a 'true community of the people'. The lifting of the ban in October 1934 led to a long editorial on the 'Church Question' in the 15 October issue. Nagel was relieved that the Confessing Church members had shown no signs of wanting to leave the *Deutsche Evangelische Kirche* and that only three provincial churches of the twenty-eight were hesitating about uniting with the Reichskirche. The crisis was still not perceived to have anything to do with freedom of belief. As an example of the mood at the time the German delegation at the ecumenical meeting on the island of Fanö are quoted as saying that 'the conditions in present-day Germany presented far more opportunities to preach the gospel than was the case in former times'.

One of the few theologians who came into conflict with the new government was Karl Barth. The *Allianzblatt* announced his removal from his post in its third issue in 1935. On 30 March 1935 readers were told that a 'Dr Karl Barth Committee' had been formed in Holland to provide Barth with a new sphere for his studies. Barth had given a series of guest lectures in February and March at the Theological Faculty of the University of Utrecht. Barth's significance for the German *Kirchenkampf* is implicitly recognised by the paper. His name continued to be mentioned. The paper was able to report on 30 October 1937 that a chair had been made available for Barth at the University of Basle. On 15 January 1939 readers were notified that the writings of Karl Barth had been proscribed throughout the Reich. It is unlikely that many evangelicals had studied Barth anyway. In 1929, however, the *Allianzblatt* had published an article by Nagel on 'Karl Barth and the Faith that Saves' which later appeared as a brochure with a preface by Pastor Brandenburg. Barthian theology was rejected for a number of reasons. Particularly obnoxious to evangelicals were views that Jesus Christ could be understood 'only as a problem, only as a myth', that the first Christian community was an object 'unworthy of any historical study', that 'assurance of salvation in the neo-Protestant sense is worse than paganism' and the infamous sentence in the commentary on Romans where Barth said he would

> in jedem Augenblick der Zeit lieber mit der Kirche (und so z.B. auch mit der Theologie) in der Hölle sein, als mit den Pietisten niederer und höherer Ordnung, älterer oder moderner Observanz in einem Himmel – den es nicht gibt.

> at any moment in time rather be in hell with the Church (and consequently with theology too) than in heaven (which doesn't exist) with pietists of the lower or higher species, whether they be the older or more recent type.

The life and work of the theologian had been followed with interest. Nagel accepted the truth of Barth's statements on the 'necessary crisis' facing the Church, yet remained very concerned about the practical effects and outworking of Barth's theology in the lives of believers. In the issue of 15 April 1936 the *Allianzblatt* reiterated its belief, and concorded with the view expressed by the Methodist paper *Wächterstimmen*, that, to date, those effects had been 'disastrous'. Barth was seen primarily as the anti-pietist, just as Bonhoeffer regarded himself as such, although the latter actually used the Herrnhut daily readings for his personal edification. Barth is quoted as saying at the conference of the Swiss Reformed Pastoral Association in St. Gallen on 23-25 September 1935 that he felt obliged to deny that liberals, positive theologians, pietists and 'enthusiasts' (the derogatory term he used, *Schwärmer*, was applied to Baptists, Pentecostals and other independent groups) were his 'brethren in Christ'. Elsewhere Barth had sharply attacked the resolutions of the Augsburg Synod of the Confessing Church; the synod, he is quoted as saying, lacked all legitimacy because it paid insufficient attention to the Reformed creed. Such unbalanced radicalism was interpreted as the reason why the Confessing Church had distanced itself from Barth. The Alliance could not be expected to have much sympathy for a man whose theology was proving not only divisive, but hostile to that movement from which it itself had derived so much hope and encouragement.

On leaving Germany in 1935, Karl Barth, who had become the intellectual and spiritual father of the Confessing Church, reproached it with having only spoken out for itself, with having no heart for millions of people suffering unjustly and with remaining silent on the simplest questions of legality and honesty. Barth was convinced that if he had stopped quoting Romans Chapter Thirteen and started quoting Revelation Chapter Thirteen or the prophets, he would have had all the influential members of the Confessing Church turning against him.[16]

In spite of the political bias of the Confessing Church, one must nevertheless note that the authorities felt it warranted to arrest and temporarily hold 3,000 pastors at various moments during this period. 125 were sent to concentration camps (the most notable being Niemöller, who spent seven years first in Sachsenhausen, later in Dachau, before being freed by American troops) and twenty-two are known to have died in camps or to have been executed.[17]

Other evangelical papers took up a similarly non-committal stance as the *Allianzblatt*. The Plymouth Brethren paper, *Die Tenne*, stayed neutral throughout the *Kirchenkampf* and even welcomed the prohibition in 1934 on all reporting of the ecclesiastical crisis. 'We have never taken part in the struggle and can only welcome this decree', the editor, Major Fritz von Kietzell said. Kietzell warned readers not to criticise measures taken by the government, but rather to show thanks for those policies which were a blessing to all: the workfare scheme, the *Winterhilfswerk*, the family policies and especially the new emphasis and support for marriage, and the prohibition of sects such as the Jehovah's Witnesses were all measures that Christians could take great pleasure in, argued the *Tenne*. Hitler was, indeed, responsible, all ecclesiastical camps believed, for the miraculous turn of events in the fortunes of the economy and the moral tone of society.

The *Allianzblatt* was not alone in portraying him as a great leader, worthy of being followed. It is generally true to say that evangelicals had supreme confidence in Hitler's piety. This was probably the key factor in determining evangelical reactions to the symbols of National Socialism and to the political aspect of the Church struggle. Salvation (*Heil*) had, in an earthly sense, come to Germany. The channel was a man who was not ashamed to use God's name and pray in public. Hitler prayed, eyewitnesses said, in such a manner that 'mightily moved our hearts', to quote the editor of the *Allianzblatt*. The paper quotes Hitler as concluding a 1 May speech in Berlin with a prayer. The 'tone of impassioned conviction' and the clear use of their own evangelical terminology, not unusual in Hitler's speeches, left a deep impression.

> Wir hörten, wie Hitler den Segen des Himmels für das Werk des deutschen Wiederaufstiegs erflehte, und er sprach Worte, die das Herz mächtig bewegten: 'Wir bitten nicht den Allmächtigen: Herr mach uns frei! Nein, wir wollen selbst arbeiten, wir wollen uns brüderlich vertragen und zusammenringen, damit einmal die Stunde kommt, da wir vor ihn hintreten und bitten können: Herr, Du siehst, wir haben uns geändert, das deutsche Volk ist nicht mehr das Volk der Ehrlosigkeit und Schande, der Selbstzerfleischung, der Kleinmütigkeit und Kleingläubigkeit. Nein, Herr, das deutsche Volk ist wieder stark geworden in seinem Geiste, stark in seinem Willen, stark in seiner Beharrlichkeit, stark im Ertragen aller Opfer. Herr, wir lassen nicht von Dir, nun segne unsern Kampf um unsere Freiheit und damit unser deutsches Volk und Vaterland'.

> We heard Adolf Hitler plead with Heaven to bless the work of German reconstruction. He spoke words which greatly moved our hearts: 'We don't just ask the Almighty: "Lord, set us free!" We want to work, too, we want to treat each other as brethren and struggle together so that one day we will stand before you and say: Lord, you see that we have changed, the German people is no longer a people of dishonour and shame, of self-laceration, of faint-heartedness and weakness of faith. No, Lord, the German people has become strong again in its spirit, strong in its will, strong in its perseverence, strong in bearing every sacrifice. Lord, we are not going to let go of you, so bless our struggle for our freedom and bless the German nation and Fatherland'.[18]

The *Allianzblatt* could only add that all Germans needed similarly to lift up their hands to God and receive the blessing 'for the struggle'. Hitler's speeches apparently left such a deep impression on his hearers in the Alliance that certain other accomodations to the regime seemed trifling. The three central symbols of Hitler's regime – the Führer title, the Hitler salute together with the greeting of 'Heil Hitler' (*Heil* meaning 'salvation' in a religious context) and the swastika – are cases in point. All these symbols seemed, to evangelicals, to have religious roots and significance. Accomodation here would most certainly signal willingness to accomodate elsewhere.

In September 1932 a report appeared in the *Allianzblatt* on the 46th Blankenburg Conference (22-27 August 1932) at which Privy Councillor Professor Müller (Erlangen) quoted Jesus as saying 'You should not call yourselves "leader", you only have one leader, Christ'. When this title only expressed 'a special confidence in a programme or a certain political leader', then a Christian need not worry. Should this confidence become, however, a 'religious faith in a messiah figure', then that clearly was wrong.[19] Whatever Müller might have intended with this speech (nowhere does he name Hitler), the *Allianzblatt* and its editor never had any scruples about using the 'Führer' title to describe Hitler's function. Even when it did say that 'what unites Luther and Hitler was their great faith in God',[20] the editors clearly did not see Hitler's role as that of a great religious reformer. They did, however, see his political function as that of a political saviour sent in a time of need.

What about the 'German greeting' and the Hitler salute? The *Allianzblatt* published a letter (dated 28 July 1933) from one of Hitler's authorised representatives in his dealings with the Protestant Church, Herr Weiss, to a missionary who had worries about the spiritual import of the greeting. Weiss says:

> 1. Die Deutung des Hitlergrusses ist ja inzwischen durch den Erlass des Herrn Reichsministers des Innern, Dr Frick, eindeutig festgelegt worden. Es dürfte also Ihre Besorgnis einer gotteslästerlichen Deutung dieses Grusses schon aus diesem Grunde hinfällig sein.
> 2. Sie wissen so gut wie jeder evangelische Deutsche, dass der Herr Reichskanzler selbst eine Einstellung zum christlichen Bekenntnis und eine persönliche Glaubensüberzeugung hat, die eine unchristliche Deutung des Hitlergrusses für ihn persönlich von vornherein ausschliessen würde. Ich würde es für geradezu unverantwortlich halten, den Gruss in entgegengesetztem Sinne auszulegen. Das wäre eine ganz grobe Missachtung des Willens unseres Führers.

1. The interpretation of the Hitler greeting has been clearly laid down in the meantime in a decree of the Reich Minister of the Interior, Dr Frick. Your concern about interpretation of the greeting as blasphemous is for this reason no longer sustainable. 2. You know as well as every Protestant German that the Reich Chancellor has made clear his position on the Christian faith and has personal religious convictions, so that an unchristian interpretation of the Hitler greeting would be ruled out from the start for him personally. I would consider it highly irresponsible to interpret the greeting in a way contrary to its original intent. That would show a complete and gross disregard for the will of the Führer.[21]

There was unrest and uncertainty in evangelical circles as regards all these symbols and the editor tried to deal with it. The questions about the Hitler greeting, about raising one's arm (in the Hitler salute), about the symbol on the flag of the new state (the swastika) concerned many believers and unsettled them. The editor considered the 'anxious questions' surrounding the greeting and the new state emblem of the broken cross to be 'unnecessary'. 'What sort of wrongdoing could possibly be involved in recognising these symbols?', they asked. It would be immature and reckless to try and produce a 'martyr frame of mind'. Christians had to submit to the authorities set over them and respect the emblems of that authority.[22]

Some evangelical leaders who were national figures saw no problem in adopting the symbols of the new regime. Friedrich Heitmüller, editor of *In Jesu Dienst* and a member of the Blankenburg Committee of the Evangelical Alliance as well as one of the four 'Councillors' of the evangelical Youth League for Committed Christians,[23] had published, in 1934, a book entitled 'Seven Talks by a Christian and National Socialist', in which he talked of the 'many honest' Christians who in their heart of hearts knew they were part of the National Socialist movement, even though they had not wanted to join the NSDAP'. This perhaps explains his talk about 'God's call to the German nation' at the 47th Blankenburg Conference (3-10 September 1933) at the Conference in which he praised God for 'the deliverance of our people and Fatherland from political and economic liberalism' and the threat of 'satanic' Marxism and Bolshevism. The divine order – marriage, family, nationhood, law, purity of blood, a willingness and fitness to fight and militarily defend oneself – had been rediscovered by the nation. Gone seemed to be the days of open godlessness, adultery and class struggle. National Socialists, men who 'speak affectionately of God', had broken with the 'French' spirit and returned to God's ways and truly German ways. It is important to keep this all in mind when considering the fact that, the following year, Heitmüller, a regional leader of the Gnadau Association and a member of its Executive Committee, took his church out of the *Deutsche Evangelische Kirche* and reorganised it on a free church basis. This move should not be seen as a criticism of National Socialism. On the contrary, it implied criticism of the Confessing Church's approach to Church-State relations, for the Confessing Church was generally opposed, as was Karl Barth, to a free church solution to the crisis. Though he later expressed support for the struggle some Confessing groups, particularly in western regions of Germany, had waged against the doctrines and practices of the German Christians,[24] Heitmüller makes clear in his memoirs that he believed the Confessing Church was led more by ecclesiastical and political considerations, rather than biblical views on the New Testament community. The root of the crisis, for him and most certainly for most evangelicals, lay in the unnatural and unbiblical links between Church and State.

At the same conference, Seminary Director Dr Melle answered a whole range of questions dealing with the 'national movement'. As far as the swastika was concerned, he referred believers to the words of Paul in Romans: 'Every subject must obey the government authorities, for no authority exists apart from God'. Now that the swastika had become the symbol of the new state, there is 'simply no reason' why one shouldn't recognize and accept the symbol. 'Whatever is said against it', Melle warned, 'is from the devil'. The decrees of the new government had to be respected. The 'Heil Hitler' greeting introduced by the new government as the 'German' way of greeting each other had to be obeyed. There should be 'no misgivings whatsoever' about using the 'Heil Hitler' greeting. Melle gave his own personal interpretation to the audience: 'The greeting means for me that I wish the leader whom God has sent us well-being and blessings'. Some Christians, worried about the spiritual implications of saying 'Heil Hitler' were in the habit, he noted, of immediately praying for Hitler after using the greeting. This was acceptable, he said. 'Hitler and his advisers will certainly be content with this interpretation of the greeting and will thank us for it'. Another delegate at the conference, Herr Hammer from Berlin, explained that the arm raised during the German greeting was an old Germanic greeting which gave expression to the wish: 'I come in peace without a weapon'. He added that believers could sanctify the German greeting because they wished others salvation in Christ. 'So we should value and esteem this greeting', he concluded.[25]

Dr Melle, Chairman of the Blankenburg Committee, said that the political changes in Germany should be seen as 'a gift of God to the German people and also a gift from God to the Church of Jesus Christ'. God hadn't sent a religious revival first, as they had hoped, but he had answered prayers in His way. 'He gave us Adolf Hitler, a great political leader'.[26] It was now the task of Christians to be faithful interceders for the government. In this regard Dr Melle reported to the Conference something Hitler had told Bishop Müller, who in turn had informed Melle. Ludwig Müller was believed to be an evangelical[27] and, in the Church struggle, a moderate. Hitler had told Müller that what had pleased him most among all the congratulations he received on his birthday was the fact that so many people in Germany, 'simple, but pious people', were praying for him. Melle commented that Hitler's words revealed a 'very high regard for prayer'. At the same time Hitler clearly recognised, he believed, the real source of strength of a government.[28] On all these points, records the *Allianzblatt*, there was a 'unanimity' at the Blankenburg Conference in interpreting current events.[29] God's Providence had 'saved the nation from sinking into Asiatic, demonic chaos'. For this 'miracle' one 'must give thanks'.[30] All these convictions were incorporated into the prayer programme conducted in the second week of January 1934 by the German Evangelical Alliance.[31]

On the basis of this particular understanding of the nature of the new regime and its symbols the *Allianzblatt* approached the Church struggle. The paper in fact devotes far more space to the German Christians than to their opponents. It is important to note that the ideology of what was to become the German Christian movement had been permeating Protestantism for decades. It predated the NSDAP. Even the slogan 'German Christians' had its forerunner, long before the First World War, in a slogan invented by Arthur Bonus, 'the Germanization of Christianity'. It was perfectly possible not to see the German Christian movement of the 1930s as a rather overt attempt on the part of one political party to subvert the Christian Church. The 'German Christian Church Movement' had been operating in Thuringia since 1927 and the Berlin pastor, Joachim Hossenfelder, had co-founded a National Socialist Protestant Pastors Alliance at the beginning of 1932.[32] In June 1932 the German Christian Movement was founded. The *Allianzblatt* first dealt with the development in July 1933, in a response to a letter written by a concerned evangelical. Nagel insisted the 'Faith Movement of German Christians' was not an arm of the state. It had shown willingness, however, to cooperate with the government in order to carry through the work of renewing the Church. This was acceptable, especially when one remembered that the country had not long ago been standing on the brink of ruin. The government had the right to call on the help of religious and church forces to protect its citizens from hostile forces. Such calls did not, he believed, involve meddling in the spiritual sphere of life. *Gleichschaltung* was desired by the government not to lame the Church, but to improve its effectiveness and increase its unity. Such a policy did not infringe the 'fundamental human rights of man' which, as all knew, were guaranteed by the Constitution and the programme of the National Socialist Party. Within this context Nagel said the present discussion about the German Christian Movement was above all an inner-church affair. He had no doubt that there were Christians in the Movement, people who truly believed in the Word of God and defended the Reformational creeds. But there were also theologically liberal groups in the Movement, too. Others accepted biblical truth but mixed it with errors. The question he had was which group would prove to be the stronger in the long run. In the 'Guiding Principles of the German Christians' there were a lot of good points, he noted, which Christians could accept. There were other points, however, which needed clarification – for example, their idea that 'the Confessional basis [of the Church] needs to be further extended'.[33] There was clearly a struggle going on in the ranks of the German Christians for the purity of the gospel; it was not the task of the government to join that struggle on either side. Issues such as church offices, appointments, or its constitution should be left to the Church to resolve. Any governmental meddling would contradict the basic teaching of Scripture as well as the Programme and principles of the National Socialist movement. This had been repeatedly and clearly stated by officials.[34]

One of the leaders of the Movement, Pastor Jakubski, an evangelical, was given space in the *Allianzblatt* to explain exactly what this 'extension' of the creedal basis of the Church meant.[35] Just as Luther, Melanchton and other Reformers had spoken out against the false doctrines prevalent in the Church at that time and had commented on them in various articles in the Creeds, Jakubski said, the Church should now condemn the false doctrines of mammonism, materialism, liberalism, pacifism and Marxism. The German Christians and their leader, Pastor Hossenfelder, had declared war on liberal theology and Marxism, he said. The Faith Movement was, he insisted, founded completely on the revelation of God in the Old and New Testaments. What individual National Socialists may have said about the Old Testament was not the fault of the Faith Movement. The Faith Movement of German Christians was simply part of the nation's revival and the renewal of German Protestantism, which the Führer had called for. It wanted nothing more than to put the Church once again into the centre of the nation's life and draw a people, estranged in the past from God and Church, back into the churches. It should, therefore, not be confused with the purely nationalist-racist ideas of Alfred Rosenberg nor with the spiritually liberal 'German Church' and least of all with Ludendorff's Tannenberg Alliance. Jakubski felt it was dishonest to confuse the German Christians with the legion of Germanic faith cults which were blatantly hostile to Christianity.

In August 1933 Bernhard Peters commented on the Faith Movement. The German Christian emphasis on nationhood and the *Volk* was, he said, 'fully in accord with Luther's teaching'. National characteristics were a gift from God and evangelical Christians welcomed the logical conclusion from this doctrine, namely that 'Germany should be there for Germans' (*Deutschland den Deutschen*). 'Those of us', he added, 'who are one hundred per cent committed to the political principles of National Socialism have the responsibility before God of helping the Party rebuild the nation'. Christians should trust in the power of the Gospel as they stood side by side with National Socialists.[36]

The Deputy Church Commissar for the Rhineland, Pastor Röttgen, is quoted as saying the Faith Movement was basically evangelical in character. He compared it with the first pietist revival of religion. 'Let's get back to Luther, let's go back to Calvin', should be the watchword for all believers seeking the nation's spiritual health.[37] In answer to a question whether the name 'German Christian' involved a programme which went beyond the Gospel, Röttgen said: 'Nothing we do will ever go beyond the Gospel; the Gospel is for us our greatest treasure'.[38] The *Allianzblatt* made a point of emphasising that, in Röttgen's address and others made by German Christians, the Gospel, and the Gospel alone, was at the heart of the matter.

The character of the Faith Movement was also discussed by Dr Melle at the Blankenburg Conference in the autumn of 1933. He accepted that the movement's theology had not yet been fully worked out. Some things had been said which even its own leaders would not subscribe to. Melle said he knew the German Christian leader and trusted Bishop Müller's judgement. It was important for Christians not to confuse the essentials with the non-essentials. They had 'every reason' to pray that God might use the movement to preach the Gospel of the cross of Christ to the German people.[39]

What evangelicals were perhaps most concerned about was a mixing of religion and politics. The *Allianzblatt* welcomed a decision taken by the leader of the German Christians in the province of Baden ordering all pastors in the Movement to resign from their political offices (local NSDAP leaders, regional NSDAP leaders, etc.) in much the same way as the Concordat (20 July 1933) forbade Catholic priests from taking up jobs in politics. This step by a German Christian leader was explicitly supported by the Nazi newspaper *Völkischer Beobachter* as a step in the right direction of keeping one's religion and politics separate. This, Nagel commented, had been frequently called for by the *Allianzblatt* 'for the sake of the Kingdom of God and the purity of the Gospel as well as for the sake of the government and the freedom of religious confession'. He welcomed the *Beobachter*'s stance, reprinting its article. 'National Socialism cannot allow itself', the *Beobachter* argued, 'to be used to give political support to any of the Church groups'. This position was in complete accordance with Paragraph 24 of its statute; the Party could not ally itself with a particular religious group. The religious groups could no longer count on the help of the government or the Party in their spiritual and intellectual struggle with each other.[40]

This 'deconfessionalisation' of the party political system was, then, a common goal of the NSDAP and the Evangelical Alliance. Leading evangelicals were convinced that their 'brother' Bishop Müller was pursuing noble, Christian goals in the German Faith Movement; unchristian ideas expressed by some members of this Movement were considered immature and sectarian points of view.[41] In the same way, other evanglicals, such as Friedrich Heitmüller, initially sought, by speeches and pamphlets, to foster the good that they saw in National Socialism and to counteract the tendencies which caused some concern.

With triumphal victories in the church elections of July 1933, the German Christians won majorities in parish committees as well as in synods (only in Hanover, Württemberg and Bavaria could non-German Christians retain the bishop's office). Many of the new synodalists publicly wore brown shirts, the National Socialist uniform, while performing their church duties and shouted down non-members during synodal discussions. In Prussia leading churchmen like Otto Dibelius were suspended from office and replaced by German Christians. The synods in Prussia, Saxony. Thuringia, Schleswig-Holstein, Mecklenburg and Braunschweig, which had German Christian majorities all passed laws in September 1933 making it impossible for 'non-Aryans' to hold church office. Protests from within the Church and the gradual withdrawal of NSDAP support prevented the National Synod from passing a similar law, but the Church as a body had accomodated itself to the new situation, intellectually and organisationally at least.

Like the German Christian Movement, the 'Gospel and Church' Group, sponsored by the Young Reformers Movement, had campaigned during the election for a Church reform, but on a more non-political basis. This did not mean that Young Reformers were opposed to the new politics. One of its leaders, the conservative Lutheran Walter Künneth, granted Hitler the right 'to solve the Jewish problem' in the way the government felt fit, but he denied the Chancellor the right to limit the pastoral office to 'Aryans'. In the new situation, however, he could accept that Church leaders might feel it necessary to take steps to emphasise the German element in the Church's character. There was, moreover, a Working Party of National Socialists within the ranks of the Young Reformers which had supported the candidature of Friedrich Bodelschwingh for the post of bishop.[42] After Müller had accused the Young Reformers of being 'reactionary' and politically suspect, he tried to calm the situation down with a speech held during Luther Week in Eisenach just a few months later. He reiterated the belief that Adolf Hitler had promised the churches his protection and that the state would be based on 'positive Christianity'. No Christian need fear persecution. The Reich Bishop went on to deal once again with the 'stupid' rumours that all clergymen not belonging to the German Christians would have to count on being removed from office or transferred. He assured people that he really meant what he said at the National Synod in Wittenberg: 'the inner-church struggle was over, the struggle to win over the soul of the German nation was beginning'.[43]

In the same issue of *Allianzblatt* another report insisted there was 'No Discrimination for Reasons of One's Faith, No Religious Intolerance'. This was based on a decree issued by the Deputy Party leader of the NSDAP, Rudolf Hess, who declared that no National Socialist could be discriminated against in any way for not adhering to a particular form of belief or confession or for not belonging to any church at all. A person's religious beliefs were said to be his own private matter for which he was 'responsible solely to his own conscience'. In matters of conscience it was decreed to be wrong to force people to adhere to any particular doctrine.[44] The *Allianzblatt* said the decree deserved the thanks of believers and would 'help to clarify matters'. It was thoroughly in accord with the Party's fundamental declarations and in harmony with the position taken in Hitler's book, *Mein Kampf*. It suggested that while godlessness should be put down by force, positive Christianity could not be decreed. Force could not change hearts.[45]

This proclaimed freedom of conscience was given added credence by Provost Lörzer, Deputy Leader of the German Christians, in the following issue of *Allianzblatt*: 'We German Christians consider it a matter of course to heartily and completely support the demand for freedom of conscience'.[46]

The Faith Movement realized it would have to change its tactics (reported in the foreign press) and Hess realized that the supra-confessional appeal of the NSDAP was being threatened by close cooperation with the Faith Movement.

The writing was on the wall and the so-called Sports Palace scandal of 13 November 1933 marked the beginning of the end of large-scale evangelical support for the Movement. In an address before 20,000 people which included leading German Christians as well as Bishop Hossenfelder, Dr Reinhold Krause, the leader of Berlin branch of the Movement, called on the Church to liberate itself 'from all that is un-German in liturgy and confession, from the Old Testament with its Jewish recompense ethic, from all these stories about cattle-dealers and pimps'. He went on: 'Our Provincial Church will also have to see to it that all obviously distorted and superstitious reports should be expunged from the New Testament, and that the whole scapegoat and inferiority theology of Rabbi Paul should be renounced in principle, for it has perpetrated a falsification of the Gospel'.[47]

The message received thunderous applause and the meeting passed a resolution unanimously adopting these ideas and calling for the removal of all pastors 'who are either not willing or not able to provide leadership for a religious renewal of our people in order to complete the German Reformation in the spirit of National Socialism'.[48] Bishop Müller, realizing the extreme unrest caused throughout Germany by the speech, distanced himself from the demands which he saw as 'an intolerable attack on the confessional basis of the Church'. He would never ever allow such false doctrines and such a spirit to influence the Protestant Church. 'Only a church which preaches the true and unadulterated Gospel in a living way can serve the German people in the Third Reich'.[49]

In spite of the reaction to the meeting in the Sportpalast in Berlin, the *Allianzblatt* deemed it fit to publish in its very next issue a speech by Bishop Hossenfelder (who had been present in Berlin and had accepted the resolution) under the evangelically sounding headline 'Jesus Christ lives, triumphs and is victorious'. The 'struggle' going on in Germany was being orchestrated by the 'old enemy', Satan, he said. Disguised as a weak-kneed bourgeois, Satan whispered:'Now the Church is surely saved. Now we can go back to sleep again and let the pastors play at church'. The spirit of Antichrist had the impudence, he thundered, to 'lump National Socialism and paganism together', although Adolf Hitler clearly wanted to govern a Christian people. His book *Mein Kampf* stated categorically that he did not want so-called religious reformers preaching old Germanic ideas. Such reformers had, in

Hitler's view, been 'sent by those spiritual forces which do not want our people to be resurrected'. Hossenfelder went on to charge that it was an outrageous sin against the commandment of honesty to say National Socialism had anything to do with Germanic paganism.[50] The choice of speech for publication would suggest a willingness to meet the German Christians at least half-way. The criticism of pastors playing at church would have recalled similar articles that had appeared in the *Allianzblatt* in the first two decades of the century. Certainly, the paper was intent on distinguishing carefully between people such as Hossenfelder and cult cranks such as Ludendorff and Count Reventlow.

The main commentary in the same issue of *Allianzblatt* ('On the Blessing of a Biblically Purified Patriotism'), which contains quotes from *Mein Kampf, Revolution der Deutschen* by Dr Goebbels, a speech by the Catholic Vice-Chancellor von Papen and Professor Stark's *National Socialism and The Catholic Church*, clearly reveals that the faith of the Alliance in the Führer and his mission was still unbroken.[51] Its attitude to the German Christians, perhaps as a result of this article on Hossenfelder, becomes, nevertheless, noticeably more reserved. In the first issue of 1934, which came out in a new format (26 pages rather than 16, in the same green cover, though it was now a weekly paper), Bernhard Peters noted that the struggle to reorganize the Protestant Church had calmed down. The Church leaders of Bavaria, Württemberg, Hanover, Thuringia, Oldenburg and Baden had handed over to the Reich Bishop a declaration demanding the elimination of the 'rival government' of German Christians. Four Tübingen theologians thereupon had announced their withdrawal from the Faith Movement. The 'Spiritual Ministry'[52] stepped down and a new Ministry was formed. The Reich Bishop gave up his patronage of the Faith Movement of German Christians as a result of a new Church law and Bishop Hossenfelder, who also resigned from his office of Bishop, gave up his leadership functions in the German Christian Movement.

With these changes an 'impetuous movement' had temporarily come to a standstill. Peters expressed his hope that German believers would now stop the in-fighting and begin to treat each other as brothers.[53] In the following month the government was called on not to give official recognition to the so-called Working Group of the Germanic Faith Movement, a medley of various groups (including the Nordic Faith Fellowship and the Germanic God Fellowship) under the leadership of Count Raventlow[54], Professor Bergmann (Leipzig) and Professor Hauer (Tübingen). On the other hand, it was noted in the paper, the way these groups denied the truths of the Gospel ('crude and violent') almost seemed to be tantamount to a violation of the dignity of Christians.[55] This 'third confession' in Germany increased worries at a time when the German Christians were breaking ranks. In December the evangelical Gnadau Association declared its separation from them.[56] The eyes of the *Allianzblatt* editors seem to have been opened to the 'German romanticism and mysticism' influencing the nation. It recognised that many evangelicals had become 'more sober in their judgement of the situation'. It recorded the declarations from brethren who now wanted to disassociate themselves from the German Christians and expressed regret that they had ever joined them during the floodtide of nationalism.[57] Some Christians were even contemplating leaving the Church altogether while others said that 'in principle we would welcome a split in the Church, however bad it might outwardly seem, as a gracious intervention on the part of God'. The *Allianzblatt* agreed that a smaller church, purified of the huge mass of fellow-travellers, would have a much greater appeal and effectiveness in the Third Reich than 'this bloated entity' called the Reich Church. Yet a surprisingly great amount of resistance in the Reich Church to attacks on the Bible was noted; this might portend a step-back from 'a Church of large numbers' to a 'smaller, healthier Church of truly Protestant believers' who would willingly accept Church discipline.[58] Such a Church would, in their view, be a real boon to Hitler. He could certainly not be happy with the Protestant Church's state in the spring of 1934, given 'the efforts of National Socialists to overcome denominational splits in the German people'.[59] The *Allianzblatt* was convinced that the controversy which had flared up within the Protestant Church was extremely unwelcome for the government. It noted growing anger on the part of Göring. It took note of disagreeable statements by other 'prominent figures' and warned of the 'wave of anti-Christian faith movements' that had cropped up following since 1933. Its trust in the Führer remained unshaken, however. Readers were reminded that Hitler had stated again and again that his desire was for 'a people with religious faith, capable of winning victories over the forces of darkness'.[60] Bernhard Peters comforted them with his view that Bishop Müller's dream of 'one People, one Reich, one Church' would probably remain a romantic German dream. Biblical prophecy did not lead him to the view that either the Papacy or paganism would one day rule the German Empire.[61]

In all these conflicts, evangelicals could 'not find the slightest reason to quarrel with the government, which has allowed us to live according to our faith'.[62] The quarrel with the German Christians was the reason, as we have seen above, Walter Michaelis led the Gnadau leadership to call on their associations to cut ties with the Movement. Believers who had already 'put their jobs and livelihoods at risk' by supporting the Confessing Front[63], Michaelis said, had set a good example. In spite of the 'admixtures' one might expect in such a large movement stretching over the whole of Germany, believers should, he said, fix their gaze on 'the spirit directing it' as well as on its goals.[64]

Evangelicals elsewhere were following events in German Protestantism carefully. The Council of the World's Evangelical Alliance, also referred to as the British Branch of the movement, sent an address to the *Deutsche Evangelische Kirche* at the beginning of 1934. This appeared on 15 March 1934 in the *Allianzblatt*. It praised the Church's holding firm to the basic principles of the Christian faith. At the same time the World's Alliance expressed its thanks for the steps the *Evangelische Kirche* had taken to 'secure the unity of Protestantism', to preserve the purity of the gospel against 'extreme viewpoints' and to guard the freedom to preach that gospel. The Alliance was well aware, the address said, of the great influence German Protestantism wielded within the world-wide Church and looked to Germany for an example of perseverence, humble faith and commitment to New Testament doctrines. In the name of the Reich Bishop, Dr Heckel wrote a letter of thanks to the World's Alliance, emphasising that the *Evangelische Kirche* would not be cut loose from the Reformational creeds.

The German Alliance, however, in contrast to the Gnadau Association and the World's Evangelical Alliance, never passed a similar resolution. It is symptomatic of the German Alliance's position on the controversy that Professor Adolf Köberle's series of four articles on 'The Gospel in The Ideological Struggle of the Present Time' (October-November 1935) not once mentions the Confessing Church. Nor is it mentioned in the article which appeared in the 2 July 1933 issue on 'The Struggle for the Church'. In complete contrast to the British Alliance's *Evangelical Christendom*, the *Allianzblatt* only twice mentions Martin Niemöller and Bonhoeffer once.[65] The resolution adopted at a meeting of the Union of Protestant Free Churches in Essen (3-5 November 1936) probably best expresses evangelicals' feelings at the time. The Third Reich was welcomed as a new beginning brought about by 'divine intervention'. The new government was 'joyfully accepted'. They prayed continually for the Führer and his fellow workers, the Conference heard. The 'controversies' going on within the provincial churches were not their business.

The crisis was a call from God to those churches to repent of their hollow spirituality and learn again to preach the true gospel which alone could 'renew and rebuild the nation'.[66]

The German Alliance's position was greatly affected by its differing perception of the threat the German Christians posed to the cause of the gospel. At their Reich meeting in Berlin (3-5 April 1933) the German Christians called for the synchronisation and coordination (*Gleichschaltung*) of Church and State. To quote the revised Guiding Principles (16 May 1933): 'The new state wants the Church. Not to be a pliable tool of her, but because it knows where the foundations of a people are laid'.[67] The German Christians wanted to unite the twenty-eight Provincial Churches into one German Protestant Church, on the Confessional basis of the Reformation, and give them a non-parliamentary, non-democratic form of electoral process and government. Ludwig Müller was given the responsibility by Hitler personally to carry out the restructuring of the Church. The President of the loose federation of the Provincial Churches, Dr Kapler, recognised too that 'the reform of the Constitution of German Protestantism is the dictate of the hour and must be initiated forthwith' (23 April 1933).[68] Hermann Rauschning, for a time Chairman of a Provincial Synod and member of the National Synod, as well as President of the Senate of the Free State of Danzig, noted in 1941 that one reason he and other nationalist Christians worked with and through the NSDAP was 'our sense of the necessity of re-Christianisation'. 'We regarded it as essential to get away from the denominations of the Evangelical churches and to found a United German Church. Our motives were not rationalistic; we simply regarded these denominational differences as wholly unimportant in face of the great spiritual crisis. It seemed necessary to us all to remove the official State character of our churches'.[69] Though not averse to an organisational restructuring of Protestantism, the Confessing Church group, by resisting, for purely theological reasons, the *Gleichschaltung* of the Church, was quite wrongly suspected by some National Socialists (and on one or two occasions by Hitler himself) of being politically disloyal.

The *Allianzblatt* followed these developments closely. 'That the new government has proclaimed it does not want to encroach upon the independence of the Church can be considered a special privilege', it said. It accepted the government's words. It also used prophetical scriptures to back the calls for a united Protestantism in Germany. To wage war on the forces of darkness, the Protestant Church had to first prevent Catholicism gaining ground in Prussia, the last stronghold keeping back the Roman Empire prophesied in Scripture. The uniting of Protestantism would mean that Rome's ancient lust for world rule could be restrained once again. It noted the fears of evangelicals within the provincial churches. The Gnadau Association was worried that a centralised Reich Church would not tolerate their independence for long. There was also talk of the possibility of a Reich Church encompassing both Protestants and Catholics. The *Allianzblatt* caste doubt on this idea. First of all, such a development had not formed part of the discussions which German ministers had conducted with the Pope in the Vatican in Rome. Anyway, how could a union of Protestant and Catholic Christians ever be achieved? A new Reformer would have to appear, a second Luther, to complete the work of Reformation. God might do such a work in their day, they thought, but it did not seem likely.[70]

A strong, united Protestant Church should, then, in Bernhard Peters' view, hold back the resurrection of the old Roman Empire and thus postpone the coming of Antichrist. On the other hand, there is a worry at the back of his mind that the Vatican (and the Catholic Hitler?) might well turn this to its own advantage. More unity seemed to be in keeping with biblical and Lutheran ideals. Yet evangelical fears that they could be submerged by a new super-church were expressed in the following issue of *Allianzblatt* too. The confidant of the Reich Chancellor, the east Prussian military chaplain, Müller, is quoted as saying that Germany needed a strong Protestant Church capable of renewing the nation's moral senses and of keeping all 'poisonous, un-German' influences like materialism, Bolshevism, and 'undignified' pacifism away from the German body politic. These modern heresies had to be dealt with. Such a Reich Church, if that was all that was intended, would have been most acceptable to evangelicals. In what way the Gnadau Associations were to be fitted into this structure had not yet been discussed, and this caused many to ponder their future.[71]

This unified Church was 'the wish of the new Government'.[72] The small Reformed Churches were the first to unite (forming the German Reformed Church[73]) followed by the Lutheran Churches. Then talks took place in Loccum (near Hanover) on the constitutional and organisational foundations of a United German Protestant Church. Many difficulties had to be overcome. Regional peculiarities had to be taken into account. The Reformed synodal structure was deeply rooted in the West and, on the other hand, the *Allianzblatt* noted that the Lutherans were ill-disposed towards the parliamentary system and were drawn to an episcopal constitution. It believed that the desire for unity was so strong in all camps that these difficulties could be overcome quickly. As the Reich Bishop was to be a Lutheran, the other confessions would be represented in a Spiritual Ministry set up to advise the Reich Bishop and ensure that the proclaimed equality of all confessions and parity of esteem was not violated.[74]

In a society of coordinated, synchronized parts executing the will of one Party, twenty-eight separate churches each embodying a particularist, provincial spirit and, superimposed upon this mosaic, the divisions between Lutherans, Calvinists and Zwinglians, must have seemed anarchronistic and the move towards unity excited widespread feelings of sympathy. The large majority of the church voters felt the type of unity envisaged by the German Christians was necessary. There was also wide support for the German Christian emphasis on a true *Volkskirche*, a church of the people and for the people. Pastor Dr Trillhaas, a university lecturer in Erlangen, was quoted as approving of their unmasking the provincial churches as relics from a bygone age. The German Christians had correctly contested the validity of the parliamentary form of government in the church and called for, and achieved, an authoritarian leadership.[75] Unity on the basis of Reformational doctrines was, of course, the central goal of the Evangelical Alliance. For evangelicals, there was no doubt that a greater degree of unity among Protestants would be a boon to the their movement.

Although the German Christians wanted the Reich Bishop to be of their own, the representatives of the Old Prussian Union churches, the Lutheran Church, the Reformed Church and the Young Reformers' Movement selected Friedrich von Bodelschwingh. Nominated by the three-man Loccum Assembly the representatives of the Church governments confirmed this choice, though not unanimously (26-27 May 1933). Bodelschwingh, too, wanted to reform Protestantism. In his Whitsun message of 1933, he declared that the Church had reached an 'historical turning point' which God had given to the German people. The German Protestant Church was being called upon to bring about a closer unity than ever before. The organisational changes would be a permanent blessing for the Fatherland only if God were not left out of the equation.[76] The *Allianzblatt* notes that the message of this deeply pious man met with protest and counter-statements. German Christians felt Bodelschwingh was a front for conservative ideas and his rigid evangelicalism made them distrustful. His election, the *Allianzblatt* reported, had been welcomed by 'all who are truly and impartially interested in the coming of the Kingdom of God', particularly by those interested in evangelism and fellowship.[77] Bodelschwingh was one of their own and in his hands, they believed, the Church, even with its German Christian admixture, was safe.

On 24 June 1933 the Prussian Minister of Culture appointed August Jäger as State Commissar in charge of the entire Prussian Churches and Bodelschwingh was forced to resign on the same day his brethren caved in to governmental pressure.[78] On hearing of this the *Allianzblatt* emphasised that the Protestant Church 'clarify' its relationship to the National Socialist state. There had been weeks of 'unbearable tensions' inside Christian ranks. Church and governmental leaders had been unable to resolve the organisational question facing Protestantism and incapable of choosing a Reich bishop acceptable to all. It noted with sadness Friedrich von Bodelschwingh's 'dignified statement' in which he offered his resignation. The *Allianzblatt* was clearly distressed by the struggle for control of the Church in Prussia, the pressures from 'political authorities' which was leading General Superintendents within the Church to speak of an 'extremely serious situation'. The Gospel, in their eyes, seemed to be 'politically adulterated and falsified' in the times of change and political passion. Dr Rust, the Prussian Minister of Culture, had been stung by this accusation and insisted he had never even thought of changing a single sentence of the Church's Confession. In one regard the *Allianzblatt* came down on the side of Rust in the debate. 'The Lords of the Protestant Church', Rust declared, 'should today stop playing the martyr'. They had had enough opportunities of becoming martyrs 'when the Godless Movement roamed proudly through the streets'. Who could deny that? On the other hand, they were worried on hearing that the government had dismissed General Superintendents from their posts and appointed Dr Jäger as Commissar for Church Affairs in the hope of resolving the key issues. These 'painful conflicts' had even led the old Reich President Hindenburg to speak, in a letter to the Reich Chancellor, of his 'great concern' about the controversies in the Church. They were doing 'serious harm' to the German nation and Fatherland. He had asked the Reich Chancellor to restore peace in the Protestant Church by starting negotiations with all the parties involved and to bring about a new constitution and union of the various provincial churches. Once again, the *Allianzblatt* reports on the events in a way that portrays Hitler's involvement as not merely constructive, but motivated by deep and genuine concern for Protestantism. His immediate instructions had accelerated the preparatory work on the constitution and his call for new church elections was seen as visionary. It noted, without any criticism, the decision to ensure that at least 70 per cent of the members of the various church bodies be National Socialists. Evangelicals wished, as much as Hitler and Bishop Müller, that the 'Church controversy' would end and that all the competing groups would finally recognise that only together could the Protestant Church 'once again become the Church as it should be'.[79]

The attempt to remain objective and fair during this ecclesiastical struggle for power which did not seem to seriously affect the evangelical cause is expressed here. Distance to Bodelschwingh, in the interest of a good working relationship with the government, had been quickly achieved. Dibelius, one of the superintendents who were dismissed, was a former member of the very right-wing German National People's Party, and was not politically suspect in the eyes of the authorities: he had given God's blessing to Hitler and the members of the new Reichstag on 21 March 1933 on the so-called Day of Potsdam[80], but he had not joined the German Christians, who Jäger wanted to entrust with the direction of the Church. Hindenburg's letter, 'forbidding such treatment of his Church', as Dibelius notes[81], led to a change of policy. New church elections took place on the day this *Allianzblatt* report was published, 23 July 1933, nine days after the Interior Minister Frick had announced this governmental decision to Church leaders.[82] Ironically, German Christians obtained an average of 75 per cent of the votes cast throughout the Reich.[83]

The new Constitution of the German Protestant Church was signed on 11 July 1933. In Article 1 the Church's 'unalterable basis' was described as 'the Gospel of Jesus Christ, witnessed to us in Holy Scripture and brought to light again in the Reformation Confessions'. The Reich Bishop provided 'a unitary leadership' and appointed the members of the Spiritual Ministry (Article 6), which governed and legislated for the whole Church (Article 7).

'Things turned out better than one had expected', noted the *Allianzblatt*, not least due to the 'effective' involvement of Hindenburg. There was to be no State Church after all. The independence of the Reformation Confessions was constitutionally guaranteed. The only authority recognized above the Confession was the Gospel as proclaimed in Holy Scripture. As the Constitution was founded on the idea of the 'Führer principle', the Reich Bishop would not be an elected representative. The *Allianzblatt* had no disagreement with the new structure. The Constitution contained no Aryan Paragraph. The 'Aryan Paragraph (Jews)'(sic) was recognised to be a 'political necessity', but not applicable to a Protestant Church based on the Gospel. This should not be interpreted, however, to mean that 'racially and culturally alien' ideas would be acceptable within the Church. At least one area would be affected:

the selection of the new generation of theological leaders. Hitler was reported to have telegraphed Hindenburg that the freedom of the Church to order its own affairs had been restored. This had always been something, Hitler said, that he had attached great importance to. 'I am happy', he said, 'that there are now guarantees that your wish and mine and the wish of all those involved for a pacification of Protestant Church life will very shortly be fulfilled'.[84] Hitler the Pacifier of the Protestant Church – this was the view from Bad Blankenburg.

Even the critics of the German Christians in the Young Reformers Movement (Künneth, Lilje, Niemöller) accepted the idea of an appointed Reich Bishop and rejected primary elections within the church as an antiquated error (Twelve Demands, 9 May 1933).[85] Whereas the German Christians hoped to exclude Jewish believers from the German Protestant Church and set up churches exclusively for them, the Young Reformers and Confessing pastors were against extending the Aryan Paragraph to the sphere of the Church. The *Allianzblatt*, in this article, accepted, too, that the exclusion of non-Aryan Christians from the fellowship of the Church was contrary to the statements of the New Testament. It accepted, however, that Church leaders should be Aryan and, like both contenders in the Church struggle, it accepted the political necessity of excluding Jews from positions of influence in society. It is noticeable that in the reports on 23 July and 6 August Adolf Hitler is portrayed as a man whose quick and decisive action brought peace to the Church. This emphasis continues on 20 August 1933 when the paper said the Protestant Church had another occasion to be thankful to the Reich Chancellor who had done his utmost to free the Church from its inner strife. He had freed it from 'the decay caused by parties', he had broken the 'chains of rationalism' which a past age had clamped on it, he had made it possible for the Church to return to its confessional foundation and, finally, he had led the Church back again into the 'great national throng'. This had been a great servive to the Church, for it was now in a position to win the masses for Christ. Hitler had also neutralised the 'bitter class hatred' once directed against the Church. If some would argue that the leadership of the Church had become subordinate to the views (*Anschauungen*) of the State, then evangelicals must remember that the Protestant Church's synchronization (*Gleichschaltung*) with the National Socialist state was an outworking of the Reformation's ideas on Church and State.[86]

Gleichschaltung, submission to the political and ideological will of the authorities, was seen to be consistent with the teaching of the Reformation.

Historically, this has been the case and it was explicitly *not* against this almost suicidal tendency of German Protestantism to sacrifice its real identity that the Christians meeting in Barmen directed their statements: 'We reject the false teaching that the Church can and must recognise any other events, powers, personalities, and truths apart from and in addition to this one word of God as sources of its proclamation' (Article l); 'We reject the false teaching that there are areas of our life which are subject not to Jesus Christ, but to other lords' (Article 2); 'We reject the false teaching that the Church can let the form of its message and its polity be determined by its own inclinations or by the ideological or political views which happen to have the upper hand at the time' (Article 3).[87] The Barmen Declaration is specifically directed at the leaders and speakers of the German Christians and criticises their errors and 'conduct'. The official commentary on the Declaration, provided the day before (30 May 1934) in a speech by Pastor Hans Asmussen, explicitly declares 'its love of our nation and Fatherland' and states categorically that this 'theological statement on the situation within the German Protestant Church' and on the 'present struggle going on within it' was not in any way a criticism of 'the events of 1933':

> Wenn wir dagegen protestieren, dann protestieren wir nicht als Volksglieder gegen die jüngste Geschichte des Volkes, nicht als Staatsbürger gegen den neuen Staat, nicht als Untertanen gegen die Obrigkeit, sondern wir erheben Protest gegen dieselbe Erscheinung, die seit mehr als 200 Jahren die Verwüstung der Kirche schon langsam vorbereitet hat.

> We are not protesting as Germans against the most recent history of our nation, nor as citizens against the new state, nor as subjects against the authorities – no, we are protesting against the same phenomenon which has slowly been ravaging the Church for more than 200 years.[88]

Hitler and National Socialism were not the problem, but the fact that the historical events of 1933 were being treated as a divine revelation of God's will, equal in authority with the Holy Scriptures.

The Prussian General Synod, the 'Brown Synod', did in fact decide to apply Aryan laws to its own jurisdiction, thus changing its own Constitution (5-6 September 1933). This event mobilised a minority of pastors to set up the Emergency League for those brethren who were being denied the use of church rooms by church councils controlled by German Christians or who were being threatened with 'disciplinary removal'(21 September 1933).[89]

Six days later Ludwig Müller was elected Reich Bishop. His speech to the National Synod meeting in Wittenberg was published in the *Allianzblatt* of 22 October and was discussed at length in the commentary ('The New Church and the New State'). In the view of the editor, a new era had been rung in at Wittenberg and the speech was felt to be of especial interest to evangelicals due to its 'programmatic significance'. Martin Luther's dream, said Müller, was being fulfilled: a unified German Protestant Church, not a loose church federation, but a new structure comprising different forms. The willingness to enter a new epoch had been brought about by the National Socialist movement, but the Reich Church was essentially 'a gift of God'. It was God's will for the Church, Müller added, to be a 'confessing church' (sic), preaching the Gospel to the nation in its own language and in a way it could identify with. To achieve that, all pastors and officers would have to be 'of German blood and rooted in the German soil'. God wanted His Church to show solidarity with the German people.[90] The new German Protestant Church could not hold to 'an indifferent neutrality' towards the State, even though it would not be a State Church. It was pleasing to know that the Church was dealing with a state which had explicitly stated its support the work of the Church and had guaranteed it the freedom it required. The state had no interest in violating a person's freedom of conscience. 'The state will remain a state', he insisted, 'and the Church will remain the Church'.[91] The two would cooperate wherever possible. Moreover, the new Church wanted fraternal relations with Christians everywhere. Denominational struggles would no longer tear apart the national community. The Church was aware of its responsibility, he concluded, to develop an 'open and honest' relationship with other churches, especially the Protestant Free Churches. They would not be expected to have to abandon traditions and doctrines they considered precious. 'We count on their cooperation wherever there are common areas of work', he said.[92]

The *Allianzblatt* felt Müller's election and keynote address would advance the Kingdom of God in Germany and, indeed, throughout the world. After the 'awful times of inner strife and unprecedented moral and religious decay' the Church had stood up and even had the magnanimity to stretch out a hand to the Free Churches. Such a step would surely be blessed by God, the paper commented.[93] It supported Müller's view that the 'hour of evangelism' had arrived. 'The struggle over Church polity is over and the struggle for the soul of the people is beginning' was a heartfelt desire of all true believers.[94] Not only the *Allianzblatt* was pleased to hear of the re-emphasis on evangelism and the parity of esteem accorded the Free Churches. The Baptist *Wahrheitszeuge*, on 15 October 1933, also rejoiced in the 'fundamentally different' relationship then developing between the provincial and independent churches. Never before had a bishop spoken with such open and candid words of the fraternal feelings that should characterise that relationship.

Two days later, on the evening of the 29th, a torch-lit procession organised by the Students Action Alliance (*Studentenkampfbund*), marched through the streets of Berlin. German Christians, the Gnadau Association, the Free Churches, the Youth Federation for Committed Christians, and the Salvation Army were all involved. Wreaths were laid at the Luther Monument and at the War Memorial and after three 'Sieg Heil' shouts in honour of Hindenburg, Hitler and Müller, short speeches were made. The third to speak was Pastor Jakubski, well-known in evangelical circles and especially among the youth. Jakubski was on the Reich Executive Committee of the Faith Movement of German Christians, where he headed the department dealing with evangelical groups. He spoke in the name of the 'silent majority' of pious believers in the country who he said could be found 'interceding for the new Government' and 'fighting for its cause' too. He rejoiced in the same faith as the Reich Bishop and politically they saw eye to eye as well. Müller, on hearing of Jakubski's greeting, replied in a letter on 30 September, saying participation in the evangelical gathering on 29th and the experience of fellowship had been 'an exhilarating pleasure' for him. Müller was particularly glad about the evangelical 'solidarity' with the German Protestant Church.[95] Müller was certainly perceived to be one of their own (he had taken part for years in Alliance gatherings) and there was initially a hope that he would be instrumental in bringing the new Reich Church into a more obviously evangelical state. Evangelicals were generally to be found among the so-called *Mitte* in the Church conflict: the silent, moderate, middle-of-the-road Christian unwilling to completely damn the German Christians and rather uncomfortable, in most regions, with the personnel of the Confessing Church. There were, however, numerous exceptions, such as Jakubski, who did play an active part in the German Christian movement.

Twenty thousand Protestants, many if not most evangelical in outlook, 'marching, cheering, waving flags' and yelling 'Sieg Heil' in a torch-lit procession marching past nationally known evangelical leaders (for example, the Reich Director of the Youth Federation for Committed Christians, Karl Gustav Schürmann, and Pastor Jakubski) who were among the guests of honour standing alongside Bishop Müller on the steps of Berlin Cathedral, was – in the dimensions of the Third Reich – a relatively minor affair. Nevertheless, the symbolic importance of the event should not be underestimated. The silent moral majority, the Free Churches and even the Salvation Army were all present to lend colour and noise to the celebration of Müller's seizure of power.

While this procession may have suggested unity and harmony the Protestant Church was in fact still in a state of ferment and unrest. Divisions festered until the Government decided to set up a Reich Ministry of Church Affairs under Hanns Kerrl (16 July 1935) and, for the Reich Church and in Provincial Churches controlled by German Christians, so-called Church Committees, to which Kerrl appointed primarily 'neutral' or 'moderate' churchmen. Kerrl was the only member of the Nazi leadership, it was said, who, as a result of an evangelical upbringing, could quote Scripture to anyone. These committees basically took over the functions of the Reich Bishop (who, nevertheless, refused to resign) and provided forums of peaceful co-existence. The government hoped thereby to defuse the situation. Unwittingly, it helped to create disunity and alienation among Confessing churchmen, who proceeded to argue with one another about the best response to these committees.[96] For at no time did the Reich Fraternal Council[97] or the five-man Provisional Church Leadership (formed on 22 November 1934 by the Confessing Church) seek to take the place of the German Protestant Church or to leave it altogether in order to set up a kind of Free Church. Confessing Church clergymen remained as paid officials of the German Protestant Church, seeking to redirect it from within and claiming all the time to be the 'true Church'.[98]

The Fourth Confessing Synod meeting in Bad Oeynhausen (17-22 February 1936) was the last of its kind: it elected a Second Provisional Leadership but this was not accepted by all the provincial Fraternal Councils because of its radical rejection of cooperation with the Church Committees. Its influence was largely restricted to Prussia. A second group, a Council of the Lutheran Church of Germany, encompassing the 'intact' Lutheran churches (those not controlled by German Christians, ie. Bavaria, Hanover and Württemberg) as well as the Fraternal Councils of those Provincial Churches which were willing to advocate cooperation with Kerrl's Church Committees (in the 'non-intact' Churches), was set up on 18 March 1936. The moderate Lutheran leaders suspended all relations with the Second Provisional Leadership once the latter's critical letter to Hitler of 28 May 1936, contrary to the authors' intentions, became public and eventually signed, on 20

November 1936, an agreement with the Reich Church Committee to support 'measures for restoring order' in the Church and further its reconstruction.99 The 'true Church' had become two rival sects, something the Alliance had always feared would happen.

The *Allianzblatt*, true to the Alliance's central goal of unity among believers, emphasised throughout 1935-1937 this key issue for the Church. It reprinted an article from *Junge Kirche* in its 30 December 1936 issue. Under the heading 'On the Paralysis of the Confessing Church' the paper noted the high degree of in-fighting within the ranks of the Confessing synods. Many, it is said, had grown weary and tolerance of brethren holding different viewpoints had been stretched to beaking level. This 'inner paralysis' hung like a millstone around the necks of Confessing pastors. In this situation the *Allianzblatt* expressed its hope, not that the organisational problem would be finally reolved (it saw little hope of that happening within a semi-State Church structure), but that evangelicals would 'be preserved from the fruitless church controversy'. Thus, it comments on the second session of the Fourth Confessing Synod of the Prussian Union (May 1937) that the 'untimely' discussion of doctrinal differences should only be within the context of a 'peaceful examination' of issues which had separated believers. 'That surely is the urgent lesson to be learnt from contemporary events by people still capable of listening', it said.100 Similarly, it rejected as 'harmful and irresponsible as far as the national community is concerned' the discussion of what was 'Germanic' or 'alien' in religion.101 The fact that many Open Brethren believers, after the prohibition of their meetings, were willing to join the Federation of Free Church Christians (16 November 1937) – breaking with a ninety year old tradition of remaining separate from any 'religious system' – was celebrated by the *Allianzblatt*. It was to be hoped that the goal of unity as stated in John 17,21 would be more greatly valued by Christians in Germany.102

In this context the *Allianzblatt* referred readers to 'events which will gain historical significance for the Church'. One such event relating to the 'remodelling of the German Protestant Church' was a declaration of the Theological Office of the German Christian Movement in the Reich. It welcomed the statement made by the Reich Church Commitee and the Prussian Church Committee on 17 October 1935 exhorting the Protestant congregations to support 'the German people, the Reich and the Führer' by their 'intercession, loyalty and obedience'.103 The German Christians further welcomed the support given by the Committees to the National Socialists' programme of 'race, blood and soil'. Race, and the German nation in particular, was a God-given reality. These were the very same concerns, the declaration said, of the German Christians, reiterating that they still stood on the 'spiritual foundation of the Gospel of Jesus Christ' as interpreted by Luther and the Reformers. The Church Press Office of the German Protestant Church responded. It dearly hoped that this declaration of the German Christians might help to unite all the 'positive forces' at work in the movement thereby serve to bring about a pacification of the German Protestant Church.[104]

Just as the *Allianzblatt* used the German Christian perspective, which, admittedly, sounded positively evangelical, to interpret the statement made by the Reich Church Committee, the German Christian response to the founding of a Lutheran Council implicitly revealed its bias. In March a 'Council of the Lutheran Church of Germany' was formed under the chairmanship of Herr Breit, a member of the Bavarian High Consistory. The Council, which cooperated with the Church Committees in the Reich, was gaining increasing importance, the *Allianzblatt* said, in the task of bringing about Church unity. In quoting the *Allgemeine evangelisch-lutherische Kirchenzeitung* it consciously distanced itself from the attempt to 'canonise the synods and results of Barmen and Dahlem'. It also refused to belittle them, for they were seen to have rediscovered 'the unique reality and independence of the Church'. The newspaper produced by the Reich Movement of German Christians *Positive Christianity* is also quoted as saying, on the occasion of the admittance of the Saxony Provincial Church to the Lutheran Council, that the 'idea of a Reich Church is invincible'. People were already saying that 'agreement has been reached between the Reich Church Committee, the Confessing Church as represented by the Lutheran Council and the Reich Movement of German Christians' (as reported in the Methodist paper *Evangelist* and reprinted by the *Allianzblatt*).[105] This latter was as example – as the headline suggests – of an 'alliance within the German Church'. Such an alliance was desirable, not least in the interests of the German nation.

In December 1936 a 'significant' declaration of the Theological Department of the German Protestant Church on the role of the Reich Church Committee during the 'state of emergency within the Church' was reprinted in *Allianzblatt*. All sides had realized, the declaration said, that the 'legal help of the state' was necessary to deal with the emergency. Help had came in the form of the government's commissioning men of the Church to prepare a generally recognized legal structure for the Church. During the interim period, these men would lead and represent the Church on the basis of its Confession and rules.

The Reich Church Committee was also expressly described as being bound by its commission and the Church's constitution to 'resist all groups which endanger the constitutional basis of the German Protestant Church'.[106] Even the radical Second Provisional Leadership had to accept that the government's pacification measures had 'put an end to some of the abuses hitherto perpetrated by state officials or Party members and tolerated by the state', but felt they had also robbed the Church of its full freedom to preach and compelled it to tolerate false teaching. The German Protestant Church had become financially and organisationally too dependent on the State.[107]

The Reich Church Committee lacked support in the Confessing Church as well as in the National Socialist leadership (Martin Bormann, Heinrich Himmler and Alfred Rosenberg were rivals of Hanns Kerrl and did everything to hinder his work). The churchmen on the Reich Committee realized they would not be able to bring about unity and resigned on 12 February 1937. Quite surprisingly, Hitler decreed, on 15 February 1937, that the General Synod would be newly elected. He was furious that Kerrl's Ministry was willing to use violent tactics at a time when 'the last thing I needed was a struggle with the Church'. Goebbels then persuaded him that free elections without Party or State interference, followed by very generous expense allowances for the synodalists, would bring about the desired result of a united Protestant Church living together with the State in peaceful coexistence.[108]

The announcement that free Church elections were to take place in Germany was welcomed in the *Allianzblatt*. It looked forward to the 'struggle for the final say' in church affairs. In this regard it gratefully welcomed the fact that the Confessing Church, together with groups closely associated with it, was going to enter the campaign as a united force. Encouraged by the Reich Fraternal Council, the Provisional Church Leadership and the Lutheran Council had entered into a working agreement, which the evangelical Work Group of Missionary and Nursing Associations had also joined. It was most pleasing for the editor that all those groups 'founded on the Bible and Confession' had thus formed an integrated whole. All this was simply due, the paper stated, to the fact that the Führer had 'really opened up a significant opportunity' for the German Protestant Church to fulfil its great task. The Church had a duty to respond in a truly Christian manner to this opportunity.[109]

A further decree passed in July announced that no election would take place after all. Various factors played a role in the change of mind, none of which were discussed by the *Allianzblatt*. It seems that the Nazi leadership was no longer sure the German Christians could extend their power in the Church and Hitler probably moved to the view that a clear separation of Church and State was in the best interests of both sides. From 1937 a number of articles appeared discussing the 'freedom of the Church from the State'. This did not seem to imply, for the NSDAP, the dissolution of the German Protestant Church. Religiosity was essential to the regime. Werner Reichelt (1990) has recently argued that National Socialism was, as Barth believed, a pseudo-Christian ideology in which the Christian elements were all-pervasive. Moreover, as Goebbels noted in his diary, if Protestantism did perish, 'we would no longer have a counterweight to the Vatican'.[110]

In the very confusing inner-Church state of affairs in the years 1936-1937 the *Allianzblatt* cautiously began to express outright support for the Confessing Church. No doubt the editors realized that some evangelicals had not taken Michaelis' advice and left the German Christian Movement; the Movement itself, moreover, noting that support for it in Church and Party circles was dwindling, had moderated its statements, as it had done once before, between May 1932 and May 1933. On the other hand, the divisions in the Confessing Church and the fact that the Evangelical Alliance, like the Gnadau Association, commanded support in the 'intact' as well as the 'destroyed' churches, meant it was forced to simply 'mark time'.[111]

The elections offered temporarily the hope of providing, for once and for all, a way out of the muddle and once again it is Adolf Hitler who is seen as the man paving the way to salvation. That this faith in the Führer and his Church Minister Kerrl survived even into the war is shown by Dr Melle's review of a booklet by Werner Haugg on *The Reich Ministry for Church Affairs* (published by the Junker und Dünnhaupt Verlag, Berlin). It appeared as one of a series of books on the governmental system of Germany. Haugg's booklet would, the titular head of German Methodists believed, help people to understand the Church-State problem and he hoped 'it would prove to be a valuable contribution to the solution of the Church question in the new Germany'. He had already recommended that Methodist pastors use the booklet as material for talks on the issue for it proved 'quite convincingly' that the Church Ministry was not only necessary but also had a significant role to play in the total State. Personal aspects of the life and work of Reich Minister Kerrl were dealt with in the booklet:'The piety of his parents was the decisive factor, leaving deep impressions on him in his childhood'. 'His job is to protect religious freedom in the Great German Empire!' Of central importance was the reiteration of the principle of religious tolerance as defended by the National Socialist Party. Neither the State, nor the Reich Ministry for Church Affairs exerted, Haugg argued, any influence whatsoever on the confessional basis of the Church and other religious groups. It was up to the individual in Nazi Germany to decide on his own personal religion. The principles of the National Socialist ideology tolerated all religious beliefs as long as they did not simply camouflage 'political demands'.[112] Although a National Socialist could not be irreligious, he was not forced to believe in any particular Church dogma; he was free to belong to, or not belong to, a religious fellowship. All the citizens of the Reich enjoyed complete freedom of belief and conscience 'within the limits of the general rules of the country'.[113]

In December 1941 Kerrl died and his attempts – as in May 1939 to get the Church to unite and provide itself with a new constitution[114] – had proved fruitless. The Church itself, as Bishop Wurm complained in a letter to German pastors (December 1941), was still in 'a state of inner strife and impotence'.[115] A certain modus vivendi had been achieved between Church and State. The *Kraft durch Freude* organization had been prohibited from conducting meetings directed against religious fellowships.[116] Discussions about religious issues and controversies in the army had been prohibited at the end of 1938, although, as the *Allianzblatt* noted, a soldier's religious convictions remained inviolable and private.[117] This policy of clamping down on the public discussion of controversial matters for the sake of peace and harmony was continued during the war, as confidential directives issued by Ley (June 1941) and Goebbels (August 1941) show.[118] Such a policy dovetailed, of course, with the strategy of the Evangelical Alliance not only in the Church struggle but in its general approach to interdenominational cooperation.

Nagel wished evangelicals to remain above the fray, neutral on issues such as the Church struggle. One reader is quoted on 30 January 1934 as saying that it was not the business of the Blankenburg Conference to discuss the 'affairs and possible future' of the provincial churches; Nagel adds that such limits to debates were 'indisputable' and valid for the whole Evangelical Alliance. Giving outright support to one or the other side in the dispute, which was, by its very nature, of minor importance to members of the Free Churches, would no doubt have weakened the unity of the Alliance and perhaps led to its fracturing into a number of different groups. As Christians could be found in all camps – on 15 November 1934 he said he had no trouble recounting the names of brethren who held diametrically opposing views in the crisis – it would have been unwise and contrary to the spirit of party-political neutrality for the Alliance to even try to bring about unity in such matters of opinion. 'Unity among us will be a long time in coming as far as political understanding is concerned', he stated in 1936, referring in particular to different views held on the issue of the *Kirchenkampf*.[119] For this reason, the *Allianzblatt* refused to take sides in the inner-church conflict and sought to remain as neutral as possible, while trusting that the government would play its role in bringing about unity between denominations and especially within Protestantism. Its editor was not one who saw the situation as being 'serious or even threatening', but a man who remained 'optimistic' about the final outcome. This confidence had much to do with his Free Church premillennialism.[120]

Notes

1. K.G.W. Lüdecke (1938, 466).
2. J.P. Stern (1979, 107, 109).
3. F. Spotts (1973, 8).
4. A.S. Duncan-Jones (1940,10).
5. A.S. Duncan-Jones (1940, 13).
6. J.P. Stern (1979, 93).
7. G. Fischer (1986, 24); C. Vollnhals (1989, 268-275).
8. F. Spotts (1973, 8).
9. *Frankfurter Allgemeine Zeitung*, 14.09.1989.
10. C. Vollnhals (1989, 26).
11. P. Matheson (1981,43); F. Baumgärtel (1976, 32-39); C. Vollnhals (1989,57).
12. F. Baumgärtel (1976, 39-41; W. Kreck (1988, 96-118); Eberhard Bethge (1985, 427, 679); Matthias Schreiber (1997, 88); Kurt Nowak (1995, 259); EA 30.01.1935 (Nr 2), 33.
13. G. Fischer (1986, 24); Document 5, in: J. Hampel, Vol 1 (1989, 203-5). Nowhere does the Declaration specifically mention National Socialism or Adolf Hitler.
14. P. Matheson (1981, 46).
15. P. Matheson (1981, 47).
16. G.F. Nagel (1929, 12, 27, 36, 38); W. Kreck (1988, 104); C. Vollnhals (1989, 23-24, 77-80); EA 15.05.1934 (Nr 9), 148-149; EA 15.07.1934 (Nr 13), 213; EA 30.07.1934 (Nr 14), 227; EA 15.10.1934 (Nr 19), 315-317; EA 15.04.1936 (Nr 7), 110.
17. F. Spotts (1973, 9); W. Oehme (1980) gives an account of the lives of 22 Protestants who, for so-called political offences, were arrested and died in confinement.

18. EA 28.05.1933 (Nr 22), 349; G. Jordy (1986, 64-65, 72-74).
19. EA 04.-11.09.1932 (Nr 36/37), 670.
20. EA 08.10.1933 (Nr 41), 670.
21. EA 15.10.1933 (Nr 42), 687.
22. EA 01.10.1933 (Nr 40), 653-654. In the *Moody Bible Institute Monthly* (XXXVIII, March 1938, 375) W.D. Herrstrom suggested that Mussolini had instituted the fascist salute there to programme people to later accept the mark of the beast, as detailed in Revelation 13. 'It is certain that the people of the world will be required to raise their right hands with a movement similar to the present Fascist salute, in order to show the mark during the reign of the Beast'.
23. EA 24.09.1933 (Nr 39), 635.
24. EA 03.10.1933 (Nr 36/37), 576-579.
25. EA 24.09.1933 (Nr 39), 639; EA 03-10.09.1933 (Nr 36/37), 593-594. Herr Hammer was a Church Superintendent and Director of the Bethany Association in Berlin.
26. EA 24.09.1933 (Nr 39), 638.
27. EA 24.09.1933 (Nr 39), 639; Otto Dibelius (1964, 141); Friedrich Heitmüller (1950, 137).
28. EA 17.12.1933 (Nr 51), 813.
29. EA 24.09.1933 (Nr 39), 639.
30. EA 17.12.1933 (Nr 51), 814.
31. EA 17.12.1933 (Nr 51), 805-810. In the section on 'Prayers for Peoples and their Governments' evangelicals were encouraged to thank God for the ' godly men' He had placed in government to save Germany from Bolshevism and lead them back to the Christian basics of marriage, family, respect for the nation and strong government.
32. G. Fischer (1986, 22); Hermann Rauschning (1941, 231).
33. The original Guiding Principles (26 May 1932) state categorically in Paragraph 1: These guiding principles are not intended to be or to replace a confession of faith, or to challenge the confessional basis of the Protestant Church'. P. Matheson (1981, 4-6). The more moderate, revised principles of 16 May 1933 state: We support: 1.The full retention of the confessional basis of the Reformation, insisting, however, on the extension of the Confession to deal decisively with all modern heresies such as mammonism, bolshevism and unchristian pacifism', P. Matheson (1981, 21-23).
34. EA 09.07.1933 (Nr 28), 442-443.
35. EA 23.07.1933 (Nr 30), 476.
36. EA 20.08.1933 (Nr 34), 544; B. Peters (1933, 113).
37. EA 06.08.1933 (Nr 32), 508.
38. EA 06.08.1933 (Nr 32), 508.
39. Otto Dibelius (1964, 141); EA 03-10.09.1933 (Nr 36-37), 593-4.
40. EA 01.10.1933 (Nr 40), 656.

41. For a short treatment of the subject, see K. Rennstich (1992).
42. L. Müller wrote to Hitler at the time, saying the 'so-called "Church struggle" is, at bottom, nothing but a struggle against you and against National Socialism', quoted in J. Hampel, Vol.1 (1989, 182); F. Baumgärtel (1976, 87); G. van Norden (1979, 341-351).
43. EA 12.11.1933 (Nr 46), 748. The bishop's initial statement on the rumours is published in EA 05.11.1933 (Nr 45), 732. This statement is 'aimed at preventing unauthorised and drastic measures being taken against our opponents within the Church' (Müller), in EA 10.12.1933 (Nr 50), 796.
44. EA 12.11.1933 (Nr 46), 749. Alfred Rosenberg made similar statements in 1934 (EA 30.03.1934 (Nr 6), 100f) and 1935 (EA 30.06.1935 (Nr 12), 191).
45. EA 12.11.1933 (Nr 46), 749.
46. EA 19-26.12.1933 (Nr 47/48), 768.
47. J. Hampel, Vol.1 (1989,183); P. Matheson (1981, 39-40).
48. Document 4, in: J. Hampel, Vol 1 (1989, 202-203).
49. The text of Bishop Müller's statement ('The Reich Bishop Against False Doctrines') is in EA 10.12.1933, (Nr 50), 794-795. In Bavaria 200 pastors left the German Christian Movement following the Sportpalast incident. Only 40 pastors remained members. F. Baumgärtel (1976, 88).
50. EA 17.12.1933 (Nr 51), 811-812.
51. EA 17.12.1933 (Nr 51), 813-816.
52. Set up (according to the Constitution of the German Protestant Church, 11 July 1933) to pass church laws in cooperation with the Reich Bishop. Essentially, it was the Church's governing body.
53. EA 15.01.1934 (Nr 1), 18.
54. On Count Reventlow, see EA 15.12.1934 (Nr 23), 382.
55. EA 28.02.1934, 68.
56. EA 28.02.1934, 70-71; EA 15.02.1935 (Nr 3), 45-46.
57. EA 28.02.1934, 70.
58. EA 28.02.1934, 69. Taken from *Licht und Leben* and *Das Zeitbild*.
59. EA 30.03.1934, 103.
60. EA 30.07.1934 (Nr 14), 232.
61. EA 30.03.1934, 103.
62. EA 30.03.1934, 103.
63. Cp. E.C. Helmreich (1970, 406). If Michaelis had seen the Confessing Church as a political opposition he most probably would not have led evangelicals into the Working Group of Missionary and Nursing Organisations and Associations in the German Protestant Church, which was under the influence of Confessing churchmen. Michaelis did precisely this on 25 October 1934.

64. The Gnadau resolution taken at Bad Salzuflen, in EA 15.02.1934 (Nr 3), 45-46. 'Foreigners say that the German Church struggle has a 'vicarious' significance in the intellectual struggle going on throughout the world. They say that what is being fought for and struggled for here is for the benefit of everyone', EA 30.06.1936, (Nr 12), 185.
65. EA 15.01.1934 (Nr 1), 15. EA 15.10.1936 (Nr 19), 308 (Bonhoeffer as part of the German delegation at the ecumenical conference at Chamby, August 1936); EA 15.04.1936 (Nr 7), 110 (Niemöller being awarded an honorary doctorate by the Theological Faculty of the Evangelical Synod of North America). Bonhoeffer, who was profoundly influenced by Bultmann, developed the idea of a 'religionless Christianity'. In one of his letters from prison (05.05.1944) he expresses the very unevangelical ideas that Bultmann's 'demythologisation' of the New Testament had not been radical enough and that the 'individualistic concern for personal salvation has almost completely left all of us'. Dietrich Bonhoeffer (1953, 125-126). Bonhoeffer at the time was still largely unknown in Germany, so it is not surprising that the *Allianzblatt* does not discuss his role at the time. Many of Bonhoeffer's statements would have caused outrage in Alliance circles. In an article which appeared in *Evangelische Theologie* in June 1936, Bonhoeffer wrote: 'Whoever knowingly cuts himself off from the Confessing Church in Germany cuts himself off from salvation'. A number of his colleagues in the Confessing Church disagreed with him on this point. Dietrich Bonhoeffer (1977, 93-94).
66. EA 30.11.1936 (Nr 22), 357; P. Matheson (1981, 52); EA 30.12.1936 (Nr 24), 389; EA 15.12.1935 (Nr 23), 367. On the function of the Council of the Lutheran Church, see EA 30.06.1936 (Nr 14), 220.
67. P. Matheson (1981, 22).
68. Peter Matheson (1981, 17).
69. H. Rauschning (1941, 230). On Rauschning see H.J. Laski (1941,79).
70. EA 21.05.1933 (Nr 21), 335.
71. EA 28.05.1933 (Nr 22), 351.
72. EA 25.06.1933 (Nr 26), 413.
73. EA 16.07.1933 (Nr 29), 459.
74. EA 25.06.1933 (Nr 26), 414.
75. EA 25.06.1933 (Nr 26), 415.
76. EA 25.06.1933 (Nr 26), 415.
77. EA 18.06.1933 (Nr 25), 394.
78. J. Hamel, Vol.1 (1989, 18).
79. EA 23.07.1933 (Nr 30), 479.
80. Dibelius' sermon on Romans 8,31 on that day is recorded in G. van Norden (1979, 52-55). On Dibelius' anti-semitism:W. Gerlach (1972, 24-29). On the conflict surrounding Dibelius, see R. Stupperich (1989, 209-219).

81. O. Dibelius (1964, 145).
82. J. Hampel, Vol. 1 (1989, 181).
83. According to another source, the German Christians 'received a little more than 70% of the votes', G. Denzler/V. Fabricius, Vol.1 (1988, 39).
84. EA 06.08.1933 (Nr 32), 509-510. On the Aryan Paragraph and the Church's struggle against its application within the Church, see G. Denzler/V. Fabricius, Vol.1 (1988, 40-48) and Vol.2 (1988, 74-87).
85. G. Denzler/V. Fabricius, Vol.2 (1988, 46-47). On the relationship between the Young Reformers and evangelicalism, see *Der Christlich-Soziale Volksdienst*, 17 June 1933. On Künneth see G. van Norden (1979, 341-351); F. Baumgärtel (1976, 87).
86. EA 20.08.1933 (Nr 34), 543. In the same article Bernhard Peters says the Catholic Church had reason 'to see God's gracious leading' in Hitler's guarantees of freedom of belief and of public worship in the Concordat between the German Reich and the Holy See (20 July 1933).
87. P. Matheson (1981, 46-47). The full text is in J. Hampel, Vol.1 (1989, 203-205) and in G. Huntemann (1985, 102-106).
88. G. Huntemann (1985, 117).
89. Niemöller's circular letter rallying oppposition to the subversion of the Church's Constitution (by the vast majority of churchmen) can be found in P. Matheson (1981, 36-37).
90. Cp.W. Künneth (Die Nation vor Gott. Zur Botschaft der Kirche im Dritten Reich, Berlin 1933): 'The Church has to ensure that Paul's method of "becoming a Greek to the Greeks" is applied to the German situation and that the Church in Germany has German features'. This, he said, was one of the 'truths in the demands being made by German Christians'.
91. One of these demands of the Young Reformers Movement as well as the Church and Gospel Group in the July elections.
92. EA 22.10.1933 (Nr 43), 698-699, 702-703.
93. EA 22.10.1933 (Nr 43), 699.
94. EA 22.10.1933 (Nr 43), 702-703.
95. EA 29.10.1933 (Nr 44), 716. According to E. Rüppel (1969, 126) Jakubski was the second to speak.
96. In an article published in the *Moody Bible Institute Monthly*, Paul Umlauf, a lay worker who had worked with children and young people for thirty years in Berlin, denied that the Nazi Government was hostile to religion. His letter is one example of how German evangelicals used the foreign press to 'correct' views held by their brethren and so help to reshape public opinion abroad. Umlauf believed, for example, that the crisis within Protestantism *necessitated* the election of the Reich Bishop and the appointment of Nazi Commissars to monitor Church life. He wrote: 'Chancellor Hitler, in his national socialist

programme, has made it clear that he looks upon Christianity as the cultural foundation on which the new state must be built up'. The Churches had proved incapable of running their own internal affairs. 'Democratic and Marxist groups' had 'used their positions within the churches' to carry on 'a kind of underhand propaganda against the state'. 'If God thinks fit to do so, He will call upon the temporary powers to adjust any errors that may have crept into the government of the Church'. The government actions had become 'necessary' to preserve the 'true interests of the Church'. The causes of the disruption had been, in Umlauf's opinion, two-fold. First, German Church leaders had 'failed to read the signs of the times correctly'. Secondly, the 'mixing up of religious and political issues could never have assumed the proportions it actually did if it had not been for the fact that certain sections abroad, especially those connected with the emigrés, had taken a hand in the dispute for purely political reasons'. *Moody Bible Institute Monthly*, August 1934, 553-4.

97. The committee of twelve men set up after the Confessing Synod's meeting in Berlin-Dahlem (20 October 1934) 'to lead and to represent the German Protestant Church as a federation of confessionally-bound Churches'.
98. J. Hampel, Vol.1 (1989, 194).
99. P. Matheson (1981, 64).
100. EA 15.07.1937 (Nr 13), 182; EA 30.12.1936 (Nr 24), 389; EA 15.12.1935 (Nr 23), 367.
101. EA 15.07.1937 (Nr 13), 183-4.
102. EA 30.12.1937 (Nr 24), 749.
103. P. Matheson (1981, 54) sets the date at 15 October 1935.
104. EA 30.01.1936 (Nr 2), 30.
105. EA 30.06.1936 (Nr 14), 220.
106. Mitteilungsblatt der Deutschen Evangelischen Kirche, Nr 4, 1936, in EA 30.12.1936 (Nr 24), 387.
107. Protest to the Provisional Leadership to Hitler, 28 May 1936, in P. Matheson (1981, 60).
108. G. Denzler/V. Fabricius Vol.1 (1988, 71-72).
109. EA 15-30.05.1937 (Nr 9/10), quoting the paper *Reformation*.
110. EA 15-30.05.1937 (Nr 9/10), 72. At a meeting with the Protestant bishops on 25 January 1934, Hitler said he himself had been born a Catholic and was thankful to Providence for this, since it had enabled him to win millions of Catholics over to the National Socialist movement. In his heart, however, he said he stood closer to the Protestant Church and expected it to have a different attitude to the Third Reich to that of the Catholics. P. Matheson (1981, 43).
111. Michaelis, letter to Dr von Thadden-Trieglaff, 27.01.1937, quoted in E. Rüppel (1969, 192).
112. On the subject of the political misuse of the pulpit EA 15.12.1937 (Nr 23), 355.

113. EA 15-30.09.1940 (Nr 17/18), 133-134.
114. G. Denzler/V. Fabricius Vol.2 (1988, 169-170).
115. G. Denzler/ V. Fabricius Vol.1 (1988, 97).
116. EA 30.10.1938, 287.
117. EA 30.12.1938 (Nr 24), 341.
118. P. Matheson (1981, 92).
119. EA 15.11.1934 (Nr 21), 348; EA 30.01.1934 (Nr 2), 38; EA 15.03.1936 (Nr 5), 76-77.
120. EA 15.03.1936 (Nr 5), 76. He asked his readers 'to be patient if not everything that is relevant to the subject can be said in the individual essays' and 'to be patient if it isn't possible to answer all questions in one essay', EA 29.10.1933 (Nr 44), 718.

Chapter Five

Evangelical Religious Concerns

Economic, social, sexual and educational issues are all issues which are dealt with in the foundational document of evangelicalism, the Bible, and are in a real sense religious matters. The Lutheran doctrine of 'two kingdoms' strictly compartmentalised Christian thinking and behaviour into a worldly-secular arena, where politicians held sway, and a private-religious sphere where the individual was alone with his God. This doctrine blurred the whole concept of the Lordship of Christ: that there is no area of human life not accountable to Christ's rule. The Confessing Church made some attempt to break through the almost schizophrenic mentality brought about by a narrow interpretation of Lutheran teaching. Modern evangelicalism is just now, in the 1990s, coming to terms with the potential consequences of accepting the view that Christ is Lord of all areas of human endeavour. Yet there remain areas of evangelical belief which retain prime importance for their adherents. The symbolic significance of apparently unimportant phenomena is not unknown to the historian of evangelicalism. Many an American politician has tapped into the evangelical subconscious by playing the 'Bible card' and reaped the electoral rewards. Whether Hitler and his party deliberately used Christian symbols for propaganda purposes is still unclear. Werner Reichelt and others have argued that they did, and with great effect.

First and foremost evangelicals have a high regard for the *evangel*, the good news of salvation, the divine message to the world. Any politics that could utilise the symbol of the Bible could be sure to win evangelical support. The *Allianzblatt* etched reports on the importance of the Bible in the minds of readers. Some reports suggested, however, a special relationship between fascism and the biblical tradition. In November 1933 a short report appeared on 'The Bible on the Stamp', taken from the Christian weekly for full-time Methodist staff. It referred to a stamp that commemorated the tenth anniversary of the victory of Fascism. A Bible is displayed. The *Allianzblatt* called the brown 30 centesimi stamp 'unique' in that the fasces were displayed under the slogan: Credere! (Believe!) In the centre of the stamp was a Bible, lying open on a lectern which has the form of a Roman eagle: the word 'Gospel' stood out. Behind the Bible, at the right, there stood a simple wooden cross; from the left the flags of Fascism bow before the Bible. The following year the Brethren *Die Tenne* brought a similar report on the stamp, saying it was proof, if proof were needed, of a desire to 'glorify the gospel'. The same denomination also helped circulate the notion that Hitler read daily in the *Losungen* (daily meditations on Bible passages) of the Herrnhut Brüdergemeine.[1]

In March 1937 the *Allianzblatt* elaborated on 'Mussolini's Attitude to the New Testament', this time quoting the paper *Reformation*. The Italian leader had apparently sent out a circular letter to all the headmasters and rectors of schools, in which he expressly ordered the New Testament to be read and used in lessons. The decree is quoted as saying that all professors and teachers should read the New Testament for themselves, should instruct children in the book and interpret it to them. They should also ensure that the children learn the most beautiful portions of Scripture by heart. The Bible, described as divine in the decree, was to be made available in every school library. The *Allianzblatt* interprets the decree as an attempt by the national government to draw the soul of the Italian people back onto the only path on which the Italian Fatherland could 'achieve true grandeur'.[2]

German Christians, too, wanted their brethren abroad to know that Adolf Hitler loved the Bible. James Gray, the editor at the time of the *Moody Bible Institute Monthly*, published without comment a blatantly pro-Hitler letter to him from Hedwig Nabholz, a German national living in Maryland, in its October 1935 issue. The letter writer, identifying herself as an old devout Christian waiting for the Second Coming, praised the magazine for not misjudging Hitler and passed on reliable information that Hitler 'studies the New Testament'. 'We believe', she wrote, 'that Christ will come soon and He will be merciful to Hitler too. Hitler's father was a drinker, but Adolf lives with his mother and is a very good son'. She said all her relatives in Germany were devout evanglicals who 'praise Hitler'. Christians should, she said, 'pray for him' and 'not believe everything that his enemies say about him'. One reason for this view was that, during a recent trip to Germany, she saw that the churches had complete freedom to preach the gospel.[3] Another report in the *Allianzblatt* shows that the editors were very careful to note any sign of Hitler's faith. 'Our readers will certainly be interested to know a piece of news circulating in the press at the moment', they said in March 1936. It had to do with Dr Hermann Menge who had translated the Bible from the original languages into German. His translation of the Bible, though not as widely read as Luther's, was and is nevertheless very popular. The editor notified readers that the Führer and Reich Chancellor had congratulated Dr Menge on his 95th birthday in a telegram. 'I hope and wish', Hitler had written, 'that you may remain in good health and may enjoy blessings in the years to come'.[4] Surely, one might think, if Hitler would take the time to send a telegram to an evangelical Bible translator who was by no means a household name even among German Protestants, then he really must be a reader of the Bible himself. That, of course, was one of the rumours that circulated in evangelical circles at the time.

Evangelicals revered the Word of God because they revered the name of God. Here, too, the National Socialist government took pains to take evangelical sensitivities into account in their formulation of public policy. The use of oaths on numerous state occasions and during Hitler Youth inductions has already been referred to. The use of the name of God symbolised, in their eyes, commitment to truth and godliness. The abuse of the Name signified corruption and decay. In his book on 'The Idea of Government', Nagel explicitly supported the Reich law forbidding blasphemy as well as verbal abuse aimed at a church or religious fellowship.[5] In Germany, in the mid-1930s, there was a heated discussion on the issue in the religious press. The *Allianzblatt* also reported on the work being done to reform the law. On 15 August 1935 it took cognizance of the new laws on violating religious feelings and places of worship. In the Reichstag debate the paper supported the draft bill, which the Nazis then made law. The relevant sections of the bill read as follows:

> Wer öffentlich Gott lästert, wird mit Gefängnis bestraft.
> Wer öffentlich das religiöse Empfinden des deutschen Volkes gröblich verletzt, wird mit Gefängnis bestraft.
> Wer öffentlich eine staatlich anerkannte Religionsgemeinschaft beschimpft oder böswillig verächtlich macht, wird mit Gefängnis bestraft.
> Wer Stätten, die zum Gottesdienst bestimmt sind, verunehrt, wird mit Gefängnis bestraft. Dasselbe gilt auch für die Gegenstände des Gottesdienstes oder der religiösen Verehrung.
> Wer den Gottesdienst oder einzelne gottesdienstliche Handlungen verhindert oder stört, wird mit Gefängnis bestraft.
> Wer eine Bestattungsfeier verhindert oder stört, wird mit Gefängnis bestraft.

> Whoever publicly blasphemes God shall be sentenced to a term of imprisonment. Whoever publicly and maliciously offends the religious feelings of the German people shall be sentenced to a term of imprisonment. Whoever publicly reviles or maliciously derides a religious fellowship which has been given governmental recognition will be sentenced to a term of inprisonment.

> Whoever treats places of worship, objects of religious veneration or objects used in worship with dishonour will be sentenced to a term of imprisonment.
> Whoever prevents or disturbs religious services or individual acts of worship shall be sentenced to a term of imprisonment. Whoever hinders or disturbs a burial service shall be sentenced to a term of imprisonment.

The *Allianzblatt* said the draft bill was proof that the National Socialists took Article 24 of their programme seriously and aimed to implement it.[6] It was also necessary to forbid these things because, it argued, 'crude blasphemy eats away at the foundations of the state and destroys the authority of the state'.[7] Blasphemy and treason were, in their eyes, bedfellows; blasphemy stained the fabric of society and led directly to anarchy. The committee set up to look at the question accepted that there was a 'respect for a higher being rooted in the character of the German people' which deserved government protection; religious views, however, which offended the German race's sense of propriety and morality 'could not enjoy the state's protection'.[8] The *Allianzblatt* did not protest against this point; evangelicals were, after all, to be protected, as long as they 'did not draw anti-racist or anti-patriotic conclusions from their faith and stand up for them'.[9]

One of the major and most publicised blasphemy trials of the late Weimar Republic was conducted between 1928 and 1931 against the painter, George Grosz, a number of whose drawings – 'Christ on the Cross with Gas Mask', 'Pouring out of the Holy Spirit' and 'Cleric balancing a cross on his nose' – were confiscated in 1928 on the grounds of blasphemy. Goebbels in fact asked for the 'Christ with Gas Mask' drawing to be included in a brochure on cultural Bolshevism and it was also to be seen in the November 1937 exhibition of 'Degenerate Art' in Munich.[10]

Paragraph 166 of the penal code was used to silence criticism of individual ministers who had not, as Gross believed was in fact the case, acted 'in accordance with their profession as messengers of divine peace and mercy' during the last war. His drawings were clearly satirical and there clearly had been Christian ministers who had given biblical justification to militarism. The Church, he felt, in bondage to the military and the judiciary, was betraying its mission.

Silencing Grosz, for whatever reason, was, on the other hand, in the interests of the government, for he was a political radical (he was a member of the Communist Party until 1923, but still gave electoral support to the KPD up to the 1930s). The interests of a nationalist Church and an anti-communist government coincided and so the law remained as yet another weapon in the arsenal of a Party claiming to be 'positively Christian' under the leadership of a Roman Catholic in a government repeatedly proclaiming Christianity to be its moral basis of action.

Evangelicals were, thirdly, adamant that the Word of God be passed on to others. Evangelicals were *evangelistic*. Evangelism was central to the Free Church tradition, the first cause of its organisational existence in Germany, but also to the pietist camp within the provincial churches, which was generally found in the Gnadau Associations for Fellowship and Evangelism, presided over by Walter Michaelis. The Nazi government was more than willing to grant to evangelicals the opportunity to evangelise, especially during the occasions when the eyes of the world were focussed on Germany, as was the case during the Berlin Olympics.

On 1 August 1936 the Olympic Games began in Berlin. In February a boycott of the Games by American athletes had seemed likely because the YMCA had refused to send its sportsmen to a country where they had heard Christians were being persecuted. The evangelical East German Young Men's Association, encouraged by German sports officials, wrote to the YMCA saying that 'we have of course gone through hard times, a few non-essential activities are no longer permissible, but we young evangelicals are still free to read our Bibles and use our song books'.[11] The Americans thereupon promised to attend.

The German Protestant Church, the Free Churches and the German YMCA formed a Church Olympic Committee which organised pastoral care for sportsmen and women and for visitors. Worship services were held to open and close the Games; morning and evening prayer services were organised on a daily basis in a special Olympic Tent; a whole range of meetings went on at which visitors could inform themselves about church activities in Germany and German missionary activities abroad; a tent mission conducted evangelistic activities in front of the main stadium.[12] A very high degree of tolerance and support was practised by the government which could not have gone unnoticed by the numerous foreigners in the German capital. The *Allianzblatt* reported on the sporting event too, contrasting peaceful athletic events with the arms race. It noted the government's interest in making the guests feel at home so they could 'see for themselves how things are in Germany'. It also hoped that the young men and women would report home that Germany is 'a country characterised by order and work'.[13]

The first week of religious events were conducted under the motto *The Work of Christ in Germany*, the second week under the slogan *The Week of Nations*. Pastors of the Confessing Church such as Jacobi, Iwand, Asmussen, Niemöller, Dibelius and Bonhoeffer all had time to explain the position of their movement's struggle. Bonhoeffer offended evangelical sensibilities by saying his study of Zinzendorf and pietism had made him 'very depressed'. Pietism, in Bonhoeffer's opinion, signified a decine from the heights of the Reformation. 'What rottenness there is beneath all this piety', he said. The idea of 'unity' among believers was emphasised by those of a more tolerant persuasion. Although the Evangelical Alliance was not officially involved, Gustav Nagel addressed the visitors in the Olympic Tent on 2 August in the name of the Alliance: 'A spirit of joy and faith flooded this first meeting', he reported later. Other evangelical leaders (Kröker, Melle) were also present. Nagel was impressed. Work had been done for the Kingdom of Christ, but he also hoped there would be political repercussions from the sporting event, while insisting the Games 'were by no means meant to be a propaganda event'.[14]

One of those responsible for organising these Christian events during the sixteen days of Olympic competitions wrote in 1980 that he, and other evangelicals, had been tricked into 'helping Hitler to document his triumph as a Chancellor of Peace before the whole world'. This, he confessed, had been preying on his mind for the last forty-four years.[15] With hindsight such a statement is much easier to make. At the time the *Allianzblatt* was very much within the camp of 'true believers' in Hitler's mission of peace and justice. The freedom to evangelise on such an occasion outweighed all other considerations; in the same way, the Confessing Church had used the occasion to put forward its goals.

Freedom to evangelise, however, was very precious to evangelicals. The struggle for the right of people to practise their religion as they saw fit was the central policy of the Evangelical Alliance in the decades after its formation. The pages of *Evangelical Christendom* have always been full of reports from all over Europe and the Middle East about the state of religious freedom. Indeed, British and German evangelicals spent a lot of time in the second half of the nineteenth century negotiating with government officials (in Spain, Turkey and Italy for example) to grant basic rights to oppressed minorities. The Alliance could indeed look back with pride on a number of remarkable campaigns. The British paper had been a great help to the Free Churches in Europe, not least by publicising their plight. Baptists, Methodists and

Independents had had to put up with a lot of discrimination and even persecution in Germany in the first two Reichs. The Baptist magazine, the *Wahrheitszeuge*, repeatedly testified to the truth that the Third Reich and, in particular, the newly created *Deutsche Evangelische Kirche* had begun to treat them in a way strikingly different from the traditional fashion. Many in the Free Churches, driven by a desire to evangelise, felt freer to work in public in Germany than ever before. Neither the Evangelical Alliance as an organisation nor individual evangelical Christians were subjected to governmental measures of discrimination or persecution between 1933 and 1945. On 15 November 1934 the *Allianzblatt* drew attention to the history of evangelicalism in Germany and claimed that the Alliance had always called for complete freedom to believe and practise one's faith. 'It has often championed religious freedom in word and deed', Nagel said. He insisted, in the same editorial, that the Alliance had a keen interest in monitoring whether freedom was being guaranteed to all religious groups. He made one rather ominous qualification however; only those groups which were not dangerous to the government (*nicht staatsgefährlich*) should enjoy religious freedom. In any situation, but especially in a dictatorial system, such a qualification was liable to mean in practice that freedom was a rather arbitrary gift from those with power to those who admired and submitted to power. It is also noticeable that whereas Nagel does talk of 'disruptions' and 'great tensions' within the Alliance caused by the Church crisis, nowhere are these divisions and tensions said to be due to the fact that some religious groups were now prohibited from meeting. Reactions to bans on esoteric groups and religious cults were similar to the reactions to the bans on political and union activity:they did not seem to concern evangelicals.

At least 37 religious denominations or fellowships were forbidden in Germany between 1934 and 1942. Some of the religious groups banned by the Nazis were the Church of the Kingdom of God (banned on 31 January 1934), the Fellowship of the Divine Word and Divine Socialism (26 January 1936), the Pentecostal Biblical Faith Fellowship (10 April 1937), the Christian Assemblies (Darbyists) (13 April 1937), the Bahai Religion (21 May 1937), the Gral Movement (1938), Christian Science (14 July 1941), the Disciples of Christ (1942).[16] The government's guidelines on combatting 'sects' included the following danger signals, any one of which could lead to prohibition and persecution:teaching members to hold egocentric views and become indifferent to questions relating to the nation and the state; involvement of Marxists and Communists; Freemasonic or Jewish links;

refusal to take oaths or give the 'Heil Hitler' greeting; rejection of military service; refusal to accept posts in governmental organisations; refusal to take part in company parades or to work in the armaments industry; faith healing; exploitation and brainwashing; rejection of the National Socialist racial theories. As long as a religious group was not guilty of any of these 'offences' it was considered harmless to the government; the more the above criteria were met, the more dangerous the fellowship would be considered. As few evangelical denominations and no branch of the Gnadau Association was banned by the Nazis, one has to accept that these features of 'dangerous sects' were not typical or noticeable elements of evangelical spirituality at the time. Pentecostals, who were not allowed to join the Alliance due to their use of spiritual gifts such as tongues, could not expect solidarity from the umbrella organisation. The 60,000 to 70,000 followers of J.N. Darby, the Plymouth Brethren (called the *Elberfelder Brüder* or *Christliche Versammlung* in Germany) were opposed to organisational alliances for spiritual reasons and, though respected in the Evangelical Aliance, did not look for or expect support from it. The leaders of the closed Brethren found it very difficult to stomach the ban. They were proud of their nationalist credentials. On hearing of the ban Dr Richter, Ernst Brockhaus and Hugo Hartnack, Brethren leaders, wrote to the Geheime Staatspolizei on 29 April 1937 calling for an end to the ban or, at the very least, an explanation for prohibiting a movement that had so many war veterans and National Socialists in it. The men categorically denied that Brethren refused to do military service or take part in the workfare scheme. Nor did they reject the Hitler salute. 'We refuse to have any dealings with people', the letter said, 'who either rejected or fought against the new state'. Brethren stood obediently and loyally behind the Führer of the German people, they added, closing the letter with a respectful 'Heil Hitler!' Numerous petitions were sent to Rudolf Hess. One such petitioner, Eugen Linder, said that he had been an early warrior for the National Socialist cause at a time when every third voter in his town, Haan, opted for the Communists. He himself had written a number of propaganda pamphlets for the NSDAP, of which he had been a member since 1930. He had never doubted that the principles and goals of National Socialism were in complete accord with the principles of the gospel. One point of agreement was the Party principle of *Gemeinnutz vor Eigennutz* set alongside the words of Christ:'Love your neighbour as yourself'. Even among those religious groups which were banned by the Nazis there were not a few members who felt offended to be even considered a critic of the regime.[17]

The religious group which met with more persecution than any other was the Jehovah's Witnesses, at the time known as Bible Students or Serious Bible Students. Their internationalist outlook and links with America, their opposition to oaths, military service and political activities made them suspect in Germany even before Hitler's appointment in January 1933. Indeed, they had been persecuted and discriminated against for some time; the Nazis simply institutionalised what had previously been a religious campaign to oust them from the country. Nobody spoke up for them; nobody defended them. As a result thousands of Witnesses were murdered because they refused to 'heil the Catholic Hitler of Nazi Germany'. They blamed the existence of the Third Reich and its persecuting machinery on the 'love affair between the Vatican and the National Socialists', the 'spiritual adultery' of Catholics and the decay of traditional Protestant values and theology. Though putting much of the blame on the Church to which Hitler belonged and from which he was never excommunicated, Witnesses note that the NSDAP had won its first absolute majority in a state that was nominally 75% Protestant and continued to poll over 20% of the vote in constituencies which had a Protestant majority. Over 95% of the citizens of the state which persecuted them had, of course, been baptised into one of the main denominations. These denominations, through their press organs, supported the ban on their activities. No other church or religious fellowship can match this record of perseverence, courage and a willingness to die before bowing the knee to Hitler. It is reckoned that of the nearly 20,000 Witnesses who lived in Germany in 1933, every second member was imprisoned and every fourth member murdered in a concentration camp. The restoration to positions of social power of both main denominations after the war, as well as the generally working class and underprivileged character of most groups of Witnesses, best explains why their courageous resistance has found so little attention among bourgeois historians and churchmen. They remained suspect in both Germanies after 1945.[18]

The *Allianzblatt* reported in February 1932 that the Police President in Munich had ordered 'the confiscation and seizure of all publications of the International Bible Students Union, Magdeburg' which could be found in Catholic Bavaria.[19] The Union, together with its allied organizations, was prohibited by a decree of the Reich President for the 'Protection of People and State' on 28 February 1933, which claimed the step was necessary because they stirred up 'ill-feeling towards the institutions of Church and State'.[20] On 4 March 1933 non-members were prohibited from spreading their tracts or talking about their doctrines in Württemberg. The Jehovah's Witnesses were prohibited in Bavaria on 13 April 1933, in Prussia on 24 June 1933. Their assets were confiscated.[21] The prohibition of the Union of International Bible Students/Serious Bible Students in Bavaria was reported in the *Allianzblatt*. It followed the reading of the ban and informed evangelicals that the Union had been working together with the Social Democratic Party and the Communist Party of Germany 'under the cover of Christianity' to demoralize and confuse the German people. At the same time the report also noted that the Commissar for Mecklenburg-Schwerin had issued an order prohibiting the Union of Freethinkers and the Union of Serious Bible Students.[22] No commentary is made on the ban. In January 1934 came another report, this time taken from the *Hamburg News*. It reported with apparent relish that the police had been observing the Union for some time and discovered that, in spite of the ban, the Union was still conducting covert activities in the Erfurt region. During a surprise action the police had managed to arrest five people including their outlawed leader. The police also confiscated large quantities of printed matter, which the group had hidden away prior to the ban, as well as a car, which was being used for their evangelistic trips. At the Erfurt police headquarters packages addressed to Union members were found to contain 'illegal, Communist' brochures sent from Berlin. These had been confiscated and six 'Communist curiers' were arrested in this regard. A large quantity of printed material, including newly written manuscripts for illegal flyers and some curier plans were confiscated. In Hochheim, near Erfurt, the police managed to arrest five 'communist functionaries', two of whom had only recently been released from protective custody.[23]

The *Allianzblatt* headline emphasised that the Bible Students were just a front organization for more sinister goings-on being conducted by Communists. Not surprisingly, there is no evidence to suggest Communists infiltrated the Bible Student's organization. This should be seen as an example of the *Allianzblatt*'s blindness to the rather obvious truth. The editors, however, welcomed legal bans on religious groups which were proving to be successful at winning converts. In an article entitled 'Against Sects which Endanger our People', the *Allianzblatt* wrote that times of political upheaval had always been favourable to the growth of all kinds of apocalyptic sects. Spiritist groups in particular seemed to profit from times of crisis and change. The paper noted the formation of a so-called 'Club of the Like-Minded' in the Waldenburg area of Silesia. The members of the sect were said to perform spiritist rituals at their meetings and claimed to be looking for the Kingdom of God. Whoever joined the sect had to fast for a week and was only allowed to eat vegetarian meals. This applied to the children too; babies were said to be weaned off milk at a tender age. As the sect posed a public danger, the Police President of Waldenburg had had its leaders arrested and put in protective custody until their sect stopped all its activities. In that particular case the *Allianzblatt* admitted that the danger of such shenanigans to the government was obvious. 'We must welcome this use of legal powers which has put an end to them!', it reported. The *Allianzblatt* then betrayed, for the first time, a worry that the same decrees would one day be used to stop evangelical work. It said it dearly hoped that the authorities were getting expert advice in their struggle against 'heretics and deluded creatures'.[24] It no doubt realised that there were many in the government who had little understanding of and even less sympathy for the differences between religious groups, and even more officials in the mainstream churches who might look for the opportunity to crack down on pietists within and without ecclesiastical structures.

In September 1933 astrology was attacked as a 'public nuisance'. The boom in the sale of astrological tracts in 1933 – 'thousands of these tracts are being sold' – was disturbing the peace of the country and their content was 'spiritually corrupting'. The editors of *Allianzblatt* welcomed the decision of a court in Saxony which deemed astrological 'propaganda' to be a 'danger to law and order' leading to disorderly conduct, unrest and agitation. On 15 March 1937 the paper praised the Romanian government for stopping the spread of occultism and banning fortune-telling. Contrary to what evangelicals assert today, Hitler did not resort to astrology. His private secretary categorically denied that Hitler had anything but contempt for spiritist practices. Astrological associations were dissolved and spiritists risked severe punishment if they practised their arts during Hitler's period of office. Nor did he welcome the resurgence of Germanic cults which one or two of his comrades dabbled in. 'Nothing would be more foolish', Hitler claimed, 'than to reestablish the worship of Wotan. [...] I especially would not want our movement to acquire a religious character and institute a form of worship. It would be appalling for me if I were to end up in the skin of a Buddha'. To demonise Hitler, as is the contemporary fashion in evangelical circles, is unhistorical or rather anti-historical. Using speculations about occult roots of National Socialism to explain a system of government which, at the time, attracted the almost unanimous support of evangelicals in Germany, does not help one to understand why Hitler was able to gain so many followers.[25]

The following month, the religious group called 'Shepherd and Sheep', set up by Friedrich August Hain in Saxony, was dissolved. Providing support to 'one of the strangest groups in the history of sects in Saxony' and seeking to preserve the fellowship amongst members would be punished, stated the Ministry of the Interior in Saxony.[26] No comments were made in the *Allianzblatt* about this further ban but another article in the same issue ('What is a Sect?') criticised the fact that evangelical Christians were 'frequently' being classified by Church authorities as sects. The effect of this ignorance was 'disastrous'. The example of a standard text (*Kirchenkunde*, published in Schwerin in 1932) written by the bishop of Mecklenburg, Gerhard Tolzien, is recited. In this 'otherwise objective and excellent study', the Baptists, the Methodists and the Herrnhut Brethren are classified alongside Christian Science, Mormons and Serious Bible Students as 'sects'. That, according to the *Allianzblatt*, was 'incomprehensible'.[27] The first named groups, however, were never banned by the Hitler government, although, no doubt, there were not a few traditional Lutherans and Calvinists in Germany who would have welcomed such measures.

In December 1935 a report was taken from the *Völkischer Beobachter* (Nr 320) in which the Gestapo announced that the Anthroposophic Society had been dissolved and prohibited. It listed the reasons given by the authorities for the ban, viz. its 'internationalist outlook' and 'close ties to Freemasons abroad, Jews and pacifists'. The anthroposophic teaching methods and goals, based on the pedagogy of the founder, Steiner, and applied in anthroposophic schools (many of which are still in operation), were, the *Beobachter* stated, 'individualistic, geared to the educational needs of the individual' and so had 'nothing in common with National Socialist educational principles'. The continuing activities of the Society would have had 'a debilitating effect' on the interests of the National Socialist state. It was dissolved because of its 'subversive and dangerous character'.[28] The *Allianzblatt* adds a short 'biblical' commentary. The paper had shown in detail that 'not a single biblical truth' was recognised by the anthroposophic system. All biblical doctrines were either devalued or rejected. 'Of course, it was not religious reasons, but reasons of another kind which have led to the prohibition of the Society', the editor argued.[29]

The joy of seeing yet one more competitor in the religious market place disappear is only slightly concealed. In February 1935, following the banning of the 'Weissenberg sect' (the Protestant Church of the Revelation of St. John) in Prussia, the editors of *Allianzblatt* were more open about their satisfaction. It said the ban was 'justified' and 'a blessing'. The 'spiritist nonsense' performed by the sect not only endangered the souls of people, it was also 'dangerous to public safety'. Once again, the editor recognised the potential dangers of supporting the banning of a religious grouping. He hoped the authorities would 'be able in future to differentiate appropriately between such a scandalous public nuisance like the Weissenberg sect and healthy Christian practices'.[30] One can here detect slight discomfort on the part of the editors, and yet the basic attack on religious freedom is welcomed as a 'blessing'. Their trust in the authorities is still unshakeable, for their own Christian faith was not under attack. Nagel and his colleagues were presumably happy that the 'party spirit' and sectarian outgrowths were also coming to an end and that their faith and the existence of Free Churches had received, after the years of Church-State collusion, public recognition. This had most noticeably been the case with the centenary celebrations of the founding of the first Baptist church in Germany (April 1934 in Hamburg) and the Baptist World Congress held in the German capital in August 1934 when government representatives had taken part in the proceedings. One of the central figures in the Baptist movement, F.W. Simoleit, who became at this time a member of the Executive Committee of the Evangelical Alliance in Germany, said in May 1934 that 'we Baptists have rarely ever taken as much pleasure in a government as we have done during the past year'. Nor could evangelical leaders forget that the Weimar Republic had tolerated not only all kinds of faith in God but also 'the crudest and blasphemous' attacks on the same.[31]

Was one perhaps satisfied that the tables had turned, that 'accounts could be settled'?[32] Did one hope that the Day of Judgement had arrived already for these sects? It was certainly not surprising that the *Allianzblatt* reported on the dissolution of Freemasonic lodges in Germany. Evangelicals would have disliked the secrecy and occult practices, even though the leaders must have known that the Alliance had been founded in Freemasons Hall in London. The German Branch was formally set up in Freemasons Tavern in London on 1 September 1846, amidst a whole range of occult symbols. One might, however, have expected a certain amount of nostalgic sympathy for the brethren. The arrest of the Grand Master of the Grand National Mother Lodge, the confiscation of the Grand Lodge's assets and the 'self-dissolution' of the old Prussian lodges (21 July 1935) which 'was carried out with the consent of the Interior Ministry' were seen as events of historical importance. For a long time the lodges had been 'concealed by a mystical darkness'. The paper was glad that the veil had been lifted. 'Research' had exposed the 'true goal of Freemasonry' to be the creation of 'a Jewish world republic'.33 The *Allianzblatt* reported in the same year on a Masonic meeting in France on 15 June 1936 ('Growing Numbers Turn Their Backs on Religion in France') which links the religious indifference in the country to the activities of Freemasons. It claims French army officers were told by Masons they would lose all chance of promotion if they went to Catholic mass. Under the 'slogan' of brotherhood and tolerance the 'poison of intolerance' was mixed by Masons with 'Russian atheism' to form a new union. The 'bacilli' of the French Revolution had coalesced with Bolshevism and been given a new lease of life. That energy was, however, 'corruptive', and 'ruinous'.34

Not until the autumn of 1940 could Germans innoculate the French, too, against these germs after troops occupied the Grand Orient de France building in the Rue Cadet as well as the headquarters of the Grande Loge de France in the Rue Puteaux. Of the 80,000 Masons in Germany at the time of Hitler's take-over, 4,800 suffered some form of persecution (53 dying in concentration camps). The German government confiscated property and monies to the value of 80 million Reichsmarks, of which only a small proportion was returned to the lodges after the war.35

The Nazi watchword was also the evangelical watchword: *Fight against Bolshevism.* The goal was the same: to protect German culture with its Christian features. The means to achieve that goal seemed, to evangelicals, to be justifiable. A clear understanding of the developing character of National Socialism was nowhere to be heard. In contrast, the Jehovah's Witnesses produced a tract entitled 'Look the Facts in the Face' which hit the nail on the head. It talked of the appearance on earth of a 'hideous monster', which – in complete disregard of the inalienable rights of man – was engaged in the 'rapid seizure of power and dominion over the world'. 'What is this hideous monster? It is the totalitarian government or dictatorship, which makes the state supreme, reduces all men to mindless obedience, rules over them by arbitrary despots and forces everyone to render them unconditional obedience. This monster is, therefore, a deceitful aping of God's righteous rule'.36

Criticism in the *Allianzblatt* of the government's religious policies was only rarely expressed. A report in the July 1935 issue shows that there was a degree of tolerance on the part of the government for muted criticism. It is entitled 'Neo-pagan Services on the Radio'. It dealt with the growing interest in old Germanic ceremonies. The radio station in Berlin had transmitted a 'German Spring Service' on Easter Monday in its programme 'Hour of the Powerful', which, as announced by the station's newsreader prior to the transmission, was organised by 'adherents of the Germanic Faith Movement'. The *Allianzblatt* recognised that radio was probably the most important means of publicity. Its significance in the life of the German people can be gauged by the fact that the number of radio owners had increased from the beginning of 1933 from 4.3 million to over 6.7 million, ie. by nearly 2.5 million or by over 50%. The editor was annoyed that the neo-pagan movement could advertise its activities and beliefs in public rooms (e.g. the Sports Palace in Berlin), in magazines and on the radio, at a time when the work of the Church was subject to various kinds of restrictions, the removal of which they felt was all-important, not least for the sake of our nation.[37]

The *Allianzblatt* reported throughout the 1930s on the resurgence of all kinds of Germanic religious sects which were tolerated by the government without receiving official support or sanction.[38] Nowhere does the *Allianzblatt* intimate that there may be a relationship between National Socialism and the Wotan cults; indeed, it quotes Göring as saying their 'ridiculous' ideas showed that they hadn't understood National Socialism at all. In fact, he said, they harmed the National Socialist movement.[39]

Evangelicals agreed with that sentiment. One was 'touched' and felt 'grateful' that the Führer was apparently concerned that evangelicals in particular contribute to evangelising and developing the spirituality of the German people.[40] Hitler, they believed, wanted the Bible-based fellowships and Free Churches to lead the German people back to Christ. They and they alone could bring about unity in German Protestantism and overcome 'the corrupting power of individualism' in the Church.[41] Declarations made by the Gnadau Association to Promote Fellowship and Evangelisation (8 June 1933) and the Federation of Independent Evangelical Fellowships (17 June 1933), in which thanks were offered to God for the 'reorganization of the State', were reprinted in the *Allianzblatt*.[42] The Baptists proclaimed that 'to profess one's patriotic beliefs is, as for as we are concerned, superfluous, because the Baptists in Germany were always nationalists'.[43] 'We declare without reserve our support for the new state, for the way it was formed and the way it has developed', the Baptists proclaimed.[44] The Secretary of the Federation of Independent Evangelical Fellowships reported to the Central Conference of the organization, which counted 12,723 members, that the political developments had in no way restricted their labours. 'Even the dissolution of our youth organisation has hardly been noticed', he said.[45] He did, however, report that 'the danger of accomodation to the new situation is extremely great' and the witnessing spirit had given way in places to spiritual self-satisfaction. During the whole of 1933 there were worries in the Free Churches, encouraged by press reports and unsubstantiated rumours, that they would be forced to dissolve or integrate themselves into the German Protestant Church. The Reich Church Minister at the time, Dr Simon Schöffel, and Reich Bishop Müller, emphasised that 'denominational struggles' would be avoided and the government 'counted on cooperation wherever common areas of work arose'.[46] From 1934 on, the *Allianzblatt* had little to report on the Free Churches for there were 'few declarations of fundamental importance made by their leaders'.[47] They had been left alone by the government to 'spiritualize' the German nation.

The *Allianzblatt* broke its relative silence with reports on a speech made by Bishop Nuelsen to the First German Central Conference of the Episcopal Methodist Church and a speech made by the Chairman of the Union of Protestant Free Churches in Germany (VEF), Dr Melle (Frankfurt), the latter speaking in the name of the Union. These speeches give a representative and valuable impression of how Free Church leaders saw the four-year old Third Reich. Bishop Nuelsen is reported to have said he was 'full of boundless appreciation for the Reich government' for the work of the Methodist Church had been limited 'in no way whatsoever' and the government 'has put no pressure at all upon us'. They had been able to continue their operations in the traditional manner. 'In fact', he added, 'we can say with thanks that we have experienced all kinds of favours and friendly understanding and concessions from the government'. Talk about a 'Church struggle' was inappropriate as for as Methodists were concerned: 'We have no conflict with the Führer or the government of the Third Reich'. There had been no occasion at all for that. On the contrary, they were glad and thankful for 'the freedom and the peace' which had been brought about. They prayed that the Lord would continue to give the Führer and his ministers 'the spirit of wisdom, of knowledge and the fear of God' to serve the German people responsibly – to promote their welfare and be 'a blessing to the whole world'. Nuelsen believed the freedoms Methodists enjoyed had to do with the fact that, as a Free Church, they did not 'covet the privileges and special rights the state churches enjoy', such as the right to financial support from the government or church taxes. 'Our pastors are not civil servants whose salaries and emoluments are financed by the government', he said, but men whose salaries were paid from voluntary contributions. As German nationals, Methodists faithfully stood by and supported their government in every way possible.[48]

Bishop Melle (Frankfurt a.M.), speaking at the annual general meeting of the Federation of Free Churches, said it was not necessary to remind people that the Protestant Free Churches believed God had intervened in the turn of events in 1933. They welcomed the new state 'joyfully and with a good conscience', praying for it earnestly. In their worship services prayers were regularly offered up for the Führer and his officials, he said, adding that 'our mission wasn't and isn't politics, but the proclamation of the gospel'. Methodists did not feel entitled to join in the arguments going on inside the Provincial Churches. In their opinion the conflict was 'partly about questions and goals arising from the ideal of a state church' – something we do not find in the Scriptures of the New Testament. The 'church crisis' was in effect a divine 'judgement' on the spiritual life of the Church in Germany. He did, however, express sympathy and prayer support for those who were suffering. At the same time Methodists generally believed they could 'join neither side in the struggle'. There had been on this matter 'complete unanimity' in the Methodist leadership from the very beginning. They relished their freedom to evangelize and build new fellowships. The authorities and the government had thankfully 'gained confidence in us'. Moreover, their contacts with Free Church groups abroad helped 'to win them over' as well and create 'understanding and sympathy' for the new Germany.[49]

Dr Melle, a leading evangelical figure, seems to have believed, quite rightly, that the Church's struggle against unscriptural ideas in the message preached (e.g. the nature of the Church or the character of the Old Testament) was over. As a result the Free Churches refused to take sides in the crisis: their relatively small size, their good relations with the Third Reich and the fact that believers and unbelievers could be found in all the various groupings of the Confessing Church (German Christian, moderate Lutheran, radical Dahlemite, conservative Lutheran) encouraged them to stick to their traditional non-interventionist stance. As for the foreign diplomacy of Free Church leaders, another report in the *Allianzblatt* may be quoted to illustrate the point. In March 1936 Dr Melle left Germany to take part in the General Conference of the Methodist Church, held in Columbus, Ohio, in May. Melle made speeches at various universities (eg. Boston, Washington D.C.) and noted the high degree of respect and esteem paid to the German ambassador, Dr Hans Luther, by Americans. As a German national, Melle said this was 'especially pleasing'. The tenor of Melle's message was everywhere the same. He spoke of the 'German renewal movement' and Adolf Hitler's role in 'inspiring the German people with new self-confidence and a faith in its mission and future'.

With reference to the religious situation Melle said one had to remember that all religious movements including the Reformation had political overtones and unleashed powerful political forces. Germany had once again become 'a battleground' for political and religious ideas which might well lead to a major extension of the influence of the gospel. The assembled, presided over by Dr Ezra Tipple, the former President of Drew University, are said to have listened with 'the utmost interest' to these remarks and expressed their thanks at the end with thunderous applause.[50]

The following year, 1937, Dr Melle gave the speech in Oxford that some evangelicals in the provincial churches felt was tantamount to an official withdrawal of support for the position of the Confessing Church. Evangelicals outside those churches were far more supportive of the Methodist position. The *Zeltgruss*, the press organ of the German Tent Mission organisation, responded to the Message sent by the Oxford Ecumenical Conference to the *Deutsche Evangelische Kirche*. Addressing in particular its readers abroad, the *Zeltgruss* emphasised that the German authorities had in no way attempted to influence or prevent the preaching of the gospel in its two huge tents. This was proof, the 6,000 readers were told, that in the Third Reich Adolf Hitler had 'truly guaranteed an unlimited freedom to preach the gospel'. The editor, R.B. Volkmann, assured them that anyone could practise their Christian religion as they so wanted and that he, as an editor of a Christian newspaper, had in no way been put under pressure. Though the stance taken by Melle's critics was a minority position and, in any case, substantially wrong, it is clear there was no evangelical criticism of Melle's patriotism and support for the Reich government. These were features that typified all kinds of evangelicals at the time. Of course, one would expect that evangelicals would take seriously biblical calls to obedience to the powers ordained by God to govern the country. Romans 13 was the lens through which all was seen. Their leaders, within the Free Church tradition at least, lacked the theological tools to justify any other course of action. Nor was there a tradition of civil and religious liberty for all in the country. There was also a willingness to give the new government the benefit of the doubt and to accept its reasoning behind limiting individual freedoms for the sake of the greater good of the nation. Even taking the restrictions on press reporting into consideration, the *Allianzblatt* seemed at times even unwilling or unable to doubt governmental policy. Many evangelical concerns had been taken seriously by the National Socialists; their 'positive Christianity' was always interpreted in a way reconcilable with evangelical doctrine and practice. The changes had occurred so quickly and, for evangelicals, painlessly, that divine blessing was suspected. This, in turn, was the reason for the propaganda campaign conducted at home and abroad by evangelical leaders. Let it finally be noted that the *Allianzblatt* was not alone in this campaign. Though a detailed study of the whole range of the evangelical weeklies and monthlies still has to be done, Wolfgang Gerlach has noted the pro-Nazi stance taken by the paper *Licht und Leben*, while Bernd Densky's minute analysis of the Baptist weekly *Wahrheitszeuge* confirms the fact that evangelicals heaped praise on National Socialist domestic policy.[51]

Notes

1. EA 05.11.1933 (Nr 45), 733. See also *Fascism and The Free Churches*, EA 30.06 1935 (Nr 12), 191. G. Jordy (1986, 64).
2. EA 30.03.1937 (Nr 6).
3. *Moody Bible Institute Monthly*, October 1935, 69.
4. EA 30.03.1936 (Nr 6), 95.
5. G. Nagel (1934, 45).
6. EA 30.11.1935 (Nr 22), 355.
7. EA 30.08.1936 (Nr 16), 253ff.
8. EA 30.08.1936 (Nr 16), 253-5.
9. EA 15.02.1937 (Nr 3), 46.
10. W. Hütt (1990, 60-67, 76, 230-271).
11. P. Meiners (1985, 142).
12. P. Meiners (1985, 145); K. Zehrer (1986, 43); see EA 15.02.1936 (Nr 3), 45.
13. EA 15.03.1936 (Nr 5), 80.
14. EA 30.08.1936 (Nr 16), 252-253; D. Bonhoeffer (1977, 72-74).
15. P. Meiners (1985, 143).
16. Gutachten des Instituts für Zeitgeschichte (1958, 46-47).
17. Gutachten (1958, 49); Friedhelm Menk (1986, 66-70).
18. *The Watchtower*, 1 May 1992, 12; *Der Wachturm*, 15 April 1989, 12. *Erwachet!*, 08 November 1989, 19; Michael H. Kater (1969).
19. EA 21.02.1932 (Nr 8), 124. At the time Witnesses were known in Germany as the (Serious) Bible Students.
20. P. Matheson (1981, 48).
21. Gutachten (1958, 48).
22. EA 21.05.1933 (Nr 21), 331.

23. EA 15.01.1934 (Nr 1), 15: *Unter der Maske der Bibelforscher.*
24. EA 03.12.1933 (Nr 49), 780.
25. EA 24.09.1933 (Nr 39), 637; Alan Bullock (1973, 389); Wilhelm Wulff (1968, 7).
26. EA 22.10.1933 (Nr 43), 688.
27. EA 22.10.1933 (Nr 43), 688. A one-hundred page report produced by an Enquete Commission established by the German Bundestag in 1997 to look into 'So-called Sects and Esoteric Groups' (sparked off by the controversy over methods used by the Scientology organisation) listed the Baptists and Pentecostals amongst the organisations worthy of surveillance and legal controls. The U.S. State Department, the United Nations Human Rights Committee and the American evangelical Rutherford Institute have all attacked discrimination of religious minorities (including Jehovah's Witnesses and charismatic Christians) in Germany. Repeating the mistakes of their past, the two main Christian denominations in Germany have given public support to the government's many-pronged campaign against Scientology. Press releases of Church of Scientology International, 2 April 1997, 15 April 1997, 19 April 1997; *Süddeutsche Zeitung*, 11 July 1997; *Die Zeit*, 16 August 1996.
28. EA 15.12.1935 (Nr 23), 267.
29. EA 15.12.1935 (Nr 23), 267. After Göring announced the prohibition and dissolution of the Federation of Non-Dogmatic Religious Fellowships (*Bund freireligiöser Gemeinden Deutschlands*) the *Allianzblatt* argued the reason was 'not religious, but related to national policy. One fears these organisations could help to achieve Communist or Marxist goals', EA 15.12.1934 (Nr 23), 384.
30. EA 28.02.1935 (Nr 4), 62.
31. EA 15.12.1934 (Nr 23), 382; Bernd R. Densky (1983, 49-51).
32. EA 07.05.1933 (Nr 19), 298.
33. EA 30.01.1936 (Nr 2), 31.
34. EA 30.08.1936 (Nr 16), 254. Professor Adolf Köberle, in a lecture to full-time Christians in Blankenburg, said the government had to dissolve the Order of Freemasons because 'their international intrigues were perfectly well-known', EA 30.11.1935 (Nr 22), 345.
35. J. Holtorf (1986, Chapter 4). Well-known victims of the Nazis, who were also Freemasons, include Wilhelm Leuschner, executed after the 20 July 1944 assassination attempt, Nobel Prize winner Carl von Ossietzky and the writer Kurt Tucholsky.
36. P. Matheson (1981, 101-102).
37. This was not the Faith Movement of German Christians, but an openly 'neo-pagan' group. It was not a government-supported movement. EA 15.07.1935 (Nr 13), 205. The various newspapers of the Germanic religious groups were *Reichswart* (circulation of 24,000), *Durchbruch* (3,000), *Der Deutsche Glaube* (5,000), Ludendorff's *Am heiligen Quell* (67,000). The German Christians produced *Das Positive Christentum* (26,000), *Evangelium*

im Dritten Reich (17,000), *Briefe an DC* (13,000), *Weckruf* (10,000) and *Reichsbote* (9,000). Statistics in EA 30.03.1936 (Nr 6), 95.
38. EA 30.12.1936 (Nr 24), 388; EA 28.02.1935 (Nr 4), 62; EA 15.07.1935 (Nr 13), 204-5; EA 30.12.1937 (Nr 24), 349. According to a report in *Die Reformation*, there were 1,000 different Christian denominations or fellowships in Germany in 1937, EA 15.01.1937 (Nr 1), 15.
39. EA 30.11.1935 (Nr 22), 355.
40. EA 25.06.1933 (Nr 26), 416.
41. EA 11.06.1933 (Nr 24), 383.
42. EA 16.07.1933 (Nr 29), 458-9.
43. EA 15.01.1934 (Nr 1), 14.
44. EA 15.01.1934 (Nr 1), 14.
45. EA 30.07.1934 (Nr 14), 228.
46. EA 17.12.1933 (Nr 51), 811; K. Zehrer (1986, 23, 27, 83).
47. EA 15.01.1937 (Nr 1), 14.
48. EA 15.01.1937 (Nr 1), 13.
49. EA 15.01.1937 (Nr 1), 13-14.
50. EA 30.06.1936 (Nr 12), 184-185.
51. Wolfgand Gerlach (1987, 31-32, 119-120); *Zeltgruss*, Nr 8, August 1937, 116; Bernd R. Densky (1983).

Chapter Six

Evangelical Social Concerns

The *Allianzblatt* looked for signs of a socio-religious awakening to follow the 'political awakening' of January 1933. The subject of 'awakening' became a key issue at Alliance meetings throughout 1933, e.g. those in Siegen-Hammerhütte at the end of September.[1] Such a revival would, they hoped, lead to changes in the realms of personal behaviour as well as social priorities. The issues of employment and poverty were only two issues that were considered of importance. Many seemingly minor concerns were of major symbolic relevance for evangelicals and they pleaded with the government to deal with these issues. No social restructuring, however, would have any long-term success in their view if it was not based on a profound reassessment of the importance of religion, or rather Christianity, for the health of society. Evangelical leaders thus looked for signs of the changing times in which they lived. A contributors to the *Allianzblatt*, Bernhard Peters, was, as has been mentioned already, just one of a whole host of amateur sociologists in the evangelical camp who wrote on the religio-prophetic importance of societal trends. They interpreted a number of such trends in a way that was quite flattering to the National Socialist government.

In an article on 'a movement to join the Church' it was noted that the political events of the previous few weeks had unleashed a movement to join the Church. A number of friends had reported to the editor that more application forms to join a church had reached church consistories in the previous three weeks than in the whole period since 1919. Such a movement, which was, however, seen to spring from political opportunism rather than from a genuine Christian revival, called for great caution. Evangelicals were less concerned about Church membership than Christian discipleship.[2]

Adolf Hitler repeatedly made mention of his faith in God and numerous National Socialist leaders (*not* Martin Bormann, Heinrich Himmler, Alfred Rosenberg or Julius Streicher, to mention just the national figures) talked openly of their Christian beliefs – which were duly reported in the press. The 'Day of Potsdam' (21 March 1933), on which the Reichstag was opened, was stage-managed to reveal the new system as 'an embodiment of the Christian conservative spirit' (C. Nicolaisen). One important example of this respect for tradition was the honouring of financial treaties signed by previous governments with the Church over a century prior to the emergence of the NSDAP. In a speech in the Reichstag on 30 January 1939 Hitler detailed the sums of money his government had granted to the Churches: in the financial year 1933 130 million Reichsmarks, growing to 170 million Reichsmarks in 1934, 250 million RM in 1935, 320 million RM in 1936, 400 million in 1937 and 500 million in 1938.[3] These huge amounts were largely the church taxes collected by the state for the Church. Clearly, the example set by most National Socialist leaders encouraged others to become Church members. In a commentary on 'The New Reich and the Church of Christ', Bernhard Peters wrote that after Hitler had taken over the reins of power, atheistic Marxism had 'soon disappeared from the public stage'. People began to talk of the return of the German people to Christianity, and evangelicals noted 'deep moral fibre' and 'high moral quality' in all the government's pronouncements. The hopes of a spiritual rebirth of the nation had been encouraged by the new rulers.[4] Yet such a rebirth faced major problems, most of which were blamed on the Weimar Republic and its system of government. Of particular interest to evangelicals was the introduction of daily school prayers, at the start and end of the day. The 'dechristianisation' of the German people had gone so far that prayer was discounted by most people as a stupid activity. Many teachers had serious difficulty praying out loud. The 'tragedy' of the German situation was summed up by the experience of a preacher in the Ruhr area: he found out by talking to a group of young workers that none had any idea who Jesus was. Not the Church, but the system of government was blamed. 'What a huge amount of guilt lies on the shoulders of the system that has now collapsed!' Much work would have to be done to rebuild the Christian edifice. The *Allianzblatt* took courage from reports that the Bavarian Interior Minister had declared in a meeting with mayors that the old-fashioned handshake as a welcome to one's new post was no longer acceptable: every mayor in future (like every soldier) would have to swear by God that he would perform his duties before God. Those unwilling to swear an oath before God would not be able to work for the state, he said. Only God-fearing people could serve the German people properly. Such statements were interpreted as signs that political leaders were once again aware of the nation's true source of strength. Such men deserved the support and prayers of Christians.[5]

Another edict relating to school education also gave encouragement. It declared that teaching young people to appreciate the value of the state and the community derived most strength from the truths of Christianity. Loyalty and responsibility towards one's nation and Fatherland were, it stated, most deeply anchored in the Christain faith. Educationists had a special duty to safeguard the Christian school and the Christian fundamentals of all education. As Adolf Stoecker had once demanded, and Bernhard Peters reminded politicians, all teaching in the Christian schools of Germany should be carried out in a Christian spirit.[6]

The importance of religious undercurrents for the initial acceptance of the Nazi Party as well as the response to apparent socio-economic successes has not always been recognised. These religious elements undoubtedly predisposed 'true believers' towards the new system of government.

There were individuals at the time who tried to explain the acceptability of National Socialism to masses of people by reference to their religio-social make-up. Wilhelm Reich, a psychoanalyst whose work – in contrast to the *Allianzblatt* – was banned by the Nazis, wrote in his *The Mass Psychology of Fascism* (1933) that Christianity (he calls it 'mystical contagion') was 'the most important psychological precondition for the assimilation of fascist ideology by the masses'.[7] If this is true, then it explains why the NSDAP was keen to keep religion as a subject on the school time-table. The Party certainly wanted, and perhaps needed, 'religious experience' and a religiously trained people. 'Religious excitation, which is anti-sexual and a substitution for sexuality at one and the same time'[8] was functionally important in fascism, Reich argued. To quote George Orwell:

> Unlike Winston, she had grasped the inner meaning of the Party's sexual puritanism. It was not merely that the sex instinct created a world of its own which was outside the Party's control and which therefore had to be destroyed if possible. What was more important was that sexual privation induced hysteria, which was desirable because it could be transformed into war-fever and leader-worship. [..] All this marching up and down and cheering and waving flags is simply sex gone sour. If you're happy inside yourself, why should you get excited about Big Brother... [9]

A Christianity gone wrong has traditionally led to sexual repression, as Karlheinz Deschner (1989) has powerfully argued. This, according to Reich, produces hysteria and can intensify the sadistic impulse. It is clear, anyway, that the Third Reich suppressed and repressed eroticism as rigorously as the Churches had in the past; this policy reaped the applause of the Evangelical Alliance.

Hitler was as concerned about sexual morality as any TV preacher today in America. In *Mein Kampf* he bewailed the fact that unser gesamtes öffentliches Leben gleicht heute einem Treibhaus sexueller Vorstellungen und Reize. Man betrachte doch den Speisezettel unserer Kinos, Varietés und Theater, und man kann wohl kaum leugnen, dass dies nicht die richtige Kost, vor allem für die Jugend, ist. In Auslagen und an Anschlagsäulen wird mit den niedrigsten Mitteln gearbeitet. [...] Diese sinnlich schwüle Atmosphäre führt zu Vorstellungen und Erregungen in einer Zeit, da der Knabe für solche Dinge noch gar kein Verständnis haben dürfte.

the whole of our public life may be compared to a hot-house for the forced growth of sexual notions and incitements. A glance at the bill of fare provided by our cinemas, playhouses and theatres, suffices to prove that this is not the right food, especially for our young people. Hoardings and advertisement kiosks combine to attract the public in the most vulgar manner. [...] This seductive and sensuous atmosphere puts notions into the heads of our youth which, at their age, ought still to be unknown to them.

As an example of cultural degeneration and national decline Hitler notes the signs posted at the doors of theatres and art centres: *For Adults Only*. He found prostitution a 'disgrace to humanity'. Such phenomena called for radical social reforms. In the mean time, however, the younger generation needed to be aware of the dangers involved in sexual promiscuity and the need to avoid temptation. Perhaps his own personal experience as a Catholic taught Hitler the solution for a man full of sexual energy but inhibited by a rigid Christian code of morality:

Der Junge, der in Sport und Turnen zu einer eisernen Abhärtung gebracht wird, unterliegt dem Bedürfnis sinnlicher Befriedigungen weniger als der ausschliesslich mit geistiger Kost gefütterte Stubenhocker. [...] So muss die ganze Erziehung darauf eingestellt werden, die freie Zeit des Jungen zu einer nützlichen Ertüchtigung seines Körpers zu verwenden. Er hat kein Recht, in diesen Jahren müssig herumzulungern, Strassen und Kinos unsicher zu machen, sondern soll nach seinem sonstigen Tagewerk den jungen Leib stählen und hart machen, auf dass ihn dereinst auch das Leben nicht zu weich finden möge.

Those boys whose constitutions have been trained and hardened by sports and gymnastics are less prone to sexual indulgence than those stay-at-homes who have been fed exclusively with mental pabulum. [...] ..the day's curriculum must be arranged so as to occupy a boy's free time in profitable development of his physical powers. He has no right in those years to loaf about, becoming a nuisance in public streets and in cinemas; but when his day's work is done he ought to harden his young body so that his strength may not be found wanting when the occasion arises.

Elsewhere in *Mein Kampf*, quoted by Nagel so often, Hitler candidly reveals himself as 'an overbearing anti-feminist, a petit-bourgeois patriarch, who looks down on 'females' who he only requires for pleasure and reproduction'.[10] Marriage has the purpose of reproducing and preserving the race, of producing 'images of the Lord and not monstrous mixtures of man and monkey'. Because of a man's potency, he should marry early. If love was not controlled and channelled into reproduction, it was debased, wasteful and lecherous.[11]

There was in this area a lot of common ground between National Socialists and evangelicals. The *Allianzblatt* had been calling for tough measures to 'clean up' the media, the streets and the beaches long before 1933. Emergency measures were needed to deal with the 'hell' of the red-light St. Pauli area of Hamburg and the 'murder of souls' in Germany's big cities which had become 'colleges for up-and-coming criminals'. A 'systematic poisoning and polluting of human souls' could not be stamped out by a 'disastrously weak and sentimental' government, cried the *Allianzblatt* in February 1932.[12] Ruthless decrees were called for to tackle 'shameful excesses' and 'unbridled sensuality'. The government was encouraged to 'go to war' against the unrestrained crudeness of the times. It hoped for a man of Mussolini's stature who would 'rule with a rod of iron' and 'declare war on public shamelessness'.[13] Words of praise were found for Mussolini's 'manly, dignified, true words' on the corruption of morals in his day. Praise was found, too, for his actions. He had banished licentiousness and the 'nonsense of beauty contests'. With one stroke of his pen Mussolini had put an end to the scandal of nude dancing.[14] One of the fatal attractions of National Socialism for German evangelicals was its 'clean' image. The advertisements pages in the National Socialist press were said to be generally of a high moral quality and free from morally offensive business. To the extent that National Socialists tried to combat 'filth and trash' in literature, the press, cinema and theatre, evangelicals stood side by side with them. Perhaps due to their study of *Mein Kampf* some National Socialists certainly took rather puritanical ideas of 'clean living' seriously. This remained one of the religious dimensions of Nazi ideology and policy. Thus, in April 1935 a number of decrees were issued to tackle the problem of sleazy, sensationalist tabloid newspapers 'in the interests of moral uprightness'.[15]

Throughout the early 1930s Nagel received letters from Christians concerned about the 'unruly and wild goings-on at beaches'. He referred his readers to a decree of the Prussian Commissar, Dr Bracht, who had forbidden 'all nude performances in the theatres and revue clubs' as well as beauty contests, which were, Nagel said, 'signs of cultural decay'. One was no longer allowed to sunbathe in the nude or go to restaurants in one's swimming costumes. Laws were needed, more laws. It was wrong to say that public mischiefs could be fought with spiritual weapons, Nagel argued. Such talk was just the 'pseudo-spiritual idiom of the devil'.[16]

Another decree 'deserving the widest publication and attention' passed on 19 June 1931 aimed to 'combat offensive displays', whereby businessman, for the sake of profit, used 'sexually arousing' materials to sell their products. It also struck at 'magazines with erotic or sexual content', with nudes on the front cover, and the way 'places of entertainment used nude pictures to attract customers'. Such a 'deplorable state of affairs' should be countered with warnings to the business owner, injunctions and even the use of police force.[17]

Ever since the Church lost its monopolistic control over knowledge and the opinion-forming process when printing was invented (1455), it has been concerned about what people read and look at. Censorship was shortly thereafter introduced. In the sixteenth century there were already a number of press laws in Germany and in 1580 Daniel, Elector of Mainz, promulgated an edict against obscene writings. Since then hundreds of laws have tried, and failed, to stop people printing and reading 'obscene' and 'pornographic' materials. In 1926 a law was passed 'to protect young people from trashy and filthy writings' but Christain groups and political conservatives remained worried that regulations were too general and ineffective. National Socialists had deliberately fed such concerns. The *Kampfbund für deutsche Kultur* (Action League To Protect German Culture), set up in 1928 by a man whose religious views were rejected by evangelicals, Alfred Rosenberg, won conservative support for its struggle against 'cultural Bolshevism' and liberalism. Some of their ideas and slogans reappear on the pages of the *Allianzblatt*. What the paper does not report is the fact that the decrees passed since 1926 were also – primarily – aimed at artists and writers not in favour with the authorities; in effect, they were conceived as instruments to suppress opposition.

Since January 1930 a National Socialist, Wilhelm Frick, had been Minister of Education and of the Interior in Thuringia. Immediately after his appointment he promised to turn his province into a 'cultural stronghold' against the 'negro culture' of the Weimar Republic.[18] This Nazi cultural experiment was sure to impress Nagel. In June 1932 his 'heart breathed a sigh of relief' when he read about the *Deutscher Frauen-Kampfbund*

(Women's Action League) in Thuringia was protesting against 'Marxist and Bolshevist trends'. He quotes one of the women as saying that the League had been 'fighting for ages against the anti-culture of negro dancing and jazz music'. Such reactions to jazz, foreshadowing the even wilder response to rock 'n roll in the 1950s, reflected the cultural insecurities of evangelicals, on both sides of the Atlantic, in a modern world.[19]

Nagel was against permitting 'this undignified form of dance and music'. One expected much from Hitler's cultural policies and in this regard one was not disappointed. In June 1933 an article appeared under the title 'Fight Against Nudism' which dealt with a 'remarkable decree' by the Prussian Interior Minister. This fashion, popular especially among city dwellers, was declared by the decree to be 'one of the greatest dangers for German culture and morality'. The *Allianzblatt* called it a 'cultural aberration' and an 'epidemic ruining the nation'. In its view, the nudist movement killed off the natural feeling of modesty in women, destroyed a man's respect for women and so undermined the preconditions for any form of genuine culture. The editor said he expected all police authorities to take all the necessary measures to support the 'spiritual forces' which had been resuscitated by the Nazi movement in order to 'eradicate nudism'. He hoped the 'sword of those in authority' would cut deep into 'this pestilence'.[20]

Not only with regards to nudism did Nagel see the cultural ideas of the National Socialists 'coming very close to values of the Kingdom of God'.[21] Here were two movements in unison, rebuilding the 'ruins' left by 'Bolshevist' influence. In its attacks on nudity in the media and cultural spheres, nudism and the unfettered licence of the large cities, the Baptist paper, *Der Wahrheitszeuge*, followed the line taken by the *Allianzblatt*. Its editors, Paul Schmidt and, from 1936, Otto Muske, supported Nagel in his desire to see his compatriots lead 'clean, pure and self-disciplined' lives. This was, however, made difficult by the 'streams of ruinous filth poured over our poor downtrodden people'. Nagel quoted from an edition of the *Völkischer Beobachter*[22] in which the Nazi paper deplored how things 'decent and proper' were covered with derision and ridicule in the press. The Nazi paper criticised the content of films. Even by 1920, it said, most of the films only aimed to keep people watching. The acting had no instructive or ennobling value. Even worse were those plays which predominantly appealed to the phantasy of those in the auditorium with exciting and provocative performances or which filled them with 'horribly frightening and morbid impressions' which are bound to overexcite them. Ruinous were also the crime and detective films. The criminal was always the hero. Extremely questionable were, moreover, the innumerable tedious love stories based on impossible assumptions. A whole range of films were aimed at the lowest of all human drives by portraying love scenes, scenes where people undress, bathing scenes, couples disappearing into bedrooms and so on. The life of prostitutes was candidly shown in numerous films, often under the guise of wanting to preach morality. Then there were those films which pretended to offer sexual education. All these films were thinly disguised attacks on moral views and laws in force in Germany. Many films made jibes at religion, faith in God, faith in justice and retribution, belief in a life after death. In the judgement of the *Beobachter*, supported by the *Allianzblatt*, hardly one tenth of the films produced in Germany had any value; nine tenths of the films were declared to be totally worthless or corrupting and pernicious. Evangelicals concerned about the corrupting effects of films and plays on young people could unite with National Socialists to fight 'this terrible abuse of one of the greatest inventions of our century'. The new government's legal guidelines had 'purified the air' and led to results which filled their hearts with joy. 'Breeding grounds of filth' had been swept away by the strong arm of the law; 'strongholds of moral pollution' had crumbled and fallen.[23]

The changes that had taken place in Berlin since the Nazi take-over of power were particularly pleasing. The city with 'a highly dubious reputation' had once had a night life characterised by 'unbridled immoral excesses'. The 'Marxist' government there, the paper claimed, had always turned a blind eye to the establishments in question. Yet just one month after the National Socialist government took over power there, a decree of 22 February issued by the Interior Ministry had closed down so-called 'restaurants'. Licences for hotels with a brothel-type character and night clubs were revoked. Twenty-one places were closed down immediately where homosexuals and lesbians used to meet. Eighteen similar night clubs had to stop serving drinks at 10 p.m. The police had stepped up its activities against pubs with 'waitresses'. They also took a close look at all places with 'lots of dark recesses'. In the harmless cases the owners were told to redo the interior design and 'replace the female staff with males'. The police had also made great use of its powers to limit opening hours. They had, in conjunction with undercover police officers, also forced small bed-and-breakfast places and massage salons to 'clean up or clear out'. These places had been advertising in the papers, renting out rooms for an hour with all kinds of benefits. The police had been ruthlessly cracking down on the immoral practice of using 'sexually stimulating advertisements'. Newspaper advertisements were also closely monitored for offensive material. Finally, the *Allianzblatt* notes that street prostitution was being successfully controlled – in contrast to the past, the streets in the centre of the city 'now look pleasing'. The paper compared the police actions in Berlin to 'the cleansing of the Augean stables'. It rejoiced that vice had ceased to raise its head in the city and added that 'if a Christian does not feel deep satisfaction about these changes then his moral senses must be sick to the core'.[24]

Not only in Berlin was National Socialism dealing with vice. 3,201 prostitutes in Hamburg were arrested between 1 March and 31 August 1933. Of these 814 were taken into protective custody and 274 were taken away to be treated for disease.[25] The *Allianzblatt* applauded these actions as victories for the moral majority in Germany and it welcomed much tougher sentences for those caught in immorality. It reflected what was apparently a widespread view that the criminal had been treated too leniently in the name of 'a pseudo-humanitarian concern'. Criminals should not be allowed to expect 'sentimentalities' and a stay in comfortable 'model institutions'. Robbers and murderers could not be 'civilised' by education programmes. The paper welcomed the fact that the new government had decided to do 'the biblical thing' by using its powers and introducing truly punitive measures. It specifically referred to the reintroduction of the death penalty. The success seemed to prove them right. Referring to his local paper, the *Hamburg News* (No. 383), Nagel notes how the number of crimes committed had dropped significantly since Hitler's appointment. In Berlin no murder had taken place since the reintroduction of the death panalty. Muggings and armed robberies had completely stopped. Tough but fair penalties were now meted out swiftly to 'professional criminals'. This, the *Allianzblatt* reported, was due to the fact that the whole 'moral state of our nation' had changed since January 1933.[26] Representing essentially a middle-class to lower middle-class readership as it did, the paper might have been expected to take such a line on crime and punishment.The measures taken were indeed draconian. A news item, dated August 1933, from Hamburg, which Nagel, who lived near Hamburg, may well have read, reported that athletes who failed to observe 'the simple rules of public morality' would be put into concentration camps where they could 'learn decency and morality'.[27] Immoral sportsmen, prostitutes and homosexuals were put into concentration camps to 'learn morality'. Laws passed in January 1934 and June 1935 gave the authorities power to sterilize prostitutes and homosexuals and other 'undesirables';

between 1933 and 1945 about 400,000 people were in fact sterilized. The contrast to the molly-coddling of prisoners before Hitler came to power was most noticeable and struck a chord with those keen on upholding moral standards.

Hitler himself was deadly serious about young people foregoing pleasure and making sacrifices for Germany. At a May celebration in 1936 he told a huge gathering of young people to be ready to make sacrifices for the nation's ideals. He expected them to develop strong characters, to think 'decently' and to reject everything that was 'harmful'. Hardened German youths were required to fulfil the tasks of the future.

The *Allianzblatt* commentary added its belief that all education of young people remain 'in harmony and keeping with these words of the Führer'. It was evangelicals' understanding that happiness was intrinsically related to sacrifice. Self-control was the core of the character-building process. This had led many to criticise Christianity as 'cheerless bigotry'. Christians and National Socialists were alike in that neither group needed intoxicating substances to forget 'the misery and emptiness of our bleak everyday lives'. National Socialism and Christianity both rejected 'everything that was indecent and shameful'. The report added that in the area of education and character-building there were 'obviously areas where Christianity and the welfare of the nation directly coincide'. Whoever called on people to make sacrifices and promise to lead disciplined lives was helping to preserve and strengthen the moral fibre of the nation.[28]

The usefulness of Christian beliefs was recognised by National Socialist leaders. Shortly after all young Germans were brought into the Hitler Youth organisation (1 December 1936)[29], its leader, Baldur von Schirach, put on record his conviction that the camaraderie of the Hitler Youth had something to do with religion. In breaking with Marxist, freethinking and atheistic tendencies he hoped to bring about a classless movement where young people could learn to 'believe in great and holy ideas' which had been dragged into the mud during the 'republican' era. He strongly criticised those 'deceived pastors who have tried to class me as an enemy of religious education'. He said he had never tolerated an atheist in the Hitler Youth. He insisted that all oaths would continue to be sanctified by the phrase 'So help me God!' He did not wish, he said, to interfere with the religious education of children: 'I leave it to the churches to bring up their young people in the way their denomination feels right'. Throughout the Reich, all leaders of the organisation, men and women, would ensure that Sunday worship and any other religious meetings prescribed by the denominations were not encroached upon or interfered with by the work of the Hitler Youth.[30] This seemed to reassure the editors of the *Allianzblatt* and accord with widespread views on the primary function of families and churches to inculcate Christian beliefs.

Young Christians, of course, like most youngsters of the time who had not been given a political grounding, were swept away by the music, banners, uniforms, camps and fellowship among the members of the Hitler Youth. There had been, even before 1933, a lot of support among young Christians for the National Socialist movement. On 19 December 1933, 800,000 young Protestants gave up their youth organisation, the Evangelisches Jugendwerk, and were incorporated into the Hitler Youth, after their Reich Bishop had signed an agreement with von Schirach.[31] The *Allianzblatt* wrote shortly afterwards of its relief that churches no longer had to perform those organisational tasks. It could now focus its attention on its God-given mandate. It did, however, seem to worry that some authorities might not be willing to grant to youths on camp the opportunity to attend a worship service nearby.[32] Some youngsters certainly were unable at times to attend services, at least if they had signed up for camps. These incidents may, however, have just been due to time-tabling clashes rather than malice. Other Christians may not have been allowed to go to church since the Hitler Youth member was not permitted to attend *in uniform*, of which nearly everyone was proud.[33]

Not only young men but also young women needed to learn sound Christian values of self-discipline, sacrifice for the sake of others, modesty and sexual restraint. Whereas these values, in the case of men, would prove of benefit in times of war, in the case of women these values would be geared to strengthening the structure of the family. The unity and strength of the nation would be rooted in the unity and strength of the family. This National Socialist goal was loudly supported in the evangelical weekly. The paper published extracts of a speech given by Adolf Hitler on 8 September 1934 on the role of women in his new Germany. The Führer had declared that the slogan and substance of 'women's emancipation' had been invented by a Jewish mind. A German woman did not need to emancipate herself in 'the good old days' in Germany, he said, for she had lived true to her nature. Likewise, the German man had never needed to worry about losing his position of authority vis-a-vis women.[34] Evangelicals like Nagel had desired for some time to return to the 'good old days' when men and women knew their roles and places in society. The Brethren *Die Tenne* also gave open support to the Nazi policies on the family. They too believed that 'women's liberation' was the perverse product of the 'Jewish spirit'; it was a dirty word in Germany between 1933 and 1945, and a dirty word in Christian circles too. Nagel had outlined these views in his work on *Das biblische Urteil* in 1920.35 Only men were allowed to lead the NSDAP and only men were allowed to govern the Evangelical Alliance. Women were expected to forego careers; only after 1937, when a labour shortage became noticeable, were women encouraged to 'serve the Fatherland' outside the home. A woman had, above all, to give birth to children: infertility or a 'refusal to reproduce' were incorporated as grounds for divorce in the new divorce law of 6 July 1938.

The NSDAP tried unsuccessfully to get a stricter abortion law passed in 1930 – 'to protect the German nation'. 'Whoever tries to artificially limit the fertility of the German people to the detriment of the nation shall be sentenced, on the grounds of betrayal of one's race, to penal servitude; serious cases shall be punished with death'. Throughout the period 1918 to 1933 an average of at least 400,000 abortions (but perhaps as many as 800,000) were performed each year.36 6,000 to 10,000 women died in the process; 60,000 to 100,000 became permanently ill, sterile or invalids every year because there was no legal, free, hygienic operation available in hospitals. Thousands of women were sentenced annually to a period of hard labour or time in prison; in 1933, when the figure dropped, the number was 3,809.

In January 1932 the *Allianzblatt* reported on an anti-abortion demonstration which had taken place in Dresden. Church officials spoke of their shock that views on the inviolability of life were weakening and women were still 'sinning against nature'. Men, however, were largely to blame; they were the ones pressurizing women to sleep with them and then they 'want to shrug off responsibility for their deeds'. Serious health and psychological dangers were involved in abortion, it was said, and the government was called upon 'to increase help for pregnant women and large families and to create housing where children can be brought up in a healthy environment'.37 There was a clear understanding that the 1871 Reich law on abortion (Paragraph 218) with its penalties of up to 5 years in prison or penal servitude had not dealt with the basic economic and social factors contributing to the phenomenon of abortion; nor had it worked as a deterrent. Here was a call for housing and better family allowances: both were provided by the NSDAP.

It is noteworthy that the Alliance at no time in the 1930s politicised the issues of abortion – as it would do in the 1970s. Abortion would, in Germany and the United States, become *the* politicising factor among evangelicals, leading to resistance to government policy and even violence done to abortion clinics and their staff. There was no such consciousness of the need to involve themselves as evangelicals in the political process in the 1930s, but the new government, anyway, introduced policies close to their hearts. When the Nazis, in 1933, made the sale of abortifacients illegal, prohibited the advertising of abortion services and closed down family planning clinics (to stop the spread of information on contraception) the *Allianzblatt* remained silent. Nor were the laws of 14 July 1933 and 26 July 1935 thematised, which gave women the right to have an abortion for *eugenic* reasons. The fifty percent rise in tough sentences handed down to women between 1934 and 1938 was not talked about.[38] When the 'law to protect marriage, family and motherhood' was passed on 9 March 1943 which introduced the death penalty for people who had repeatedly had or performed abortions, the *Allianzblatt* was no longer being published.[39] The view that these measures were largely in keeping with evangelical thinking on these issues at that time is probably correct. Certainly, Nazi calls for 'chastity before marriage as being absolutely necessary'[40] were in complete accord with biblical teaching. Dr Saul spoke on 'The Position of the Christian Woman and her Tasks in the Present Day' at the 46th Blankenburg Conference (August 1932). He emphasised that a woman's place was in the home. Political involvement was contrary to a woman's nature; a woman lost all 'feminity' when she 'meddled in' public affairs. When a woman rejected a man's headship and worked outside the home she was in fact forsaking the 'biblical path'.[41]

The opportunities for women at the time to 'meddle' in male affairs were slight anyway. Their situation deteriorated in the Third Reich. The percentage of female students, for example, dropped from 15.7% in 1932/33 to 11.2% in 1939.[42] Governmental recognition was given to a narrow-minded chauvinism. 'German women don't smoke' proclaimed the *Allianzblatt* over an article in September 1933. It drew attention to and positively welcomed the instructions given by State Commissar Dreher to all owners of restaurants in Ulm not to tolerate the presence of women who smoked in their establishments. The 'revolting' sight of a woman smoking had always seemed to Nagel and his fellow believers to be a true symbol of the 'glorious' republican era which was now in the past. Smoking was tantamount to the self-abasement of women for it had been learned from 'savage Indians and prostitutes'. Then came the health warning: 'Do we have to repeat at length here the harmful effects of tobacco use, e.g. anaemia, the poisoning of babies as well as the effects on population policy?' No German, the editorial continued, should be expected to have to put up with the sight of a German woman smoking.[43]

The Gauleiter of Nuremberg, Julius Streicher, taking heed, propagated a smoking prohibition for women – less to protect the health of women than to help save the hard currency needed to pay for the import of tobacco.44 Such an anti-smoking campaign could expect evangelical support. There is, however, something perverse about publishing articles critical of the sight of a burning cigarette while remaining silent about the sight of burning books, piled high in all major cities and university towns on 10 March 1933. Such events had failed to evoke protest in the *Allianzblatt*. What people then thought to be a victory over 'cultural Bolshevism' we now know to be just a dress rehearsal for Auschwitz.

One more example of the *Allianzblatt*'s commendations of the 'new morality' is an article entitled 'Women and Morality' in January 1934. It approvingly quoted Dr Krummbacher, head of the National Socialist Women's League, who had criticised the fashion among women of shaving off their eye-brows, dying their hair, smoking in public, and powdering their noses. Such practices were deemed unnatural, unhealthy and should be rejected and scorned by all young women. The paper blamed the French for the fashion.45 The same article quotes the Chief of Staff of the SA, Röhm, who had said his army of men would refuse to be used by 'bigots' who wanted these fashions stamped out. Athough it is unclear which 'bigots' Captain Röhm had in mind at the time of this decree, it is interesting that the word he uses (*Mucker*) was originally used – in the seventeenth and eighteenth centuries – as a term of abuse for pietists. It implied hypocrisy. Röhm was not happy about his troops patrolling beaches to keep prudes happy. Dr Gottfried Krummbacher, the man who was in charge of the NS-Frauenschaft from the summer of 1933, felt that women should look naturally feminine just as the National Socialist believed that specifically feminine duties and behavioural patterns were God-given and to be upheld in public. Women had to be modest, unobtrusive and, above all, controllable. Foreign influences and fashions were deplored. Here too there was a connection with the Christian tradition, going back to Tertullian, of rejecting make-up and hair-dye, as well as the Apostle Peter's command that a woman's beauty 'should not come from outward adornment, such as braided hair and the wearing of gold jewellery and fine clothes'(1 Peter 3,3). The behaviour criticised here can well be seen as early acts of resistance to the new political atmosphere. After 1937 growing numbers of young women, especially in the cities, rejected the German greeting, preferring '*Servus*' or '*bye, bye*'. They wore red neckerchiefs and skiing shirts rather than the uniforms of the BDM, the National Socialist Girls' League. They listened to jazz and swing and they smoked in public – at least until Heinrich Himmler issued a decree on 9 March 1940 making smoking in public illegal for young people under 18 years of age.[46]

The *Allianzblatt* also had praise for the respect shown to the institution of marriage by the new regime. It took especial note of trials where individuals were sentenced to months of imprisonment for adultery. It approved of such sentences for violation of holy vows was unacceptable in 'these times of national and racial resurrection'(sic). The *Allianzblatt* blamed the undermining of the 'ethical conscience' and the breakdown of marriage on the 'weak-kneed attitude' of organs of state during the Weimar Republic. It particularly welcomed Adolf Hitler's words on the subject in *Mein Kampf*. Hitler had called on the German people to control its sexual passions or perish. It denied that supporting the sanctity of marriage was an issue for 'bigots' and 'obscurantists' and deplored the fact that even so-called Christians did not listen to the Bible and condemn divorce and adultery. The paper called on Christians to learn from the 'heathen Teutons' who 'didn't laugh about vice'. In ancient German society the adulterer and adulteress were publicly ostracized. In that society moral health was the precondition of health per se and of strength, national advancement and fitness for military service. The keys to the future once again lay in the past.[47]

These reports were, to the editors of *Allianzblatt*, clear signs of the advancing moral rearmament of the German people. Just as the laws controlling abortion and contraception would mean more little boys would be born who would one day become big soldiers, so the strengthening of the family unit and warning women to stay clear of Western decadence would help strengthen the moral fibre of a nation, making it 'fit for military service'. On 12 January 1934 evangelicals all over Germany raised their voices in prayer to thank God for His gift of the family, the 'place we learn self-discipline, the place of blessing and of joy'. They expressed thanks for the government's encouragement of family life, helping to put it back on a moral, Christian basis. Thanks were offered to God that the government was once again aware that the protection of young people from the 'poison' of literary 'trash' was one of its duties. They were grateful, too, that a sense of discipline, order and self-denial was being reawakened and encouraged by the Nazis.[48]

Apart from the National Socialists' emphasis on clean living, morality and religious faith (which were taken at face value by evangelicals), their criticism of vivisection and support for animal rights also met with the approval of the *Allianzblatt*. In July 1932 the *Allianzblatt* had talked of 'devilish practices' such as docking and warned that God would judge cruelty to animals and condemn those responsible.[49] The NSDAP seemed to hear the yearnings of created animals for freedom and fair treatment. The paper reported in detail on Minister President Göring's lecture on 28 August on vivisection, which was broadcast on all radio stations in the evening. Göring had issued a decree severely punishing cruelty to animals, experiments with animals and vivisection. Protective custody and imprisonment in concentration camps were provided for. Germans' healthy common sense and an ancient tradition of treating animals as co-workers and even co-combattants were recalled. Arguments about the use of experiments for humanity would no longer be tolerated. The only exceptions would be tests to help combat epidemics and to produce serums like insulin. Only scientists who had been carefully vetted would be allowed to perform such experiments. 'There can't be a single Christian who reads this article', the paper believed, 'who would not welcome the changes with a very thankful heart'.[50]

A period of confinement in a concentration camp may well have been seen as God's judgement on such cruelty to animals: a place of reform and reeducation. Ever since the *Münchener Neueste Nachrichten* and the *Völkischer Beobachter* reported, on 21 March 1933, the opening of a concentration camp near Dachau (which had space for 5,000 people at the time), the existence of such camps became common knowledge. One newspaper for young Christians, *Der Junge Tag*, which had a circulation of 10,000 in 1932, published a detailed report on life and conditions in a camp in its July 1933 issue.[51] In this report it was emphasised that prisoners and guards ate the same food and the relationship between them was friendly. The commandant is quoted as saying: 'We treat the people well, and they accept that. They've all really gone astray and been deceived and we want to win them all over to the nationalist cause for the sake of the Fatherland! And we will only achieve that if we treat the people in a friendly manner while keeping strict discipline at the same time'.[52] The following month, November 1933, the *Allianzblatt* published another long article on 'The Protection of Animals' which claimed that Christ himself loved animals. Christ spoke disparagingly of the shepherd who left his sheep in times of danger rather than lay down his life for them. As Christ gave recognition to the animal world, the editor argued, then it was obvious that it was the duty of politicians and animal rights organisations to do likewise and to stand up for animals whenever they were used inappropriately and improperly. 'We sin against and violate the law of God – that at least is certain – whenever we torment animals', the article stated, for animals were 'created with a nervous system our own and so felt pain just as we do'.53

Such support for animal rights groups and laws against cruelty to animals seems quite progressive. Why, though, did the *Allianzblatt* at no time support the idea of a *human* rights organisation concerned with the protection of the dignity of political prisoners? It clearly lacked the theological armoury for such an undertaking. Having internalised the ruling ideology, including its conspiracy theory, one accepted that some people were in fact unworthy of mercy. Ernst Röhm was a case in point.

The 4.5 million SA Storm Troopers were led by Ernst Röhm, a minister without portfolio in Hitler's government. In the eighteen months after securing supreme power in Germany, Hitler, seeking to gain the support of the conservative establishment and especially the army under von Blomberg, felt increasingly threatened by Röhm's willingness to stand up and complain of the Party's discrimination of his troopers, of their being underpaid and inadequately armed. At the beginning of June, the Party leaders held numerous speeches discrediting the remaining critics of the regime – 'grousers, bleaters and spoilsports', as they were termed – and warned of the dangers of a 'second revolution'.54

The Vice Chancellor, von Papen, called for a renewal of national life on the basis of Catholic conservatism. In spite of warning against further revolution von Papen was nevertheless put under house arrest for 4 days during the crisis. Under the pretext of putting down a coup d'etat, perhaps as many as 401 people were murdered between 30 June and 2 July 1934 – including a group of Jews in Silesia, killed for the entertainment of the local SS, and Father Bernhard Stempfle, who had revised the proofs, corrected the grammar and even written parts of *Mein Kampf* for Adolf Hitler.55 Hindenburg, revered by evangelicals as the epitome of the Christian statesman, thereupon thanked the Chancellor for his 'determined action and gallant personal intervention which have nipped treason in the bud'.56

On 13 July, before the Reichstag, Hitler gave prominence to the charges of corruption and homosexuality which had been made against Röhm and his associates and stressed that his government was not in favour of permanent revolution (as Röhm and others in the SA perhaps were). Posing as the guardian of the nation's moral health, he pushed through a law, on 3 July, exempting all acts committed in the previous days from prosecution. The army was happy that it was once again the sole armed force in the country; conservatives were happy that the revolution was over and an evolutionary stage had begun; and Christians were happy that a stand had been taken against homosexuality.57 The *Allianzblatt* reported on these incidents in its 30 July issue under the heading 'Preserving the Country from a New Revolution'. It spoke of the 'uncertainty' felt by all in the previous months and the sense that 'subversive activities' were about to erupt. 'We knew nothing about the conspiracy against the Führer and we would never have imagined that men who the Führer has trusted could have been plotting treason', the article stated. The quick and decisive actions of their Führer were applauded. The news of the events of 30 June 'took our breath away'. Röhm had been removed from his post for 'serious offences' and had been replaced by the Oberpräsident of Hanover, Lutze. The 'shocking' demonstration by the SA 'traitors' on the streets of Munich revealed an appalling degree of self-deception. Fortunately, the Führer then 'came rushing in from above' in his plane. Like 'a flash of lightning', he struck at the conspirators in their hideouts. He personally entered Röhm's apartment, the report said, and arrested the treacherous Chief of Staff. Hitler dragged the conspirators out of their beds.58 The *Allianzblatt* records the fact that seven SA leaders as well as Röhm had been shot dead by order of a court martial. These were not the only judicial murders noted approvingly by the paper. In Berlin General von Schleicher, the former Reich Chancellor, who had been accused of being a go-between between Röhm and a foreign power, was shot while resisting arrest; his wife was also shot dead while trying to protect her husband. The commentary on these events is introduced by the fatalistic words 'What a tragedy!' Clearly evangelicals were content that a potentially egalitarian 'second revolution' had been averted. The moral lessons drawn from the events were, however, perceived to be even more important. The 'purification' of the Storm Trooper organisation, the removal of 'questionable characters' from their ranks, the ending of all 'carousing and feasting' would, the paper hoped, mean that the SA could once again become 'an example for others' in terms of self-control and morality. It hailed the Führer for his 'death-defying' resistance to those who had betrayed his friendship and quoted the revered German President as saying to Hitler: 'You have saved the German people from the greatest of dangers!' The *Allianzblatt*, too, believed that God had preserved the country on 30 June 1934 from unimaginable horrors. Referring to the first chapter of Romans, it declared that God had brought judgement down upon the sexually immoral and the homosexuals. They had received 'the due penalty for their perversions'. It even felt the Apostle Paul was describing the moral decay in the SA base near Munich. It expressed complete understanding for the Führer's 'indignation' at these goings-on.[59]

The article goes on to detail General von Schleicher's alleged links with groups in France which sought to 'overthrow Hitler'. These 'mercenaries' had been corrupted by 'luxury' and 'bribes', but God had brought to nothing 'their struggle against the Hitler regime'.[60] None of these accusations had any basis in fact: Hitler simply used the occasion to get rid of 'difficult' people like General Kurt von Schleicher (Hitler's predecessor as Chancellor) and General Kurt von Bredow. The politically naive writers for the *Allianzblatt* had no inkling that the Machiavellians around them could have anything but noble motives. Even a bloodbath detailed on its pages does not seem to have led them to question the increasingly lawless nature of the regime. On the contrary, the strike against homosexuality seemed to be an almost divine intervention, in the person of Hitler, in the affairs of the nation and a reassertion of the claims of the divine law which, as outlined in the Old Testament, called for the death of practising homosexuals. Evil conspiracies, once again having a base in France, were, in their view, diabolical attempts to disrupt the moral rejuvenation of Germany. Fortunately, as in Bismarckian times, *Gott mit uns* had become more than just an empty slogan on soldiers' belt-buckles; it was seen very much as a reality.

Evangelicals had traditionally been concerned about sexual promiscuity, but there was also a growing realisation, particularly in the Free Churches which attracted a far higher percentage of members from the 'lower orders', that hunger and poor living conditions only encouraged immorality and radical politics. The works of Nagel are a testimony to this. There was also, then, a concern about the economic reality surrounding and impinging on the lives of millions of Germans and a willingness to support measures to alleviate suffering. There were 6,014,000 unemployed people in Germany when Hitler came to power. His movement's success can be attributed in part to the worldwide economic crisis between 1929 and 1933. Fortunately for Hitler, the recession had already bottomed out when he took power. This fortunate circumstance, coupled with the government's willingness to pile up debts (from 2 million Reichsmarks in 1933 to 42 billion Reichsmarks at the end of 1938), to employ men in road construction (115,000 in 1935) and, above all, to invest massively in the military complex, created jobs. Spending on the Wehrmacht rose from 720 million Reichsmarks in 1933 to 15.5 billion Reichsmarks in 1938; put another way, 1.3% of the national income was spent on armaments in 1932, in 1938 19%. This all led to a drop in unemployment: from 6.2 million in 1933, to 3.8 million in 1934, to 2.1 million in 1935, 1.4 million in 1936, 0.5 million in 1937 and 0.3 million in 1938.[61] Jobs legitimated Hitler's power and strengthened his image of 'saviour' in the minds of Germans.

How did the *Allianzblatt* react? The problems caused by unemployment as well as the causes of unemployment itself were nowhere analysed in the paper; unemployment was simply a 'natural' phenomenon, a cross to be borne by some. Mention was made of numbers out of work, but the paper's spotlight in the early thirties was on the struggle for power in Germany. In a 1932 report casually mentioning 5.6 million unemployed men, the *Allianzblatt* talked of the fact that 'not a day goes by without National Socialists falling victim to Communist attacks' and of 'Jews joining the ranks of the Centre Party'.[62] The creation of jobs was not, prior to 1933, a subject of discussion.

Hitler's ascension to power changed this. May Day – 'The Day of National Work', as it was renamed on 10 April 1933 – became a paid holiday for the first time, but it was not celebrated, as it had been since 1899, as a day of celebration of the struggle of the workers' movement. That change pleased the editors of the paper. Hitler's speech on that May day closed with the prayer which was quoted earlier. It also announced a new law aimed at fundamentally changing the economic and social system. An obligatory workfare scheme would be introduced to give hundreds of thousands of unemployed Germans the opportunity of doing an economically useful job for the community. The *Allianzblatt* compared the scheme with conscription and the use of mercenaries in times of crisis. It hoped all unemployed Germans would feel an obligation to take part in housing and other construction projects. Mass unemployment had to be ended somehow, but socialist strategies had to be rejected in principle.[63]

Initially, this scheme of giving unemployed young people work was voluntary (law of 26 June 1935). They earned a very small wage, but many had a meaningful occupation. 300,000 people were sent to work in the agricultural sector; another 350,000 did work on roads, canals and on the coast.

The soldier analogy which Bernhard Peters uses in the report was actually quite prophetic, in more ways than one: Dr Robert Ley, who set up the *Deutsche Arbeitsfront* in 1934 to replace the unions, described workers in his book *Soldaten der Arbeit* (1938) as 'Hitler's soldiers' fighting 'a battle [in] the service of the Führer and the nation'. Later, this workfare scheme became obligatory as the government began preparations for war.

A second point to make here is that although the Nazis called themselves 'socialists' and their programme contained a number of 'irrevocable' clauses which were clearly socialist, not one of these goals was ever achieved or even considered desirable once power had been gained. The NSDAP, whose election campaigns had been financed by big business, rewarded big business with huge contracts after 1933.[64]

The *Allianzblatt* and evangelical papers produced by groups not supportive of the Alliance, such as the Brethren's *Die Tenne*, welcomed the government's attempts to provide bread and work to the whole population. It reported with satisfaction that after four months of his government there were already 1.4 million fewer unemployed people in Germany. Real progress had been made with the help of the Almighty. The editor hoped that God would indeed grant Hitler's prayer request that the German people might 'one day live in a free German Empire' utilising all the economic resources at its disposal.[65]

By the end of 1938 the 'soldiers of work' had lost rights won in decades of struggle, for example the right to strike, contractual wage scales and the freedom to choose a profession and one's workplace. For the worker the idyllic national community as portrayed in the *Allianzblatt* meant he practically had the same status as a soldier, with the one 'freedom' of not having to wear a uniform. In its view, however, not the workers but the managers should be free to work out the economy's salvation. Governmental intervention in the free market would, it said, only be disruptive.[66]

The economic miracle was portrayed as the work of a single man, Adolf Hitler. His genius continued to amaze middle-class Germans. It was down to his 'supreme personal efforts' that 2.5 million Germans were soon back in employment. Nobody could deny that Adolf Hitler had achieved something that wouldn't have occurred to anyone in their wildest dreams just one year ago. He had promised that those who wanted to work would find work, and he had kept his word. This evangelical 'trust in the Führer' had banished despondency and despair. It was 'simply wonderful' that Hitler had succeeded in giving back to the German people faith and confidence.[67]

One example of how people were put to work was given a prominent place in the pages of the *Allianzblatt*. At the beginning of the year, there was talk in the paper of 'about half a million uprooted people along with almost 100,000 young people mostly living in an advanced state of pauperization and depravity'. These were not only an eyesore – these 'beggars' were working as 'Communist agitators'![68] Clearly, the government had to do something.

An answer came in October. The campaign to eradicate the sinister activities of beggars in Hamburg led to the arrest of 1,350 beggars and tramps. Those capable of working had been transferred, with the agreement of the Welfare Authorities, to the workfare scheme in Farmsen. Those beggars not able to work would, the paper informed readers, be transferred to the respective Public Relief offices, should it be discovered that they were in need of help. The *Allianzblatt* titled this article on the homeless and destitute 'A Great Clean-Up Operation'.[69]

Two reports in *Allianzblatt* published during the war show how completely the Alliance had imbibed National Socialist thought patterns and interpretations of events and accepted the economic system under the Hitler regime. One discussed plutocracy, the rule of the rich in the interests of the owners of the means of production. Such a system, widespread in the democratic countries, was opposed by the rule of God, it argued. The social, economic and moral consequences of the rule of the plutocratic spirit were horrendous. It undermined the individual's sense of belonging to a community. It produced miserable housing conditions and mass unemployment. Those without capital were the helpless victims of those with money. The whole community, but particularly young people, became 'spiritually degenerate' in such a system. The scriptural principle of putting the welfare of the community before that of the individual (as was being practiced, in their view, in the economic life in Germany) had been turned on its head. The struggle with the Western democracies was in fact a struggle with a destructive plutocratic spirit. 'We can only hope and pray that the result of the present struggle will be the overthrow of those spiritual powers which are ruinous to nations and states', the writer said. For only then was there hope that God's order could be set up on earth.[70]

Germany, itself a capitalist country, had by no means become a fairer, more equal society in the thirties. In 1934 wages were frozen and remained stagnant throughout the period. Wages and salaries sank from 62% of the national income in 1928 to 57% in 1938 inspite of full employment. Of the growth in income between 1933 and 1938 a full 43% consisted of capital and company profits which belonged, as ever, to a tiny number of people.[71] These men (Stinnes, Thyssen and Kirdorf in mining, Flick and Vögler in steel, Hugenberg and Schacht and their banking contacts, just to name some) remained powerful in Germany because of their wealth. The *Allianzblatt* was blind to these facts and was content to pass on the ideological nonsense of the Nazis to evangelical readers. Even the word most hated by the editors of

Allianzblatt prior to 1933 – socialism – became a concept to be proud of. The January 1941 issue of *Allianzblatt* brought a short article on 'the new social welfare system' as its bi-weekly 'Word on the Current Situation'. Germany's social system presented a stark contrast to that prevailing in England. 'We Germans are a thorn in the English flesh', for the simple reason that justice was a guiding principle in German social policy. This was most clearly shown when the insurance and pension systems were compared. Germans had no need to fear old age as the English did and should be 'grateful to the Führer' that he had introduced a comprehensive scheme prepared in the middle of the war. 'We don't just talk about socialism – we live it and set an example to others'.[72]

The 'law to enlarge the pension insurance system' was passed on 21 December 1937 and it was the final attempt to reorganize the system in the Third Reich.[73] The important point here, however, is that the editors of *Allianzblatt* still express a confident trust that their benevolent leader is already thinking about their old – age in the middle of a war which, admittedly, seemed to be going very well at the time. The open confession of faith in socialism – albeit a 'nationalised' variety – is nevertheless remarkable. 'Nobody should be hungry or cold': one thanked God that this National Socialist slogan was being taken seriously.[74] It was, after all, only what the early church practised. Indeed, Werner Reichelt has suggested that National Socialism appealed to many believers precisely because it seemed to take aspects of the gospel *seriously*, at least more seriously than the Churches.

This was certainly what Gustav Nagel believed, and he was by no means the only Christian editor who held this view. Press legislation in the autumn of 1936 required all editors to be members of the National Press Association: political reliability was a condition of membership. Nagel must have passed the test; his work did not come to an end, as did the journalistic activities of numerous Church and parish magazine editors.[75]

One small sign of press officials' being well-disposed to the *Allianzblatt* is the fact that at a time when the censors in the Reich Press Office were nit-picking in Catholic periodicals, asking what advertisements for *Dr Oetker's pudding* or articles on *The Dream Coffee Warmer* or *Everything you need for a Baby Doll* had to do with religion – only adverts and articles dealing with religious issues being permissible in a *Catholic* magazine[76] – evangelicals were being granted the freedom to order woollen underwear from Garn-Koch in Erfurt, herbal medicines to treat gall stones, Dr Franck's book on *Healthy Eating* (Munich 1937), Beeinda teas (against constipation, varicose veins, haemorrhoids, asthma 'and other ailments') and a whole host of other consumer products.[77]

The views of NSDAP leaders on religious issues were often printed verbatim without commentary, revealing the loyalty and good-will felt by Nagel. At the same time he played down difficulties and painful experiences made by some. 'We do well not to stop and think about particular aspects of current events, but to keep our eyes on the general scheme of things', was the advice offered by the editor to a reader concerned about 'certain phenomena accompanying the patriotic, national movement'. In particular, Nagel was adamant that a 'strong state conscious of its own authority', willing to 'resist all those denying its right to exist', had to be supported whole-heartedly by Christians. Nagel saw no reason not to trust the Government's 'clear statement that it does not want to violate the rights of Christians to practice their religion in accordance with the dictates of their conscience'.[78] This even led him at times to defend the state against those Christians who were critical of developments. On 1 October 1933, in an editorial on 'A Fanatical Martyr Spirit and True Martyrdom', Nagel referred to 'members of Christian circles' who had made ironical or disparaging staements about 'certain events' in the ecclesiastical and political realms. These 'critics' had, as a direct result of such behaviour, been 'transported to a concentration camp'. Nagel said such criticism was 'regrettable' and 'stupid', 'immature' and 'fanatical'. Christians needed to ensure that they remained submitted to those in authority and did not allow such a silly 'martyr mentality' to take root in their midst. A Christian only had a responsibility to help reform structures and correct mistakes if he was a minister or journalist or civil servant. Otherwise, a Christian's responsibility was limited solely to praying for the government and to supporting the government (as long as it did not require him to do things his conscience would not tolerate). A Christian only had responsibility, he said, referring to 1 Corinthians 5,12, to ensure no evil was done *within* the church; evil doers outside the church should be of no concern to him.

Nagel outlined one goal of his editorial policy: 'We do not want to be justifiably accused of having a biased view of events or of glossing over the situation. After all, we all know that things are critical and difficult'.[79] Difficult for whom? Nagel was not concerned about 'enemies of the state', unless they were to be found inside the church, in which case he saw a need to rebuke them. Above all, he was concerned about preserving the bond of unity in the Spirit of peace amongst believers. 'One of the painful accompaniments of the current developments is the fact that Christians who were once one heart and one soul have become hard-hearted to one another because one thanks God for the national uprising while the other experiences only anguish and rage. One sees a great work of God, another a mere futile work of man if not something worse. We shall see who is right, but it is important that believers, united in God, should not become alienated from one another'.[80]

Politically, the *Allianzblatt* swam with the patriotic current. After ten months of National Socialist rule it could boldly proclaim:

> 'Umzustellen' brauchten wir uns zu dem Zweck auf die Wendung unserer vaterländischen Geschicke hin nicht. Einen 'Kurswechsel' in grundsätzlicher Hinsicht brauchten wir nicht zu vollziehen. Wir waren nicht in die Lage versetzt, ein politisches Dogma oder Parteiprogramm, das wir verteidigt hätten, gegen ein anderes eintauschen zu müssen. Seit Jahren lag es uns am Herzen, gegenüber der 'Entartung des deutschen Denkens in vaterländischen Dingen' einfach den Staats- und Obrigkeitsgedanken nach dem Schriftwort leuchten zu lassen. Das ist in ungezählten Zusammenhängen unser Bemühen gewesen. Unser Anliegen war, dass Staat und Obrigkeit zu der ihnen nach dem Schriftwort gebührenden Machtstellung gelangen möchten. [...] Nach der geschehenen Wendung können wir nun, ohne irgend etwas in unserem Denken 'umstellen' zu müssen, ruhig fortfahren, nach 'Licht und Recht des Wortes für die Fragen der Zeit' zu fragen.

> We did not need to readjust to the change in the fortunes of our nation. We did not need to change course as far as our principles were concerned. We were not suddenly in a position where we had to swap one political dogma or party programme which we had defended for another. For years we had been keenly interested in stressing the biblical ideas of government and authority to counteract the 'degeneration of German thought on national issues'. In numerous contexts we strove to achieve this. It was our longing to see the state and the concept of authority regain the position of predominance, which, according to the Bible, is due them. [...] Following the turn of events we can without hesitation continue to search in the Word for light on, and answers to, the questions facing us today. We do not have to readjust our way of thinking at all.[81]

Can one reproach a 65 year old man with not recognising a need to rethink his political philosophy and theological interpretations? Nagel clearly never accepted that a situation of *status confessionis* had approached. In March 1936 he wrote that, should the values of the Gospel ever be seriously encroached upon, then this would certainly not be left unsaid. 'Then all of us should form a common defence, a community testifying to the truth, fighting for it and, if necessary, suffering for it'.[82]

Were these statements simply banal platitudes? Not once did a leading evangelical say that Christian values were being threatened, let alone violated, in the Third Reich. The *Allianzblatt*, like other church publications, including *Junge Kirche* of the Confessing Church, remained patriotically devoted to the Führer. As Victor Klemperer wrote in 1946: books, newspapers, all printed matter 'swam in the same brown gravy'.[83]

Notes

1. EA 17.09.1933 (Nr 38), 624.
2. EA 14.05.1933 (Nr 20), 316. In 1932 107,164 people renounced their membership of the Protestant Church and 23,770 joined; in 1933 26,483 people left the Church and 138,035 joined. F. Baumgärtel (1976, 85).
3. W. Reichelt (1990, 108). Church lands and forests, valued at 10 billion Reichsmarks, yielded annual rents of about 300 million Reichsmarks – the Church remained the second largest landowner, after the state, in Nazi Germany. Moreover, between 1933 and 1943 the Reich and the Provinces had provided the Churches with subsidies totalling 956 million Reichsmarks, P. Matheson (1981,l00-1). According to the Ministry for Popular Enlightenment and Propaganda, the income derived by the Churches from the Church tax amounted to 316 million Reichsmarks in 1938, 333 million Reichsmarks in 1939 and 355 million Reichsmarks in 1940.
4. EA 28.02.1934 (Nr 3), 69.
5. EA 28.05.1933 (Nr 22), 351. One sign of the political loyalty of the Confessing Church (and other sections of Protestantism) is the fact that only one theology professor (Karl Barth) refused to swear an oath of loyalty and only a handful of pastors refused, in 1938, to swear the following oath of loyalty to the Führer and Reich: 'I swear that I will be loyal and obedient to the Führer of the German Reich and German People, Adolf Hitler. I will abide by the law and carry out the duties of my office conscientiously, so help me God!' G. Denzler/V. Fabricius, Vol.1 (1988, 75). F. Baumgärtel (1976, 52) contends that Barth was in fact willing to swear the oath of loyalty.
6. Quoted by W. Reich (1978, 148); B. Peters, Arier und Jude (1934, 61).
7. W. Reich (1978, 147).
8. W. Reich (1978, 178).
9. G. Orwell (1981, 109).
10. W. Reichelt (1990,131-146); Adolf Hitler (1939, 277-8).
11. H. Glaser (1986, 147-148).
12. EA 28.02.1932 (Nr 9), 142-144.

13. EA 28.02.1932 (Nr 9), 142-144.
14. EA 28.02.1932 (Nr 9), 142-144.
15. EA 20.03.1932 (Nr 12), 188; K.-D. Bracher (1993, 298).
16. EA 04.12.1932 (Nr 49), 796f.
17. EA 17.04.1932 (Nr 16), 254-255.
18. W.Hütt (1990, 73).
19. EA 05.06.1932 (Nr 23), 363-365. B. Peters criticises 'negro music' as 'crude, insipid, animal-like and Bolshevist', EA 23.07.1933 (Nr 30), 480.
20. EA 02.07.1933 (Nr 27), 430.
21. EA 07.05.1933 (Nr 19), 299.
22. The official NSDAP newspaper. The Party acquired the *Münchener Beobachter* in December 1920 and renamed it *Völkischer Beobachter*. Dietrich Eckart (1868-1923) was its first publisher.
23. EA 07.05.1933 (Nr 19), 298-299; G. Jordy (1986, 61).
24. EA 01.10.1933 (Nr 40), 654-656
25. EA 22.10.1933 (Nr 43), 699.
26. EA 01.10.1933 (Nr 40), 653-654.
27. W. Reich (1978, 148).
28. EA 15.06.1936 (Nr 11), 173.
29. EA 30.12.1936 (Nr 24), 387-388. Denominational youth groups were still allowed to exist as purely spiritual-pastoral communities.
30. EA 15.01.1937 (Nr 1), 12-13; EA 15.03.1936 (Nr 5), 78.
31. J. Hampel, Vol 1 (1989, 185); J. Hampel, Vol 2 (1989, 295); P. Matheson (1981, 40-41).
32. EA 15.01.1934 (Nr 1), 18.
33. The Persecution of the Catholic Church in the Third Reich (1942, 374-377).
34. J. Hampel Vol.2 (1989, 314).
35. G. Jordy (1986, 64-65, 250).
36. Beilage, *Kriminologische Monatshefte* 1936 (Berlin), pp.1-16; *Deutsche Zeitschrift für öffentliche Gesundheitspflege* (Berlin 1925/26, Heft 1/2, July/August), 7ff; *Die Christliche Welt*, 1926, Nr 18, 917-919. 80-85% of the women were married. The *Christliche Welt* said 'the health of the woman, fear of childbirth, but, above all, the lack of food and the miserable living conditions, as well as the attempt to preserve the quality of the upbringing of the other children' were the main causes of abortion.
37. EA 10.01.1932 (Nr 2), 29.
38. D. Klinksiek (1982, 70-71).
39. Claude Chabrol made a film (*A Woman's Matter*, 1988) about Marie-Louise Giraud, who was the last French woman to be guillotined (in 1943). Marshall Petain had condemned her as the 'murderess of the Fatherland' because she had performed 27 abortions. In

Germany, the law does not seem to have made any difference: 500,000 abortions still took place annually. The arrival of British, American, French and Soviet troops pushed the number of women requiring abortions up: between 1945 and 1947 2 million (criminal) abortions were performed annually, *Der Tagesspiegel*, 9 March 1947. During the Third Reich thousands of women (gypsies, prostitutes, Jews, handicapped women, Eastern European slave-labourers) were forced to have abortions for 'eugenic' reasons.

40. Nationalsozialistische Frauenwarte 1935/36, 447, quoted by D. Klinksiek, (1982, 7).
41. EA 04.-11.09.1932 (Nr 36/37), 574ff.
42. J. Hampel Vol.2 (1989, 319).
43. EA 17.09.1933 (Nr 38), 620.
44. H.-J. Winkler (1961, 37).
45. EA 15.01.1934 (Nr 1), 14.
46. On youth resistance to the ideology and puritanism of the Nazi regime, see A. Klönne (1982, 228ff). In February 1934 Dr Krummbacher was replaced by Hitler's personal nominee for the post of Reichsfrauenführerin, Gertrud Scholtz-Klink.
47. EA 29.10.1933 (Nr 44), 716-717.
48. EA 17.12.1933 (Nr 51), 807.
49. EA 17.07.1932 (Nr 29).
50. EA 01.10.1933 (Nr 40), 652.
51. P. Meiners (1985, 36-7). According to Meiners, 'concentration camps in the early period had nothing to do with and were nothing like the death camps of the later period'.
52. *Der Junge Tag*, July 1933, 108 .
53. EA 05.11.1933 (Nr 45), 734-735.
54. J.P. Stern (1979, 159). Cp.EA 17.12.1933 (Nr 51), 814.
55. A. Bullock (1973, 133,302-309). Father Stempfle was a member of the Hieronymite Order and also edited an anti-semitic paper in Miesbach.
56. A. Bullock (1973, 304).
57. Hitler had known about and tolerated for years the homosexuality of Röhm and other SA men; it would remain one of the features of life in the SS. Glaser says 'homosexuality no longer played a major role within the National Socialist movement after the murder of Röhm and other SA leaders' (1986,101). On the treatment of homosexuals in concentration camps, see E. Kogon (1979,284-5). Hormones were used in medical experiments on homosexuals in Buchenwald in an attempt to 'heal' their 'disease'; no positive results were achieved. In Auschwitz lesbians were castrated and submitted to x-rays and chemical treatments under the supervision of Professor Clauberg.
58. The *Allianzblatt* here is caught in the myth-making propaganda of depicting Hitler as a demi-god, appearing from above, and showing great courage and heroism in the face of a deadly enemy.

59. EA 30.07.1934 (Nr 14), 229-231. The laws against homosexuality were toughened up on 26/28 June 1935, H. Bergschicker (1982, 78,188).
60. EA 30.07.1934 (Nr 14), 231. The *Allianzblatt* here simply reports 'what we are told in the press'.
61. J. Hampel, Vol.2 (1989, 83ff).
62. EA 24.07.1932 (Nr 30), 477ff.
63. EA 28.05.1933 (Nr 22), 349. According to Peter Meiners (1985, 17-19) a similar scheme had been operating ever since 1927 under the auspices of the evangelical Young Men's Christian Association in Germany; this scheme inspired governmental efforts in 1931 and 1933 to provide meaningful work and a goal in life for thousands of unemployed people.
64. E. Czichon (1989).
65. EA 19.07.1933 (Nr 28), 448.
66. EA 06.08.1933 (Nr 32), 511.
67. EA 03.12.1933 (Nr 49), 782.
68. EA 12.02.1933 (Nr 7), 127. The EA report is itself an excerpt from an article in the *Volkskirche*.
69. EA 22.10.1933 (Nr 43), 699. Title: *Die Grosse Säuberung*.
70. EA 01.-15.06.1940 (Nr 11/12), 93.
71. H.-J. Winkler (1961, 29).
72. EA 15.-30.01.1941 (Nr 1-2), 6-7.
73. Heinz Lampart, in: K.-D. Bracher/M. Funke/H.-A. Jacobsen (1986, 193).
74. EA 10.12.1933 (Nr 50), 796.
75. *Evangelical Christendom* , 1937, 15.
76. P. Matheson (1981, 57).
77. See the advertisement pages at the back of the *Allianzblatt*.
78. EA 18.06.1933 (Nr 25), 392-393. 'The coercion which he [Hitler] uses is good and wholesome', EA 17.09.1933 (Nr 38), 623. Reports on Nazi leaders' speeches making reference to Church-State issues are found in EA 30.06.1935 (Nr 12), 191 (Rosenberg); EA 15.12.1937 (Nr 23), 334-335 (Karl Holz, Deputy Gauleiter, Franconia); EA 15.03.1936 (Nr 5), 77-78 and EA 30.12.1937 (Nr 24), 347-348 (Kerrl).
79. EA 01.10.1933 (Nr 40), 656.
80. EA 18.06.1933 (Nr 25), 394. This excerpt is taken from a report on the longing for a united Protestant Reich Church entitled '*Gleichschaltung* of the Members of Christ under One Head is Necessary'.
81. EA 29.10.1933 (Nr 44), 717.
82. EA 15.03.1936 (Nr 5), 77.
83. V. Klemperer (1982, 18).

Chapter Seven

The Jewish Question

The widespread anti-semitism within both major denominations in Germany has been well documented.[1] Evangelicals demonstrated a double-mindedness during the 1930s on the subject. On the one hand, it seemed to be a just punishment for Jewish sins, prophesied in Scripture. On the other hand, one believed it was necessary for God to use persecutions to draw His people back into their homeland, Palestine. Distinctions were also made between Jewish Christians (good Jews), religious Jews (acceptable Jews) and apostate, anti-religious Jews (bad Jews). Finally, there were those evangelicals who detested anti-semitic persecutions while adhering to numerous anti-semitic prejudices.

Evangelicals wondered whether Zionism was the beginning of Israel's conversion to Christ, their Messiah, and thus their return to Palestine.[2] The Jewish Christian, Pastor Moser, talked of 'wrong attempts' to force a solution to the Jewish Question, referring obliquely to various governments' measures to repatriate immigrant Jews. Another, Pastor Parnes, explained the biblical solution at the 7th Jewish Christian Conference in Barmen (September 1932).[3] Arthur Ruppin noted that the number of Jews in the world had increased in the previous thirty years from 11 million to 16 million; their annual rate of increase had been, according to Ruppin, 180,000 annually from 1900 to 1930. Numerically, the Jews had never been stronger.[4] The numbers of Jews in Palestine, according to one Arab Christian, had, however, not increased fast; there were still only about 174,000 Jews in the country.[5] Herr von Harling noted that Jews throughout the world were rather opposed to Zionism. The unrest in Palestine had not helped the situation. Arabs were resisting the presence of the 'Jewish intruders' and after an English Commission had found out that, among Jewish immigrants, there were a good deal of 'Communist elements', the numbers being allowed into the country were curtailed. In the first few months of 1932 the number of returning emigrants had actually surpassed the number of immigrants into Palestine. Zionism stood, according to von Harling, for 'one-sided national ideals' and as such signified a 'secularisation of Jewry', just as the Jewish pioneers in Palestine were mainly 'representatives of a religion-less radicalism'. There were 'no hopeful prospects of a Jewish Palestine'.[6] Religious indifference, areligion or even radical atheism, especially among Zionists, typified the Jewish community there. Pastor Paetzold (Jaffa) summed up: 'The Jew today is only interested in his national culture; he is not interested at all, or only slightly, in questions about God and religion. The denial of God's existence predominates'.[7]

In spite of this feature the *Allianzblatt* expressed praise for the 'economic miracle' taking place in the Jewish settlements: an excellent educational system had been set up and all Jewish children attended school in contrast to only 20 per cent of Arab children; building projects were in progress everywhere; huge streams of capital were flowing into the country, not least because of 'the deteriorating economic and political situation of Jews in Poland, America and Germany'. With great energy, national dedication and excellent educational backgrounds, the Jews had created a model economy of a European standard in the middle of a very poor country. There was no unemployment or fears of unemployment in the Jewish region of Palestine, not least because Jewish capital was streaming into the country to provide jobs for the immigrating Jewish workers.[8]

The success of Jewish colonisation was due, Bernhard Peters argued, to the friendly attitude of the English government, whose Foreign Minister was himself a Jew, as well as to the huge amount of capital coming into the country. Whatever the causes of colonisation, behind human history stood a God whose 'prophetic Word is beginning to be fulfilled'.[9] Prophetical scriptures, which had been studied by Christians for centuries, were taken as the compass for one's actions. All events related to the Jewish people were seen through those verses. Even the anti-semitic movements throughout the world told believers that the day was soon coming when God would gather together again the Jews out of all the nations to lead them back to Palestine.[10] Palestine was once again to be 'the land of the Jews'. It had to be, for otherwise the 'Jewish Antichrist' could not make his appearance. The persecution of the Jews was serving to 'fulfil the prophecy'; everything that the Word of God says would happen, will happen.[11]

German evangelicals like their brethren overseas firmly believed that the Jews were a special people, God's people – the 'apple of His eye' (Deuteronomy 32,10; Zechariah 2,8). It is also clear, however, that they, as evangelicals, were not immune to the major conspiracy theory of the time – the Jewish-Masonic-Bolshevist threat to world peace and freedom. Privy Councillor D.K. Müller (Erlangen), in a February 1932 article on 'The Onslaught of the Godless', talked of Stalin as being 'the Pope of the Communist Church' fighting against all religions 'with the possible exception of Judaism'. He believed Moscow was showing favouritism towards Jews, when one considered the government's treatment of Christians. While church buildings were being pulled down in their hundreds, Moscow had suddenly issued counter-orders when, he said, local authorities in an eastern region were about to tear down synagogues. This almost certainly had nothing to do with the religious faith of Jews, he explained, but rather with the fact that at least three-quarters of the Bolshevik leaders belonged to the same race.

> Muss doch ohne jeden Rassen-Antisemitismus gesagt werden, dass das auserwählte Volk, welches seinen Messias verstossen hat, mehr und mehr zum zersetzenden Element im Völkerleben und zur oft verborgenen Triebkraft aller Revolutionen geworden ist. Und der ungläubig gewordene Jude wandelt sich in den zynischsten und fanatischsten Gottesfeind.
>
> Without wanting to be anti-semitic, it must be said that the chosen people which has rejected its Messiah has become more and more a corrupting element in the life of the nations and the often hidden driving force behind all revolutions. The apostate Jew turns into the most cynical, fanatical enemy of God.[12]

Bias also comes out in little comments made throughout the period. In a book review in the 3 January 1932 issue, the critic notes that the author is a 'Jewish socialist' but 'we would rather call him a socialist Jew'.[13] Those resisting Hitler in the period 1930-1932 were 'internationalist Jewish financiers'.[14] Special mention is made of the fact Jews were allowed to go through the first three degrees of Freemasonry in the United States.[15] Behind the Bolshevik movement there stood 'World Jewry' and it was a Jew who shot dead Wilhelm Gustloff, a representative of the NSDAP, in Switzerland.[16] Yet, as Pastor Lüdecke (Finkenwalde) from the Gnadau Association stated in October 1932: 'A converted Jew, Frenchman or Englishman is spiritually and mentally closer to Christians here than the most racially pure German who is far from God and Christ and wants to stay that way'.[17] In theory, this might well have been true; in practice, however, a number of leading figures in the Alliance were keen to remove the traditional prayers for Israel and mission among the Jews from the programme during the annual Alliance Prayer Week, or at least to hide it among other prayer subjects.[18] They achieved this in 1934 and 1939-1941. The prayer programme for 1933, produced before Hitler's appointment, reveals the growing influence of National Socialism over the Alliance Executive Committee.

> Wir haben uns anzuklagen ob des Ärgernisses, das die christliche Gemeinde vielfach den Juden gibt, wie andererseits anmassendes Wesen der Juden einem unevangelischen Antisemitismus neue Nahrung gibt. Wir beklagen alle Ablehnung der Judenmission durch einen falschen Rassenbegriff.
>
> We in the Christian Church must stand accused of frequently giving offence to the Jews, just as the arrogant, impudent character of the Jews, on the other hand, is nurturing an un-Protestant anti-semitism. We deplore the rejection of all mission among the Jews caused by a false concept of race.[19]

One felt it was necessary to change the text of the prayer programme (it was produced in London by the British Evangelical Alliance and translated into German) and to abridge reports dealing with the subject of Jews so as not to cause the censors offence.[20]

This did not prevent the *Allianzblatt* from responding to the measures taken by the Nazis to roll back Jewish influence in society and the economy. The paper was not alone in giving voice to deep-seated prejudices. Otto von Harling, in an article on 'Anti-semitism in the Christian press', published in 1920, had regretted the presence of such prejudice in the evangelical *Licht und Leben*. According to von Harling Jewry had repeatedly been presented in this weekly as an 'alien body, which the German people had to get rid of' and as 'the most dangerous opponent against which it was imperative to struggle to the utmost'. After 1933 *Licht und Leben* became notorious for its attempts to spread anti-semitism amongst Christians. On 9 April the paper claimed that anti-semitism was justified in view of German Jewry's 'brazenness'. Two months later, on 18 June, Dr Walter Michaelis had written in *Licht und Leben* that he and his organisation had 'nothing against stemming Jewish influence and treating Jews as non-Germans'. Nothing could be said against such action 'from a Biblical point of view'. On the contrary, he said, such treatment of Jews 'was part of the divine plan for them'. The Austrian Baptist paper, *Der Täuferbote*, also praised the German government in 1933 for raising a 'mighty dam' against the Jewish flood and claimed that all talk of persecution of Jews was simply a pack of lies. That was the line taken by the large Protestant denominations in Germany. The Brethren *Die Tenne* referred also to the fact that Jews were leaving Germany but failed to tell readers why that was the case. Any mention of ill-treatment in the paper was linked to the 'accursed' nature of the Jews. In an article on the return of the Jews to Palestine, the *Tenne* talked of the 'cleansing of Germany from elements hostile to the state, especially Jewish immigrants'. The other main

Brethren paper, *Der Botschafter des Heils in Christo*, explained that the fate of the Jews was proof that the Bible was not a product of human thought, but rather divine in origin.[21]

The boycott and plundering of Jewish shops began on 1 April 1933. So-called 'non-Aryan' civil servants were removed from office after laws passed on 7 April 1933 and 31 December 1935. Jewish artists and writers were forced out of their jobs following a law passed on 22 September 1933. In all, 250 different laws were issued in order to exclude Jews from nearly every profession. In his work on the Jewish Question, Bernhard Peters (1934) had called for such laws. Only if the government took the advice of Adolf Stoecker and excluded Jews from the legal and educational professions could 'teaching be conducted in Christian schools in the Christian spirit'. The *Allianzblatt* added its weight to the views of Stoecker and Peters. It too supported measures to restrict and even eliminate Jewish influence, at least in the economic and cultural fields. There may have been some doubt about certain excesses taking place. In February 1933 August Grünweller of the Gnadau Association said 'the Jewish threat was being answered by a kind of anti-Semitism which went far beyond Biblical limits as far as the choice of means is concerned'.[22] This theme would be referred to over and over again in the next few months. On the one hand, the Jews were seen, in great measure at least, to be responsible for the cultural and economic decay in the country. On the other hand, they were clearly a people with whom God dealt in a special way. Persecution could be used by God to fulfil His purposes, but Christians had no right to be involved in that persecution.

On 2 April 1933 the paper said the 'reformation' of the political and economic structures of the country had involved the closure of numerous Jewish department stores around the country. It added that Hitler had fortunately used all his authority to put a stop to some of the riots against the Jews. There followed a matter-of-fact account of some elements of the wave of persecution. The dismissal of Jews from posts in the whole civil service and the legal system was being 'vigorously continued'. Many Jews were accused of having supported the Communists. They were also being made responsible for having encouraged cultural Bolshevism in Germany. Anti-semitism had, the paper noted, been given a fresh impetus but the national Government was determined to neutralise the 'great influence' which Jews had under the previous democratic system. Hundreds of them were said to have already left Berlin and had flooded back to Eastern Europe. For many Jews, then, the first few days of the national revolution 'were a bitter foretaste of the distress which the Word of God says they will be made to suffer at the end of our age'. For the Jews would be hunted, the word of prophecy taught, all over the world until they returned to Palestine.23

On 16 April 1933 Christian readers were encouraged not to 'pass judgement' on the Jews; that was a matter which God had reserved for Himself. A similar appeal was made in America by the *Moody Bible Institute Monthly* in May 1933, basing its neutral position on its German 'private sources, more than one, and worthy of respect'. It was true, the *Allianzblatt* said, that the State 'should not shrink back' from measures relating to national policy which it felt were necessary. It should, however, take care not to 'perpetrate injustices'. Limits on the influence of Jews were recognised as necessary to 'strengthen' the German middle class. A 'healthy cultural policy' would have to 'roll back the pernicious influence' of Jewish Bolshevism in education, the theatre and cinema. 'We know only too well that persecutions of Jews will come and that they are provided for in God's plan for them', the article stated. Hundreds of Jews had already left Germany and thousands more who had come to the country after the last war would be forced to follow them. They knew they were all 'undesirable foreigners' who would one day be deported. The problems rocking the American economy were equally designed by the Lord to gradually 'drive the Jews out of their last place of refuge'. The measures taken by the German and American governments were 'signs of the end-times'. Jews were being forced by their God to go back to Palestine. 'We should not become proud when we recognize these signs', the writer added, 'for they remind us that time is running out for all the nations and that God will soon settle accounts with them, too'.24

On 23 April the same theme was taken up again. The editor voiced his opinion that the removal of Jews from public office and the opposition to their department stores was not simply due to anti-semitic thinking; the root cause was the 'distress of the middle classes and the young academics'. The self-employed and small businesses were being forced more and more out of business. Anti-semitism, then, had real economic causes. The so-called 'boycott movement' is portrayed as a spontaneous reaction to the economic crisis, focusing its wrath on the victors of the economic struggle. The *Allianzblatt* felt the boycott had taken a firmer public stand than the government at first would have liked. The government had in the end felt obliged to organise the movement only after Jewry had been mobilised abroad. There seemed at the time no end in sight to the 'bitter struggles'. There was an eschatological interest in the persecution. The scenes 'full of great tragedy' reminded all believers of the end of history; they were a 'foretaste of the last struggle which the ruler of the world will wage with the Whore of Babylon'. In this cosmic conflict the Jewish people was merely a pawn in the hand of spiritual forces. Germany was the battleground, Hitler the saviour. The German government would have to wage the struggle, the paper said, with 'a pitiless determination', for the Jews had brought their 'immense influence to bear' in many countries. Orders placed with German companies had been cancelled. Jewish efforts to move the American Congress had failed so far; the Congress was said to be 'very cautious' about submitting to Jewish demands for sanctions to be imposed on Germany. England was also trying to 'carefully disassociate herself' from the Jewish campaign being conducted throughout that country. In France there was talk of reoccupying the left bank of the Rhine. Russia was also being dragged into the campaign. The Communists would like to 'move heaven and earth', the *Allianzblatt* noted, to be rid of the hated Hitler government. All over the world, in this evangelical perspective, the 'powers of hell' were mobilising against Germany.[25]

Given their knowledge of Scripture, Bible-believing Christians were 'not surprised' by the government's policy of removing Jews from the fields of medicine, law, education, culture, the media and politics:the persecution had long been foretold in Scripture. The views of the Court Chaplain, Adolf Stoecker, on the dismissal of Jews from public office and discrimination against them in the professions – views written down for the followers of this Christian Party forty years prior to Hitler's measures – are granted three columns in the *Allianzblatt* of 14 May 1933 to justify the new attempt to 'smash the influence of Jewish mammonism'. According to Stoecker real Christians would 'certainly remember' the persecutions of Jews in the past with feelings of 'great compassion'. But they would not forget that the Albigenses and Waldenses had also been persecuted and that heretics and witches had been murdered in their thousands and burnt at the stake. 'It is unhistorical', said Stoecker, 'to single out the Jews in such an era and present them as victims of Christian cruelty'.[26] There was a spiritual and an economic reason for anti-semitism, in Stoecker's opinion. Spiritually, Israel was a 'stranger' among the nations. Because she failed to accept the Messiah she would always suffer persecution and contempt. Economically, the Jew had attained enormous power, particularly in America, and the world economy was controlled by the Jews. But the pursuit of dollars had not only led the Jew more and more into a Babylonian captivity, it had poured oil on to the fire of envy. With the growth of social conflicts came the growth of anti-semitism. 'We will soon see that the Jews will have only one place of refuge: Palestine!', he said. One day, the Bible said, the Beast would tear the Whore to pieces.

> Das Schlimmste für Juda kommt noch. Das Schlimmste wird sich am Ende des Zeitalters ereignen, wenn die grosse Drangsal kommt, von der der Herr sagt, dass grösser keine je gewesen sei und auch nicht wieder sein werde.

> The worst is still to come for Judah. The worst things will happen at the end of our age when the time of great distress comes, of which the Lord says that it will be unequalled from the beginning of the world until now and will never be equalled again.[27]

Karl Engler's essay on 'Present-day Jewry and Biblical Israel' which appeared in the 18 June 1933 issue of *Allianzblatt* was perhaps the most blatantly anti-semitic article to appear during the period. It contains most, if not all, of the prevailing prejudices found among certain economic classes in the German population at the time. He started by referring to the 'fatal and corrupting influence' exercised by Jews over the life of the German nation. Christians had difficulties reconciling what they knew of the Jews of this world with the Israel of the Bible. Farmers were ill-disposed towards Jews, because they were 'often duped and cheated' by them. Some had been 'robbed' of all their possessions. 'Jew' and 'rogue' meant the same thing to the farmer. Nobody, Engler said, could haggle like a Jew. Town dwellers had a similar relationship to Jewish shops. They grumbled about them but nevertheless went in droves to do their shopping there. 'The Jew is, after all, the best businessman there is'. Many Jews had become rich businessmen; big business is 'largely in Jewish hands'. As money meant power, Jews had had a controlling influence over economic and political life in Germany. As a result, Jews not only robbed Germans of their material goods, but also of their 'intellectual and ethical assets'. Jewish business speculated on the 'most dangerous and vulgar passions' of man. Jews were behind the worst kind of trashy literature. Wherever 'shameless' pictures were exhibited as art, wherever 'rotten' comic and satirical papers were being produced, wherever people were writing anarchist and socialist newspapers and books, wherever people were 'formenting and stirring up trouble', wherever things are being undermined or pulled to pieces – mainly Jews could be found doing business in these areas. When the Great War broke out, the Jews were the first who made money out of it and grabbed the 'war profits'. It was mainly Jews involved as ringleaders in the small-scale and large-scale revolutions. About eighty per cent of the members of the 'Workers and Soldiers Councils' were, according to Engler, Jews. Trotzky and Lenin, the leaders of the Russian Revolution, were Jews. One could, he said, quite properly cry out with indignation: 'Evil comes from the Jews!' even though the Lord Jesus said of them: 'Salvation is from the Jews' (John 4, 22). He wondered how this people would one day be converted to their God, Jesus Christ, given their notorious greed for money and estrangement from God. The Scriptures foretold, however, the spiritual restoration of Israel and the setting up of His kingdom in Palestine. The Last Judgement would primarily befall the Jews living there, he believed. The 'great plague' spoken of in Zechariah 14, 12-15 would strike Judah. According to Zechariah 13, 7-9 Engler said two thirds of all Jews would be 'exterminated' (*ausgerottet*) and only the remaining third would, as a purified people of God, inherit the promises. 'Reformed Judaism' will then be consumed by the wrath of God on the Day of Judgement at the end of time.[28]

Such eschatological interpretations were, and are, by no means uncommon among evangelicals. With hindsight an analysis such as the one Engler presents appears almost prophetic. The prejudices, however, help to explain why evangelicals felt unable or unwilling to stay the hand of judgement that crashed down on the Jewish people in the period under consideration. There was a real belief that God was purifying His people and drawing it back to their promised land. At the same time they were also convinced that the removal of Jews from positions of influence would indeed help to bring about a political and moral recovery. In this regard they were particularly sensitive to foreign criticism of the measures taken by the government. In July 1933 the editors denied that a massacre of Jews had either been planned or carried out, and claimed such rumours were being fabricated by the press organs of the 'Red and Golden Internationals'. Provincial church leaders such as Otto Dibelius as well as Methodist leaders like Bishop Nuelsen and Otto Melle also referred to the 'wild stories' and 'propaganda lies' circulated by foreign papers.

Evangelicals were anxious to use foreign media outlets to question such reporting. In May 1933 the *Moody Bible Institute Monthly* admitted 'there are times when all of us are in a quandary whom or what to believe' about the situation of Jews in Germany. One letter from Berlin of 22 March 1933 to the editor complained of 'how misinformed our American friends and Christians are by the latest revolution in Germany'. 'All reports', the writer claimed, 'of bloody attacks, circulated in foreign papers, were inspired by a social-democratic or communistic press in order to depreciate Hitler'. The *Moody Bible Institute Monthly* published in July 1934 a letter of 6 April from Ernst Modersohn, editor of *Weg zum Glück* and *Heilig dem Herrn*, to an American friend in Bloomfield, New Jersey, denying that Christian Jews were being excluded from the churches and that the Old Testament could no longer be read in public, as had been reported to American Christians. Such statements were among 'the many lies' being circulated to 'find fault' with and 'arouse suspicions' against the new regime. Modersohn said he at least was very grateful for the 'peace and harmony' that Hitler had brought to the country.[29] In August 1933 Social Democrats and Jews were accused of being behind the 'campaign' to stir up hatred of Germany. The *Allianzblatt* recognised that, for the Jews at least, an 'extraordinarily great deal' was at stake. They were faced with 'encirclement' and the 'destruction of their means of livelihood' in all the European countries. 'They are learning', the report said, 'that no country likes them so much that it would be willing for their sakes to wage war against Hitler'. Only prayer and supplication could now help them, the article concluded.[30]

A speech made by Dr Goebbels in October 1933 is published approvingly in the *Allianzblatt*. The speech actually reiterates points that the *Allianzblatt*, Bernhard Peters in particular, had been making throughout the year. With reference to the Jews the Reich Minister rebuffed the argument that the way the Jewish Question was being dealt with ran counter to the laws of humanity. He said it was 'incomprehensible' why people were protesting abroad but at the same time countries were refusing to accept the 'surplus' Jewish population emigrating from Germany. He took exception to the reports about atrocities and admonished all the journalists present at the meeting not to allow themselves to be used to do the shameful work of spreading such lies which only endangered world peace.[31]

In December 1933 an article appeared which traced the history of the Jews in Europe. It talked of how they had been persecuted at the time of the Black Death in 1348 and at the time of Columbus' voyage around the world in 1492. Only with the French Revolution had the Jews in Western Europe succeeded in asserting themselves and gaining a measure of power and wealth. It said, however, that a new age had begun in 1933. 'A new spirit is knocking at the gates of all the nations' and once again the 'eternal Jew' had to 'take to the road'.[32] They were clearly hoping that they would in fact return to Palestine.

On 15 September 1935 the Reichstag passed laws on German citizenship and the 'protection of German blood', the so-called Nuremberg Laws. Jews became second-class citizens, marriages and sexual relations between Jews and people with 'German blood' were forbidden. There were no Church protests against the new laws. A note sent with 'a deferential greeting' to their Führer was sent by the Provisional Leadership of the German Protestant Church on 28 May 1936. The leaders tucked away in the fifth section on 'National Socialist ideology' the statement that 'where anti-Semitism is forced upon Christians, obligating them to hate Jews, the Christian commandment to love one's neighbour is opposed to this'.[33] No specific reference is made to the Nuremberg Laws, nor had this principle ever led to criticism of *Mein Kampf*, which had appeared in 1924/1925, or of the policies of Stoecker's Christian Social Party. Most Protestant Church leaders in the first half of the twentieth century had internalised anti-Semitic prejudices. Otto Dibelius' words in a letter dated 3 April 1928 to pastors of his parish, the Kurmark, were fairly representative of a latent, widespread attitude: 'In spite of the wicked sound which the word has generally taken on, I have always known myself to be an anti-semite. One cannot fail to notice that the Jews play a leading role in all the morally corrupting phenomena of modern civilisation'.[34]

The *Allianzblatt* reported on the new legal restrictions on Jews without, however, detailing how the Alliance perceived these measures. This reservation in speaking about the laws was characteristic of evangelical circles, irrespective of the denomination. On 15 September 1935, the day the laws were promulgated, the Baptist *Wahrheitszeuge* told its readers not to forget that the hearts of Jews had been hardened by God following their rejection of the Messiah. Under God's judgement they had become a curse for the world. On 6 October the *Wahrheitszeuge* reminded readers that the Führer had given orders that 'actions against Jews be avoided, as they had been up till now'. The final articles in the Baptist paper which dealt with the issue were titled 'The Struggle against the Jews', and related that friendships with Jews had been declared to be *Rassenschande* by a court in Breslau and that Jews were no longer permitted to use the town archives in Magdeburg. The Elim Pentecostal Church, on the other hand, had to defend itself against what some government officials perceived to be a friendly disposition towards the Jews. Yet in his defence, the founder of the church in Germany, Heinrich Vietheer, insisted that he had 'warmly welcomed' the Nuremberg Laws and knew that they did not violate God's Word 'in any way'. In similar fashion one of the papers produced by the Gnadau Association, *Heilig dem Herrn*, accepted and welcomed the laws as being in accord with the Bible.35

The report in the Alliance paper took note of the 'significant' commentary published by the Departmental Chief of the Reich Interior Ministry on the Nuremberg Laws. The editor felt the core ideas contained in the official commentary deserved to be reproduced in the *Allianzblatt*. The commentary talked of the beginning of 'a satisfactory settlement' of the relations between the German and the Jewish peoples and says 'racial hatred will vanish'. Every Christian in Germany would be able to 'give hearty assent' to the new laws. The Führer had insisted that the measures would end racial hatred for ever. The laws signified 'the beginning of peaceful relations' between the German people and the Jewish people. The *Allianzblatt* said these laws were in effect the same as those provided for the Jewish people thousands of years ago to ensure their racial and religious purity. Just as the laws contained in the Old Testament had brought about 'the miracle of a strong Jewish people' which had for centuries kept its blood 'unadulterated' in the midst of foreign cultures, one could expect similar results from the new German laws. It quoted the *Hamburg News* as saying that the separation of the Jews from the German people meant 'legal protection' for them. In future, Jews would be able to live in the German state 'in a way their nature dictated'. The Jewish 'guest people' (*Gastvolk*), whose members comprised little more than one percent of the German 'host people' (*Wirtsvolk*), would in future be separated politically, culturally and biologically from the German people. There was now hope that 'the healthy feeling of being alien to one another', free of passionate emotions, would gradually develop in both camps. The solution to the 'Jewish Question', the editorial continued, would only be a Jewish state, a homeland for most of the Jewish race. It was believed that this was the reason why committed Zionists had protested *least* against the ideas of the Nuremberg Laws. They were not the only ones who had come to realize that the Nuremberg Laws were 'the only correct solution for the Jewish people'.36

Legal experts like Dr Hans-Maria Globke, who is referred to in the article above, gave respectability to the dictatorial measures by drafting them and writing the official commentary on them. These Nuremberg Laws were characterised during the trial of Adolf Eichmann as the 'basic laws of the final solution of the Jewish Question'.37 They were a milestone on the path leading to the extermination of not two-thirds, as Karl Engler had expected, but one-third of the world's Jews.

Six weeks after discussing the Nuremberg Laws the *Allianzblatt* invited Christian singers and choir members to take part in a two-week trip on the *Monte Rosa* to the Holy Land:'Limited number of places available. Extremely low prices. No foreign currency problems. Full eight days' stay in Palestine with good board and lodging. Sight-seeing tours and cross-country trips with knowledgeable travel guides'. The American Express Company in Berlin was waiting, the evangelical paper said, to process applications. Christians were encouraged to make 'all necessary sacrifices in terms of money and time' to ensure they were part of a tour group. They would, the *Allianzblatt* told them, experience days 'full of indelible memories'. Older people and women travelling on their own would be given 'special care and attention' in the Holy Land. Such study trips had been taking place for decades and were geared to helping Christians gain a 'deeper understanding' of the land and people of the Bible.[38]

In this connection the *Allianzblatt* was continually reporting on the political and social changes taking place in Palestine. There was a particular interest in the orphanages in Jerusalem, Nazareth and Bir Salem which, in 1938/39, had to be closed due to the 'bitter power struggles' and 'desperate struggle of the Arabs' against the Jewish immigration policy of the British military authorities. German and Arab workers had had to be made redundant. Arab Christians were said to be in 'indescribable need'; many Arab Christians had simply 'disappeared' – nobody knew where they were. The British Prime Minister, Chamberlain, had been called upon by the Arab Christians in Palestine to 'not allow the land of Christ to be ruled by a people which crucified him'. Christian leaders there strongly condemned the 'prejudiced' and pro-Jewish involvement of American Church leaders in the 'Palestine question'. On 1-15 June 1940 a further report appeared on these orphanages. Fifty German workers had had to leave the country after war broke out in order to avoid being interned. The orphanages were then being managed by Arab Christians. The English 'oppression' of Arabs in Palestine is said to be continuing and at least 15,000 Arab children could be seen roaming the streets.[39] In these reports there remained the obligatory reference to Biblical ideas on the end-times, yet no concrete details as to when the Jewish state would, as prophecy indicated, come into existence.

In Germany the first fruits of the Nuremberg laws were statistically recorded. While the number of Catholic schools in the Reich fell from 15,231 in 1936 to 13,025 in 1937 and the number of Protestant schools declined from 28,308 to 26,204 in the same period, the number of Jewish schools grew from 65 to 69 over the year. The number of Jewish schoolchildren had fallen from 17,397 (0.22% of the total) to 13,988 (0.18%).[40] Anti-semitism, of course, had not been eliminated from social life as a result of the laws. It was given further nourishment. Martin Sasse, the Bishop of Thuringia, published a selection of anti-semitic quotes from the writings of Martin Luther under the title *Martin Luther and the Jews: Away with Them*. In the preface to this work, the bishop rejoices in the fact that on 10 November 1938, Luther's birthday, synagogues all over Germany were burning. His joy was due to the macabre fact that Luther had once called upon Christian statesmen to burn down the synagogues and Jewish schools. Sasse recommends the works of a man he calls the 'greatest anti-semite of his time, warning his people about the Jews'.[41] In hindsight 9/10 November appears as a turning point. At the time Christian papers took as little note of the event as they had done of the bookburning incidents a few years earlier. The *Allianzblatt* failed to report the arson attacks but, significantly, the traditional prayer for Israel, which had always been part of the programme of the Alliance Prayer Week, was dropped in January 1939 and did not reappear until after the war. The organ of the Confessing Church, *Junge Kirche*, did not mention the conflagration. Bonhoeffer wrote nothing about the incident, though he did, some time later, jot down the date '9.11.38' in the margin of his Bible against Psalm 74,8 ('they burned all the meeting places of God in the land', *Gotteshäuser* being translated 'synagogues' in the King James Version). Bonhoeffer's disappointment with the compromised position of the Confessing Church at this time seems to have led him to break what links he still had with it.[42] The one evangelical paper which did refer to *Kristallnacht* was the *Deutsches Gemeinschaftsblatt*. Wilhelm Goebel justified the attacks on synagogues as a correct response to the murder of the German embassy official in Paris, von Rath. The German government's 'war against world Jewry', he said, had to be fought with weapons that were effective against a people which ruled no territory. The Jews had to be hit where they could be hurt:their money and their synagogues. He claimed that Christians should *not* judge wars and political affairs on the basis of the word and spirit of the New Testament. Christian thinking on such issues should not forget that the peoples of the world, in contrast to the New Testament church, were ruled by laws and customs which did not concern the Apostles. Using Scripture to guide thought on these matters would only lead to confusion and uncertainty, he said. Christians had to learn a two-track approach to politics: on the one hand, to make judgements 'as German citizens (*Volksgenossen*)' whenever German issues and concerns are considered, and, secondly, as Christians whenever the Church was in view. Wars had to be fought in a way that Christians had to accept as valid, even though, as Christians, they might have reservations. Burning synagogues was, in this view of events, one of those unfortunate measures that were necessary to confront 'the truly impudent manner in which [world Jewry] had thrown down the gauntlet' in Paris. 'That meant war', Goebel explained. He added that it was also because of his 'trust in the Führer in all matters concerning our people' that Goebel had found peace of mind on the matter. Once Christians had placed their trust in the Führer (and he encouraged all his readers to do so at once) they would have that certainty that all was well, 'irrespective of whether one can understand the measures taken or not'.[43]

The Baptist newspaper also failed to mention the burning synagogues. On the 4 November 1938 the monthly report produced by the directing body of the Baptist Church had – one more macabre fact in the history of evangelicalism during the Third Reich – reported on the favourable terms under which synagogues could at that time be purchased. The very next *Kurzbericht* recommended to congregations that, in view of the 'latest incidents', no further Jewish buildings be bought. In Osterode in East Prussia one such building was purchased by the local Baptists which was to be destroyed during the November pogroms. The Baptist congregation thereupon started legal proceedings against the Jewish community in Osterode to force it to return the money used to purchase the building. The titular head of the Baptists, Bundesdirektor Paul Schmidt, wrote to the Reich Ministry for Church Affairs, insisting that something be done to recover the money. The official at the Ministry with whom Schmidt enjoyed a trusting and close relationship, Werner Haugg, supported the case, saying that repayment would contribute to the 'removal of Jews (*Entjudung*) from German soil'. Ironically, the Interior Minister informed the Baptists on 23 September 1940 that the Baptist demand for compensation had been rejected as the government did not wish to aid the 'growth of sects'.[44]

Even as war approached there was growing interest in National Socialist ideology. On 23 January 1939 Bible Courses were held in the Diakonissen-Mutterhaus in Breslau. Experts were employed to give seminars on genetics and race, as well as on the 'colonial question' and Germany's progress through the centuries. One of the last reports in the *Allianzblatt* which refers specifically to the Jewish question appeared on 30 May 1939. Church leaders in the Old Prussian Union, Saxony, Hesse-Nassau, Schleswig-Holstein, Thuringia,

Mecklenburg, the Palatinate, Anhalt, Oldenburg, Lübeck and the 'East Mark' appended their signatures to a series of principles which would guide the work of those pastors and lay groups within the *Deutsche Evangelische Kirche* who were seeking a modus vivendi with the National Socialist government. The struggle of National Socialism against 'Church claims to political power' was declared to be the 'continuation and completion of the work which the German reformer, Martin Luther, began'. This separation of politics and religion, a key issue for Free Church evangelicals, was welcomed. The second principle claimed that 'the Christian faith is irreconcilably opposed to Jewry (*das Judentum*)'.[45]

The *Allianzblatt* does not seek to clarify whether Jews as people, or Judaism as a religion or Jewish culture and customs are meant here. By this time, perhaps, such distinctions had become purely academic. It is known that Jewish Christians experienced rejection in Baptist, Brethren and Free Evangelical congregations; some were encouraged or pressurised to resign membership.[46] Such reactions to Jews in their midst and support for racist laws were partly conditioned by a belief that Germany, like other nations in the world at that time, had a right and even a duty to protect its national character and particularly its economy, and partly by a certain reading of the Bible. Hartmut Weyel points out that the 'economic blackmail' of Germany after Versailles was perceived in Free Evangelical churches as a ploy of finance capital and bankers, some of whom were known to be Jewish. He feels that evangelicals were 'certainly not wrong' in making this equation. In the religious sphere, there was a widespread view that the Jews, in calling on Christ's blood to come upon them, had brought such a 'judgement' upon themselves. Added to this was a strong millennialist view that the Jews would have to face persecution before returning to their promised homeland. Such interpretations of Scripture clearly helped to undermine any sense of solidarity which undoubtedly existed among those Christians who had not forgotten that they actually worshipped a Jew.[47]

Notes

1. On Protestantism and anti-semitism, J.C. Kaiser/ M. Greschat (1988). On the Confessing Church and anti-semitism, W. Gerlach (1987).
2. EA 24.01.1932 (Nr 4), 61.
3. EA 16.10.1932 (Nr 42), 680-681.

4. EA 16.04.1933 (Nr 16), 252.
5. EA 01.05.1932 (Nr 18), 283.
6. EA 22.05.1932 (Nr 21), 333-334.
7. EA 24.01.1932 (Nr 4), 1.
8. EA 14.05.1933 (Nr 20), 319.
9. EA 14.05.1933 (Nr 20), 319. For an evangelical interpretation of Israel's role in world history and God's dealings with His people, L. Lambert (1988). On the plan in 1937 to divide Palestine into three parts, EA 15.01.1938 (Nr 11), 14-15.
10. EA 17.09.1933 (Nr 38), 624.
11. EA 24.09.1933 (Nr 39), 640; Bernhard Peters (1934).
12. EA 07.02.1932 (Nr 6), 84-91.
13. EA 03.01.1932 (Nr 1), 15.
14. EA 10.01.1932 (Nr 2), 31-32.
15. EA 15.12.1935 (Nr 23), 369.
16. EA 15.03.1936 (Nr 5), 79.
17. EA 23.10.1932 (Nr 43), 703.
18. E. Beyreuther (1969, 107-110). According to Beyreuther, the faint-hearted and fearful brethren were those members of the Alliance Executive Committee who came from the Free Churches. Friedrich Heitmüller (1950, 129).
19. E. Beyreuther (1969, 107).
20. E. Beyreuther (1969, 109-110). Nagel said that, for the 1938 Prayer Week, the suggestions made by the Executive Council in London would be used as the basis of prayer and 'a few footnotes, especially when we pray for missionary activities, will take the German situation into consideration', EA 30.12.1937 (Nr 24), 346-347. Nagel emphasised the unity of the Body of Christ:'There is neither Jew nor Greek, neither slave nor free'. There is neither Provincial Church nor Free Church nor Christians who reject organisation, there is neither theologian nor layman, for you are all one in Christ'. Compare Galatians 3,28 to which Nagel refers here.
21. W. Gerlach (1987, 31-32,119-120); G. Jordy (1986, 69-71); Friedhelm Menk (1986, 41).
22. EA 05.02.1933 (Nr 6), 95f. He hoped the National Socialist movement would remain a purely political movement and not become 'a Church in any sense' with a 'pseudo-religious cult of race'. If it became a 'Party-Church' that would only hamper the 'desperately necessary reorganisation of the state'. B. Peters (1934, 61).
23. EA 02.04.1933 (Nr 14), 223; B. Peters (1934, 65-7).
24. EA 16.04.1933 (Nr 16), 255.
25. EA 23.04.1933 (Nr 17), 269. On 2 April the *Allianzblatt* said: 'In the middle of these struggles God would be close to Germans'. 'Is He close to us because He takes special delight in the new national movement?', the editors wondered.

26. *Die Judenfrage in biblischer Beleuchtung*, EA 14.05.1933 (Nr 20), 316-319. The *Allianzblatt* reported in Febraury 1936 on Adolf Stoecker's relationship to the Gnadau Association (15.02.1936, Nr 3, 44f) and in July 1940 on the founding of an Adolf Stoecker Society (1-15.07.1940, Nr 13/14, 110). The *Allianzblatt* praised Stoecker as 'a man of the people' and a 'social thinker' in February 1936. 'It is unmistakeable that his massive influence sharpened consciences, clarified ethical views and brought salutary results'. The long quote from a Stoecker speech in the May 1933 issue is proof enough that Stoecker and his Christian Party helped to create the spiritual atmosphere in Germany from which Hitler was able to profit.
27. EA 14.05.1933 (Nr 20), 317. The references here are to Revelation Chapter 17 (The Woman on the Beast) and Matthew 24,21 (The Great Tribulation). B. Peters (1934, 67).
28. EA 18.06.1933 (Nr 25), 389-392; B. Peters, Arier und Jude (1934, 93); B. Peters, Im Umbruch der Zeit (1934, 53).
29. EA 02.07.1933 (Nr 27), 431. Evangelicals used Christian media abroad to counteract what Free Church leaders like Bishop Nuelsen and Dr Melle as well as Provincial Church leaders like Otto Dibelius described as 'propaganda lies'. *Moody Bible Institute Monthly*, May 1933, 392; July 1934, 506; T.P. Weber (1987, 194-195, 198-200).
30. EA 06.08.1933 (Nr 32), p.511.
31. EA 22.10.1933 (Nr 43), 704.
32. EA 24-31.12.1933 (Nr 52/53), 832-833.
33. G. Denzler/V. Fabricius Vol 2 (1988, 102); P. Matheson (1981, 61).
34. Hier spricht Dibelius. Eine Dokumentation (Berlin 1960), 101; J.-C. Kaiser/M. Greschat (1988, 221). The Confessing Church synods in Prussia decided not to protest against the Nuremberg Laws; passivity remained the dominant characteristic of the 'only true Church', J.-C. Kaiser/M. Greschat (1988, 242).
35. A. Strübind (1995, 267-8); B. R. Densky (1983, 15-16); E. G. Rüppel (1969, 218).
36. EA 15.02.1936 (Nr 3), 45.
37. After the war Globke became the grey eminence in the Chancellor's Office, the most important and influential civil servant in the Federal Republic of Germany until his resignation in July 1963, following the publication of incriminating documents in the German Democratic Republic. Braunbuch. Kriegs- und Naziverbrecher in der Bundesrepublik (Nationalrat der Nationalen Front des Demokratischen Deutschland, Berlin 1965); Globke und die Ausrottung der Juden. Über die verbrecherische Vergangenheit des Dr Hans Globke (Ausschuss für Deutsche Einheit, Berlin 1960).
38. EA 15.02.1934 (Nr 3), 56; EA 15.03.1934 (Nr 5), 87; EA 15.03.1935 (Nr 5), 77; EA 30.03.1936 (Nr 6), 95.
39. EA 30.01.1939 (Nr 2), 31; EA 28.02.1039 (Nr 4), 56; EA 1-15.06.1940 (Nr 11-12), 94-95.

40. EA 15.08.1938 (Nr 15), 215.
41. W. Gerlach (1987, 236-250).
42. Eberhard Bethge (1977, 511-512).
43. E.G. Rüppel (1969, 219-220); E. Beyreuther (1969, 110).
44. A. Strübind (1995, 271).
45. EA 30.05.1939 (Nr 10), 134; EA 15.03.1939 (Nr 5), 68.
46. G. Jordy (1986, 70,265); A. Strübind (1995, 268-271).
47. *Der Gärtner*, Nr 6, 6 February 1983, 88.

Chapter Eight

Hitler's Foreign Policy

Pacifism or resistance to their country's foreign policy were both equally unheard of and unthinkable to a traditionally patriotic German Protestant. The *Allianzblatt* had, like most Christian newspapers, vigorously supported the German war effort between 1914 and 1918, fully identifying itself with the interests of the German army. Christian ideals and values had quite openly been manipulated for the patriotic cause. The support given to the German war aims in the Second World War was, given the history of German Protestantism, the most natural thing in the world. During times of national emergency verses such as the one reminding the Church that in Christ there is 'neither Jew nor Greek' were seen to be of no practical consequence. The slaughter of the baptised by the baptised had been a perennial feature of European history which no Christian denomination, as a denomination, had seriously challenged.

The post-war diabolisation of Hitler's policies, especially his foreign policy, stands in marked contrast to the reactions and statements made at the time in all Christian publications in Germany. Everywhere the hand of God could be seen. Hostility to the new German government abroad was met in Germany with incomprehension. On 17 September 1933 the *Allianzblatt* noted a great ignorance of German affairs among foreigners. The German revolution had thoroughly 'upset theories' abroad about what was considered 'true and proper' for a government and a people. Even Christians abroad shook their heads and talked about 'the Antichrist' in Germany. This was felt to be rather hypocritical and self-righteous. The rhetorical question was asked:'Where then are the truly Christian nations?' In the whole of the West there seemed to the editor of the *Allianzblatt* to be a 'complete indifference' to the Christian faith and in Eastern Europe 'the hatred of God' had thrived and produced all its 'cursed results'. Hitler, on the other hand, had publicly recognised that 'a spiritual change is the only way to salvation' for nations and this, the Führer knew, could not happen without God's help. At the end of time Scripture prophesied a period in which 'the parts of Europe will be synchronized (*gleichgeschaltet*)'. Western and Eastern Europe would one day be spiritually united. Referring to the Book of Daniel, he said the five 'toes' of the Western 'leg' and the five 'toes' of the Eastern 'leg', ie. Western and Eastern Europe,

Western Rome and Eastern Rome, would be reunited.[1] Only then, in his view, would the Antichrist appear. Hitler could not be the Antichrist for he believed in the Lord. 'But who, according to the Bible, is the Antichrist? He who denies the Father and the Son'.[2] Scripture, moreover, gave clues about the nature of the Man of Sin. There could scarcely be any doubt, the *Allianzblatt* reported, that the Antichrist would be born a Jew and would appear during the final world empire, when 'Babylon will once more raise its head'. That time had not yet come, for the Jews still rejected the Lord, more furiously than ever.[3]

Not Germany, but the rest of Europe was considered to have an unchristian mentality. Germany was seen as a country which would make a major contribution to the solution of the world's political problems. Germany was, however, not being fairly treated by the great powers. The League of Nations and other European nations had been trying for decades to impede Germany's growth, fearing her economic potential. Millions of skilful hard-working people who would 'love to settle on new land' were crowded together in a 'diabolically cramped space' (*Lebensraum*). In spite of this, the German demand for colonies had gone unheard. Even the Archbishop of Australia had called on restrictions to be lifted so that Germans could settle in his country and so 'preserve Australia for whites and help defend it against the yellow peril'. Nor were Germans being allowed into America even though that country was beginning to feel 'the onslaught of the coloured race'. When would these nations begin to see the light, Nagel wondered, and wake up to the threat that hung over all. Though he found it incredible, Nagel still heard people in the West saying a 'Bolshevist Germany' was preferable to a 'nationalist Germany'. Given this treatment from other nations, it was the duty of National Socialism to do all in its power to ensure that Germans prospered again.[4]

In this struggle for equality on the world stage, Hitler is not seen to be the anti-Christian leader of an empire which would 'devour the whole earth and tread it down and crush it' (Daniel 7, 23); rather, he is seen as a man of peace, a man with vision, whose ideas were gaining adherents. It claimed the American President, Roosevelt, had taken Germany as his model in working out his measures to combat unemployment. The English too had begun to use 'increasingly friendly expressions' to describe what they saw in Germany. The *Allianzblatt* quoted the rich and famous in England who found the greatest respect for what the National Socialists were doing. Lord Rothermere is said to have declared before a large gathering that the 'victory' achieved by the young men of Germany had changed the face of the world. He said he could only hope a similar victory might be achieved by young Englishmen. Nagel hoped the truth would soon dawn on England. 'Marxists will cause that country no end of trouble', he said, 'so much in fact that the English too will one day beg God to raise up a Hitler for them'. Hitler was gradually being perceived as a 'friend, a helper and a saviour'. Nothing could be further from the truth to claim, as some foreigners did, that 'Hitlerism' brought terror to the world.[5]

As leaders of the Alliance were convinced that the National Socialist state was 'a system of peace and social justice',[6] one was equally convinced Hitler represented these values in his foreign policy. In the 11 June 1933 issue Bernhard Peters wrote about the 'Peace Speech' the Führer had held in the Reichstag on 17 May 1933 and stated the Alliance position. It believed that the speech had in fact convinced people that Germany 'wouldn't dream of seeking to dominate the world' by force of arms. A war, the Chancellor had said, could never solve the problems of Europe. Peters concurred that war could only make the problems worse and encourage the growth of 'anarchical Communism'. Peters agreed that Germany was simply fighting for its 'right to life' and for 'equality among the nations'. 'Precisely because we love our fatherland with all the strength of our being', evangelicals understood the love Poles and the French felt for their fatherlands. Neither country should feel threatened. Germany, after all, had no offensive weapons. Only Germany had grounds to fear an invasion. 'We will no longer work together with the other members of the League of Nations', Hitler had said, 'if we are not respected as a people enjoying the same rights as others'. The division of Europe into victors and vanquished had to come to an end. Peters felt the speech had banished the danger of war and dispersed the storm clouds. He noted the increased enthusiasm with which government officials had restarted work at the disarmament conferences.[7]

At the New Year's reception for diplomats in 1935 Hitler emphasised in his speech that Germany would always be a 'reliable guarantor of peace'.[8] In the summer, in a speech in the Reichstag, he 'solemnly affirmed the passionate love of peace of the National Socialist Reich'.[9] His Thirteen Point Programme, aiming to 'bring about European understanding' and set up a 'system of collective cooperation', was reported in detail in the *Allianzblatt*. Whoever lifted up a torch of war in Europe, Hitler said, could only want chaos. 'We are searching for peace because we love peace' he is quoted as saying. 'Germany will be as peace-loving as any people can be as long as Germany's honour is not offended'. In response to this the editor petitioned God to allow 'this

193

hope of the Führer' to be fulfilled.[10] The *Allianzblatt* called on witnesses to testify to Germany's desire for peace. Lord Rothermere is reported to have said that 'Hitler *is* peace' and Europe could only have 'peace with him, not against him'. The paper also quotes a statement by Cardinal Faulhaber who had gone on record as saying that the Führer's 'courageous, fearless confession of his love of peace had twice, perhaps three times kept the horrors of war away from us'. Such a viewpoint was, according to the *Allianzblatt*, 'completely true'. It was a truth that the peoples 'are beginning to understand'.[11]

Neither Nagel nor Peters nor any other evangelical leader expressed doubts about Hitler's foreign policy goals, although, as we know from their books and articles in the *Allianzblatt*, they had all carefully studied *Mein Kampf* and the NSDAP Party Programme. Just as National Socialism meant total control and unlimited despotism at home, abroad it meant conquest and world domination.[12] The latter grew naturally from the former, war was its natural child, even though this aim was hidden from many observers by the smoke-screen of peace-speak. Some key elements of National Socialist foreign policy have been touched upon in the excerpts above: land or colonies, equal rights for the German people, the restoration of German honour. A number of milestones in Hitler's foreign policy were faithfully recorded in the *Allianzblatt*, not, however, as milestones on the road to war, but as steps towards maintaining peace and restoring justice and equality in international relations.

The Versailles Teaty limited the size of the German Army and the type of weaponry it was permitted to have. At the Geneva disarmament talks the German representatives strove to restore their country's military equality. They argued that restrictions placed on Germany could only be justified and tolerated by the German government if the other European powers embarked on comprehensive disarmament. When this step was not taken, Germany left the League of Nations and the disarmament conference (14 October 1933). The *Allianzblatt* agreed that the step had been 'absolute necessity'. In its view, the League had never accepted in principle Germany's claim to equal rights because one of its key goals had been to prevent Germany's recovery. The great powers had submitted Germany to a control system for eight years. Germany would no longer submit to a dictate; it had been humiliated for long enough. The decision to leave the League of Nations was, in its view, the answer to 'the deceitful game being played in Geneva'. Support for Hitler on the issue was unlimited. Their Reich Chancellor had emphasised again and again that Germany 'wanted nothing but the peaceful cooperation of peoples' and disarmament. 'What England is now doing', it noted, 'is very far away from showing a desire to negotiate'. Germany's withdrawal from the League was a 'clear rejection of a useless debate'. Nobody needed to feel threatened as a result. The hostility against Germany predominating in the world needed to be corrected, for people were 'irritated' and 'prepared to insinuate things'.[13]

As Hitler and many other Germans saw it, heavily armed nations were seeking, by treaty, to confine their country to second-class citizenship in the European community of nations. The *Allianzblatt* strongly supported the call for peace on the basis of the equality of all nations, implicitly rejecting a supposed French claim to leadership.[14]

Hitler readily spoke of peace. His efforts to bring about arms limitation being rejected by nations, conscious perhaps of their inferiority in terms of industrial potential and human numbers, Hitler could appear as a statesman acting quite ethically to revise an unjust peace settlement. As no one was disarming, he withdrew to work out a strategy of making Germany strong again.

In an article published in November 1936 the *Allianzblatt* asked the rhetorical question: 'Must Christians boycott the League of Nations?' The reason provided to justify such a protest is the League's apparent indifference to the 'spiritual interests of Christianity'. It offended Christian feeling by refusing to listen to 'the just demands of the Christian world'. Hopes had been dashed. The League's 'anti-Christian influence' could be seen in the fact that nations such as Russia, Mexico and Spain, where believers were being persecuted and churches destroyed, were allowed to remain influential members. Was a total boycott necessary because the League had proved to be 'a useless, if not a harmful instrument of policy?' 'Will those with responsibility comprehend this warning?'[15] Not only the demand for equality, but also the need for religious separation from the League seemed to necessitate withdrawal.

Internationally, however, this was a step leading to isolation; domestically, it helped to underline and strengthen the unity between Führer and Volk. A referendum was held on 12 November 1933 which proved that a vast majority of Germans (96.3%) supported his foreign policy; a second plebiscite, on 29 March 1936, produced a similar affirmative result (90% of the total or 38 million in favour). How did evangelicals react to the referendum? They were rather surprised initially for they 'had got used to the idea that Reichstag elections were a thing of the past'. The significance of the new election was seen in the value of 'a great proclamation of trust' expressed by the German people in their leader. Adolf Hitler required proof, before the whole world, that the German people was completely on his side. 'The vote will express the German people's total agreement with his decision to put an end to the hypocrisy of Geneva', it said in an editorial. The Christian had to 'stand up bravely and gallantly for his people' at such a time, willing to share its fate. 'Our conviction is firm', it went on, 'that Germany's recovery can no longer be prevented by France'.[16] All the reports were concluded with a rather pious-sounding prayer for divine guidance.

In the same issue the editors reminded readers of their duty to vote on 12th November and reminded them of the issue: 'It's about our struggle for peace and the equal treatment of Germany'. Readers were 'earnestly admonished to give unanimous support to the government'.[17] Germans should 'affirm without reservation' the step taken in Geneva. It was important to 'open the door to German freedom' by asserting one's right and defending one's honour. 'This policy is to be motivated not by hatred for other peoples, but by love for our people'. Equality 'moves the German heart'.[18] After the referendum the vote for 'this unique man' who had restored Germany's honour was, described by the *Allianzblatt* as 'overwhelming, powerful, leaving nothing to be desired in terms of clarity'. This vote of confidence in Hitler was 'a station on the path of the German people's rebirth'. The German people had grown to 'love him'. They knew that he had 'welded them together' and that he was striving for their 'welfare' with 'total dedication'.[19] Given this basic trust in their leader, they were now open to be led to further foreign policy successes.

The Treaty of Versailles (28 June 1919) restored to France the provinces of Alsace and Lorraine, bound Germany not to fortify the left bank of the Rhine or a zone, fifty miles wide, along the right bank and ceded the coal-mining Saar region, to be administered by the League of Nations, to the French for fifteen years after which a referendum would decide its future status. The *Allianzblatt* expressed worries that France might introduce sanctions or other measures 'to solve the Saar question in accordance with their interests' but prophesied that the region would once again become part of Germany.[20] No further claims would then be made against France, just as the Chancellor had said.[21] This one issue separating the two countries was decided by plebiscite on 13 January 1935. The return of the German West March to its home in the Reich was announced on 15 February 1935 to readers. More than 90% of the people of the Saar (477,119 votes in total) had proclaimed their desire to be citizens of Germany. Only 46,513 votes were cast in favour of preserving the regime of the League of Nations and only 2,100 people declared they wanted to belong to France. The *Allianzblatt* found reasons for these 'no' votes. The 2,100 'Frenchmen' were in all probability 'employees of the French Mining Administration', the paper suggested. The status quo was only wanted by 'Marxist, Bolshevist, Jewish and other opponents' of Germany, it said. They had, however, failed miserably. The 'joy' on the day the election result was announced, 5 January, had been for all observers 'overwhelming'. Torch-lit processions had moved through the streets of the towns and villages and people were clearly 'deeply moved' by the experience. Thanksgiving services had taken place everywhere. 'One senses', Nagel wrote, 'that the fortunes of the German nation have taken a decisive turn and that European politics have changed for the better'. Imitating the German Christian view that God's will was discernible in history, Nagel said that God 'has spoken clearly' through the events of that historic day. The surprise all over the world was noticable. Hitler's Germany had been slandered so much everywhere that one had thought the people of the Saar region would seize the opportunity to turn their backs on the new Germany. The near unanimous vote to become a part of Nazi Germany revealed that 'this Germany of Hitler's has become a stronghold of German culture' and had given back to its children 'a joyful faith in the future'. As for peace in Europe, the Saar referendum had clearly dealt with one source of conflict that had disturbed Franco-German relations for centuries. The *Allianzblatt* quoted Lord Rothermere again, who had said that Germany had become the strongest power in Europe. A South African Minister is also quoted as saying that Germany was 'on the way to becoming a world power'. This was cause for the world to rejoice, he had said. 'May God allow Europe to achieve true peace', the article concluded. 'May He keep His hand over Germany just as He has done in the struggle for the West March'.[22] One of the Versailles 'chains' was thus thrown off; another was shortly to follow.

Hitler could count on widespread support for his measures to rebuild the armed forces. The military tradition had deep roots in all classes, pride in the army and resentment at the restrictions enjoined by the Versailles Treaty were widesprend. The number of soldiers had been reduced to 100,000, recruited voluntarily for a twelve-year period of service. Tanks, military aircraft and heavy artillery had all been forbidden.[23] Hitler was also encouraged by Britain's willingness to accept the National Socialist regime as a bulwark against Bolshevism and to tolerate its rearmament although the latter violated

Part V of the Versailles Treaty. On 9 March 1935 the German government announced that a German Air Force already existed; foreign governments remained inactive. Finally, on 16 March 1935, Hitler, pointing to the doubling of the period of military service four days earlier in France, declared his intention to reintroduce conscription and build up and army of 550,000 men.[24] Once again, Britain and France did nothing. On the contrary, without consulting Italy or France, Britain signed a naval agreement with Germany on 18 June 1935, 'the first great act of appeasement', says Karl Dietrich Bracher.[25]

On the same day Hitler held a two and a half hour speech in the Reichstag, putting forward the German proposal (Thirteen Points) to achieve European understanding,[26] the new National Service Act was announced:the period of active service was fixed at one year. 'On the very next day all men born in 1914 were called up and men born in 1915 were mustered'.[27] Shortly before Christmas the *Allianzblatt* noted that, in a world of unrest, Germany had 'raised up its banner and formed a bulwark by the heroic spirit of her reawakened military traditions'.[28]

The diplomatic manoeuverings of the French Government also seemed to justify defying the 'Versailles dictate' and end demilitarization. The *Allianzblatt* had in February 1933 expressed its hopes that Hitler would put an end to a situation which was 'completey irreconcilable with the principle of equality' and which provided France with a 'bridge-head from which they can march unhindered at any time against Germany'.[29] When Sarrant's government signed a military pact with the Soviets (May 1935) and Czechoslovakia, France's ally, did the same, the old fear of encirclement resurfaced on the pages of the *Allianzblatt*. 'The whole thing is one huge encirclement manoeuvre against Germany, led by World Bolshevism and supported by World Jewry'.[30] The two-year period of conscription was seen by the paper as necessary. Germany needed to feel secure in the face of a Red Army 'standing ready' to export revolution. Germany was, in its view, being 'threatened by invasion'. Germany took the step, secondly, 'for the sake of peace', which could only be maintained if 'we are strong enough to protect our country'. The world had understood this very well. The 'threat' of the Franco-Russian alliance behind which stood World Bolshevism, lying in wait for its hour, was the real source of tension in Europe.[31]

Having repudiated the military clauses of the Versailles Peace treaty, Hitler went on to denounce the Locarno Pact (1925) and occupied the demilitarized Rhineland (7 March 1936) to secure the Ruhr industrial area and the Rhine valley. No sanctions were even called for. 'Easy-going British statesmen, after suitable verbal rebuke, assured the agitated French that, after all, German territory must be the subject of German decisions', wrote Harold Laski in 1941.[32] The *Allianzblatt* saw the end of an epoch in which France led Europe. Rather than hinder the Bolshevisation of Europe, France had seemed bent on encouraging it. Hitler had now given back to the Reich its 'military freedom' and taken back the 'demilitarised zone' into the jurisdiction of the Reich. Germany's moral right to do as it has done was 'so obvious'. Almost 100 percent of the German people gave their vote to the Führer on 29 March and this was surely proof to the world that 'there are no differences of opinion, nor can there be any, in questions relating to our nation's freedom, honour and dignity'. The Führer had put 'his peace plan' before European statesmen, a sign that Germany had grown in inner strength at a time when Moscow was 'busy preparing graves' in the the western world.[33]

The third anniversary of Hitler's appointment as Chancellor was celebrated and one gave thanks to the Führer for 'freeing [the country] from the fetters of the Versailles treaty' and for ensuring that the country 'might enjoy peace and security in a troubled world'.[34] The Germans were morally right to 'isolate' themselves from the Versailles treaty, wrote Bernhard Peters in the *Allianzblatt* at the beginning of 1935.[35] The British naval agreement helped Germany shed the sense of isolation. Many Germans, including evangelicals, had, however, already proceeded to insulate themselves from the terrible reality looming on the horizon and already being practised in the heart of a nominally Christian state.

Relatively little was reported on the situation in Catholic Spain, either before the counter-revolution began on 17 July 1936 or afterwards. The first article on the war, which lasted until General Franco captured Madrid in March 1939, appeared in the *Allianzblatt* in October 1936. The article was full of the ideological phraseology typical of Nazi newspapers. Germany, the report said, had initially been selected by Moscow as the 'springboard' to conquer the West. Adolf Hitler had exorcised that spectre. From that moment on Moscow had invested all its strength in 'softening up' the west of Europe prior to what it said would be an encirclement of Germany. The 'most experienced strategists of bloody terror' had been let loose in Spain and a 'Bolshevist republic' seemed close. The same forces had succeeded in forming a People's Front government in France as a precursor of Bolshevist rule there. Resistance to such a future was organised, at a time of the greatest need, by the Spanish military. The Civil War, the paper believed, would decide whether the country would 'ward off Bolshevism' or submit to it. The terror, all of which seemed to have been perpetrated by the republican forces, raged with 'unheard-of cruelty'. Priests and nuns were being executed and churches continually destroyed. Moscow broadcast unremittingly its messages 'calling for even greater atrocities': 'Kill the priests! No mercy! No sentimentalitities!' Barcelona was in the power of 'red tribunes'. The *Allianzblatt* wondered whether the European nations realised what was at stake. Initially, the article claimed, Germany was only concerned about getting her 'endangered national comrades out of the Spanish inferno'. Germany had sent war ships to the region simply to rescue those fleeing the country. 'Many a young German lost his life while attempting to escape, many a young German was cruelly executed by the Revolutionary Tribunal', it noted. France stood alone in calling on the nations to undertake not to interfere in the troubles in Spain. Italy and Germany had promised not to involve themselves. The 'terrible scenes' from the Spanish Civil War, the 'Bolshevist atrocities', still had not taught some nations that what Moscow was 'orchestrating' in Spain, she intended to carry out in other countries. 'Radical changes are once again taking place in world history', said the editorial.[36] An immersion in the National Socialist *Weltanschauung* prevented the *Allianzblatt* from seeing what changes were in fact taking place. Europe was drawing ever closer to a total war fought in the name, as usual, of freedom and justice. General Franco was praised in a number of reports, not least for his assurance that, after the fighting was over, he would guarantee freedom of religion in a nationalist Spain.[37] That, however, remained an empty promise.

In the Versailles Treaty of 1919 Germany renounced all ideas of a union (*Anschluss*) with Austria. Remmer, the Chancellor of the new state of 'German Austria', as it was called, also had to accept the Allies' prohibition of any future union (Treaty of Saint-Germain, 10 September 1919).[38] It seemed the end of the dream of extreme German nationalists in both countries. Chancellor Brüning was forced to give up his plan for a customs union with Austria (12 March 1931) when foreign creditors withdrew their monies fearing a future political union.[39] Chancellor Hitler, however, was able to reverse the decision taken by Bismarck to exclude Austrians from the Second German Reich. Hitler, himself Austrian-born, was later to say in Vienna on 9 April 1938:'I believe that it was God's will to send a boy from here into the Reich, to let him grow up and to raise him to be the leader of the nation so that he could lead back his homeland into the Reich'.[40] Close collaboration in this endeavour was offered by the Austrian Nazi Party, which, in 1930, numbered 100,000.

Bernhard Peters spoke in December 1932 of the changing structure of the German Reich which was sure to come and might involve 'perhaps a union with Austria'. 'May God help us to achieve this new synthesis', he said, and 'may it not have to be achieved by great sacrifices'.[41] This idea gained massive momentum after January 1933. The *Allianzblatt* had kept a careful eye on the structural changes taking place within the country. It sensed that the 'German Question' was once again open following the ending of the rivalry between Prussia and Austria. Another impediment, tradition in southern Germany, had been 'torn away from the grasp of Catholic leaders'. It probably would not be long before a National Socialist majority arose in Austria and 'the Reich and Austria can come together under the common leadership of Adolf Hitler'. In its view, 'the fate of Austria is no longer in the hands of the Vatican, but in the hands of Hitler'.[42] It would not be long, it said in April 1933, before he would rule Austria and Danzig. 'Everything is now working to exterminate (*Ausrottung*) the spirit of Marxism and atheism' and to unite the German people. Unity was, however, only a means to a goal. The German people was being prepared for 'a new task'. The editor sincerely believed that God had called Germany 'to save the western world' from the moral and spiritual destruction threatening it from the West and the East. The rest of Europe, ruined by the Versailles Treaty, had no strength to do this. Germany, however, had grown in strength and confidence; it alone could resolve the tensions on the continent. 'It is simply wonderful', the paper rejoiced, 'to see how, in spite of all kinds of resistance, the German people is continuing to make advances'.[43]

The internal political struggle in Austria was also reported on by the *Allianzblatt*, the situation being compared with the situation in Germany under Brüning who, like Engelbert Dollfuss in Austria, issued a decree prohibiting the use of uniforms by political groups.[44] The movement towards an *Anschluss* was portrayed as inevitable, the outworking of a moral principle in human history. Austria's ill-treatment was about to end.[45] In spite of Christian-Social resistance to National Socialism the 'movement' there made great and rapid advances: 'no power could prevent the Austrian people being synchronised (*gleichgeschaltet*) with the German people'.[46] France, Italy, Russia, the Little Entente[47] all knew that the day of the *Anschluss* would arrive. The decision would be no different to the ones made in the referenda in the Tyrol and Salzburg:99% in favour of the union with the Reich. The signing of the Concordat with the Reich had, in the paper's opinion, sealed the fate of the resistance to the change.[48]

The Vatican had indeed accepted the prohibition of the Catholic Centre Party in Germany and the Concordat was of decisive importance to Hitler, not only for domestic reasons but also as a tool of his foreign policy. The Catholic bishops in Germany had supported Hitler's position on the League of Nations and a number of them were ecstatic about his reoccupation of the Rhineland.[49]

One of the other organisations responsible for the death of democracy in Austria was the Heimwehr, an army of patriotic conservatives led by the authoritarian Prince von Starhemberg which also found a place in the Dollfuss government. The *Allianzblatt* was able to report that Prince Starhemberg had returned home from an audience with the Pope with the conviction that only a fascist system could still save Austria. He did not necessarily want to join forces with the National Socialists; he planned to turn himself into the fascist leader of Austria. Dollfuss was said to have the same goal. One of his speeches at a Catholic Festival in Vienna was described as 'a fiery message directed against Marxism' and a declaration in favour of of the 'leader principle' and an authoritarian state. The *Allianzblatt* saw proof here that Catholicism had realised that Austria's independence could not permanently be maintained by struggling against National Socialism. Austrian Catholicism also desired freedom from Marxism. Dr Dollfuss began to 'sound like a fascist in order to take the wind out of the National Socialists' sails'. Neither Dollfuss nor Starhemberg would, according to the *Allianzblatt*, in the long run be able to govern in opposition to a movement like National Socialism.[50] 'The days of the Dollfuss system are numbered', the Reich would be restructured with or without these self-appointed leaders and a last period of grace would begin, in which not only Germany but also the Church of Christ 'will receive its final temporal form'.[51]

There is a sense that these evangelicals at least knew the end from the beginning. Their study of prophetical books in the Bible led them to expect a redrawing of state boundaries and they fatalisticly accepted National Socialism as, in some sense, a key player in the divine game. Nothing would or could prevent its onward march. It noted that the Austrian Government's ban on public demonstrations of joy following 'the victory of German culture on the banks of the Saar' could not be enforced everywhere. Germans were experiencing something of the patriotic mood felt in the middle of the nineteenth century. 'Tumultuous joy broke out far and wide', the *Allianzblatt* said of the reactions in Austria to the result of the Saar referendum. The 'day of victory' in the Saar region had 'united everything German in the world' and 'caused German hearts everywhere to beat again in unison'.[52] Hitler too is quoted, outlining his government's policy on Austria (the 'Danube Question'). Germany had 'neither the intention nor the wish' to interfere in the internal affairs of Austria, to 'annex or incorporate' (*anschliessen*) the country into Germany. The German people and government had, however, an 'understandable desire', resulting from the simple feelings of solidarity arising from a common national descent, to see that the German right of self-determination was guaranteed.[53]

After sending his troops into Germany's back garden, the Rhineland, Hitler was invited, by the Austrian Nazi Minister, Arthur Seyss-Inquart, to send a few more troops into Germany's front garden, Austria (12/13 March 1938). Italy was alarmed and the other European nations were shocked, but 'their anger had no sequence in deeds'.[54] The outside world tried to persuade itself that the annexation was in fact an internal German issue related, as Hitler said, to the right of self-determination. Everything seemed legal and constitutional, and plebiscites in Austria and Germany in April revealed nearly total support for the *Anschluß*. The Catholic bishops in Austria – Cardinal Innitzer of Vienna being particularly vocal in his support – called on all Christian believers to do their 'patriotic duty' by supporting Austria's absorption and praised the 'outstanding achievements' of the National Socialists in the fields of economic and social policy as well as their fight against 'godless Bolshevism'.[55] Austrian Protestant leaders (Superintendents Beyer, Eder, Heinzelmann and Zwernemann) expressed publicly their joy, which the *Völkischer Beobachter* and the *Allianzblatt* reported: 'We believe that this hour has been blessed by God'. On 13 March they announced the 'incorporation (*Anschluss*) of the Protestant Church in German Austria into the German Protestant Church'.[56] Pastor M. Monsky wrote to Nagel requesting the absorption of the Austrian Evangelical Alliance into the German branch (6 March 1938). Monsky wrote that there was rejoicing over 'this miracle' which the Lord of human history had granted to our German nation, a nation which had been 'reduced to material and spiritual poverty'.[57] Nagel concurred. It was, he said, as clear as daylight that 'God's wisdom and blessing were at work in these events'. The union with Austria had been 'an object of hopeful yearning' and a 'matter of prayer' for years, he admitted.[58]

Another foreign policy success received the adulation and thanks of Protestant ministers. When German troops also marched into the Sudetenland (1 October 1938), where 3.5 million Germans lived, Dr Erich Wehrenpfennig, the pro-Nazi President of the Protestant Sudeten Church, sent a telegram to

Hitler, thanking him for freeing the Sudeten Germans from the 'Czech yoke'. The German Protestant Church in Bohemia, Moravia and Slovakia saw in the occupation of these lands a 'work of incalculable and eternal value, a work blessed by God'. The incorporation of the Sudetenland into the Greater German Reich had brought about 'real peace', they said.[59]

Along with the Catholic and Protestant Churches, the Free Churches rejoiced over the 'victory' of their Führer. They praised his 'manly and peaceable presence' at the Munich negotiations preceding the annexation and called the result of Hitler's diplomacy an 'achievement full of promise and peace'. The Methodist song-writer, August Rücker, who also wrote for the Alliance, penned a five-verse hymn to commemorate the 'great victory'. God had directed the heart of the Führer and blessed his work. Fellow Germans had been liberated from oppression, Rücker wrote, peace in Europe had been secured, and now the German people came 'rejoicing and supremely blessed' to 'God and Führer'.[60]

In the Versailles Treaty Germany also ceded the so-called 'Polish Corridor' (most of Posen and part of West Prussia) to the newly created Polish state, giving it access to the Baltic Sea. Danzig became a Free City, administered by the League of Nations. One million Germans now lived in the Polish state. These losses were bitterly resented in Germany and tensions between the two countries festered on. General Joseph Pilsudski (1867-1935) made himself Minister of War and Premier in the Polish republic in 1926, changing the constitution to set up his own dictatorial rule. Civil war was only narrowly avoided in 1937 when the Camp of National Unity, the fascist grouping in the government, promised electoral reforms. Politics in the country remained turbulent throughout the 1930s. This is reflected in the reports in the *Allianzblatt*. The Polish Corridor was described in March 1933 as a major 'trouble spot' (*Brandherd*) in Europe. The 'differences between Poland and Danzig' caused tempers to run high. 'Just a little spark would suffice to unleash a world conflagration'. The editor did not believe Christians could do anything to prevent such a catastrophe. 'If God doesn't help, further catastrophes of the worst kind will erupt'.[61]

The 'danger of war breaking out' was real, the *Allianzblatt* wrote in May 1933. Germans were being persecuted in Poland and in France troops had been transported to the German border. 'Threatening speeches' had been made in the English Parliament and in America the Jews were 'stirring up hatred of Germany'.[62] The European powers were not listening to calls for the German right to self-determination to be respected. Germans in Danzig wanted to be reunited with their national comrades and 'Poland can't prevent it'. The struggle was being waged 'not with weapons, but in the spirit'. What could evangelicals do in this situation? 'We can only pray and support the government with our intercession'.63 The ten-year Non-aggression and Friendship Pact between Germany and Poland (26 January 1934) seemed to be an answer to the prayers. Was this not proof of Hitler's peaceful intentions? The *Allianzblatt* reprinted articles which suggested that this was the case. 'Hitler – he is peace', wrote a Polish newspaper in its review of 1934. This unnamed source claimed that Hitler's foreign policy had prevented potentially threatening developments in connection with the Austrian and Saar Questions. Germany's agreement with Poland had also consolidated peace in Europe. The Polish paper said claims of aggressive German intentions should be discounted. Europe had 'almost certainly ten years of peace' to look forward to.64 The 'horsemen of the Apocalypse' had not yet been let loose, the paper said. Poland, with the backing of a strong Germany, would defend civilisation from Asiatic Bolshevism.65

Though many Poles and Germans may have been lulled into a false sense of security by the non-aggression pact, the four horsemen appeared with 'power to take peace from the earth and to make men slay each other' (Revelation 6,4). On 15 March 1939 Germany invaded Czechoslovakia and dismembered the country. On 1 September 1939 Hitler sent German soldiers into Poland, provoking what the historian S.H. Steinberg in 1944 called 'an international civil war in which Christianity, civilization and humanity are arrayed against the hosts of wickedness everywhere throughout the world'.66 German evangelicals did not interpret the events quite in this way. Dr F.H. Otto Melle, Chairman of the Blankenburg Committee, said Christians had a 'holy duty to intercede and pray for the Führer of our people, for his advisers and all our national comrades'.67 Even though it was not in their power to 'interfere in the decision-making of statesmen', Christians did have a responsibility to pray for them. 'We ask Him who has all power in heaven and on earth to give to the Führer wisdom and strength for his great tasks', Melle reported. He prayed that the sacrifices which Germans might have to make, would 'bring forth the fruits of peace' for our nation.68

The *Allianzblatt* had to accomodate itself to the new situation. The newspaper could not appear in November and December 1939 and the war clearly affected the writing of contributions, printing and distribution. An Alliance Conference in the Palatinate, planned for the autumn of 1939, could not take place. By the spring of 1940 the situation had once again normalised, though 'certain restrictions' were in evidence. The editors 'submitted willingly to them, in accordance with biblical guidelines'. There remained, in spite of the war, 'vast opportunities to continue our work within the existing limits'. Nagel was able, for example, to take part in a number of Bible retreats and Alliance Conferences which were 'completely undisturbed'. The *Allianzblatt* continued to appear until the spring of 1941, though essays and articles became much shorter and concise.[69]

The effects of the war on church life are only touched upon in a handful of articles. Evangelicals presumably followed developments by reading the secular press; the *Allianzblatt* reports nowhere on battles, victories or deaths of brethren. One article in February 1940 mentions the 'return of many national comrades (*Volksgenossen*) to their new, and yet ancient homeland'. The first Baltic Germans had left their homes in Estonia and Latvia to settle in the regions of Posen and West Prussia, after these areas had been 'liberated'. The *Allianzblatt* described the population transfer as a 'determined rescue operation'. The measure had given German Protestant churches in the Baltic states the chance to start again, said the report. Bishop Poelschau of Riga is quoted as saying that, in the light of the Word of God, God was clearly calling on Germans to leave their fatherland, leave their friends, leave their father's house and 'go into a country that I [God] will show you'. God would bless those who obeyed and make them a blessing to others. 'When the Lord God commands, one cannot object; one has to obey Him unconditionally', said the bishop.[70] The clear implication was that God was working in a situation which a later generation would describe as 'ethnic cleansing' to bring blessing to Germans and, through them, to other nations. Germany had, in effect, become the chosen people.

It was reported in June 1940 that fifty German missionaries who had been working in the Syrian orphanage in Jerusalem had to leave Palestine in order to avoid being interned by the British, who, it was added, 'continue to oppress the Arabs in the most awful manner'.[71] German missionaries elsewhere – East Africa, British India, West Africa, the Gold Coast – were already in internment camps by the end of 1939. They were not forgotten, at least not by missionaries of other nationalities. Friendly missionaries sent by non-German Societies gave assistance to them in 'an exemplary manner', reported the *Allianzblatt*.[72]

In spite of such international solidarity, Nagel was very critical of statements made by English statesmen and English newspapers to the effect that 'England was waging the present war in order to defend Christianity and religion'. Nagel was obviously stung by such a self-righteous approach to a serious issue. Such a view 'contradicted the teaching of Scripture'. Nowhere did the Bible condone the use of the sword to protect Christianity; the opposite, in fact, was true. These politicians failed, moreover, to take note of the 'shocking, absolute indifference to Christianity predominant in wide sections of English society'. He began a campaign in the *Allianzblatt* to show that Germany was in fact more Christian than England. It was a contribution of the Evangelical Alliance to the wider propaganda battle being waged. His paper noted that most of the children evacuated to the rural areas of England had been found by Church of England clergy to have 'no idea why Christmas was celebrated'. Most of them thought it wasn't even a Christian festival. Christian England, it seemed, was no longer Christian. The *Times* was also quoted as reporting that, according to the inquiry carried out among the children, 60 per cent of English boys and girls had no contacts whatsoever with Christianity, that they knew 'absolutely nothing about the Bible' and 'had not learnt how to pray'. He quoted the *Times* as asking 'how can England tell the world about its struggle for Christianity, as Mr Chamberlain has recently done once again, when a majority of the young people in England does not even adhere to Christianity?'. It was a fact that most English children grew up in 'a heathen atmosphere'. Nagel insisted he was not alone in attacking such a blasphemous mingling of religion and politics. The Lutheran Church of America had also made 'loud protests against the erroneous identification of English democracy with Christianity'. One of its leaders, Professor T. Graebner, had declared that the goals of the Christian Church could never be equated with the goal of democracy or any other political system. 'The Church's programme was to preach the gospel of Jesus Christ – in war-time and in peace-time'.[73] The English government made such pseudo-religious statements purely 'for reasons of war propaganda'.[74] Similar statements made by English clergymen were picked up by the *Völkischer Beobachter* and quoted in the *Allianzblatt*. Pastor Hüfner cited such an example of an 'unchristian attitude which completely denies the Saviour'. An English vicar, who is named as Mr W.C. Whipp, had called the Germans an 'evil race' and exhorted the English to 'exterminate the German devils', in fact to 'kill the lot of them!' Hüfner said he had never read anywhere that a German pastor, whatever his denomination, had moved so far away from the Christian ethic as this 'servant of Christ' had done on the other side of the Channel.[75] Such English Christians were Christians in name only, representing a 'Christianity without Christ'. Others, like Reverend Rowland Jones, criticised the pronouncements of Lord Halifax and his social circle, reminding him of the slums, the unemployment before the war, the 'intolerable gulf between the poor and the rich' in England. 'Is this Christianity?' he is reported to have asked the Lord.[76]

Eighteen months into the war, in one of the very last issues of the *Allianzblatt*, Nagel justified what he called 'total war' against England. England had, in his view, 'forced the conflict upon us' and Germany was now completely absorbed in 'a great work, namely the re-formation of Europe, which for once is to live free of all English tutelage'. Nagel said that there could be 'no higher or more sublime goal' for Germans. Under the 'brilliant leadership' of Hitler, Germany was struggling to bring about 'a genuine and real peace' in Europe. The organ of the Free Evangelical congregations, *Der Gärtner*, confirmed that the German people could look forward to the 'last battle' against England 'with a good conscience and complete faith in our leaders and armed forces'. It, too, thanked God for the political leadership, 'men who are really free of all craving for fame and self-interest', and wondered whether God was, through Germany's war effort, 'preparing the way for the promised millennium'. First, Germany would have to struggle for its rightful place among the nations. Fierce resistance was expected from England, for, as Wilhelm Wöhrle, its editor, explained, the German army was 'not simply fighting against human forces and passions, but against demonic powers'. The initial 'successes of the plans of our Führer', said the *Gärtner* on 19 May 1940, particularly the fact that Holland and Belgium had been occupied without even a declaration of war, were surely God's answer to their longing.[77]

A long article in the June 1940 issue of *Allianzblatt* on 'Can a Christian be a Soldier?' sought to dispel doubts on the matter expressed in readers' letters to the editor. Nagel called on believers not to misunderstand the commandment *Thou shalt not kill*. Two books were recommended for careful study: Otto Borchert's *War with a Good Conscience*, which was based on the premise that 'in the world as it is God needs wars – and he needs them for all kinds of different purposes'. The other author was, and is, very well known to German evangelicals: Lieutenant-General Georg von Viebahn. In his book *Military Service and Biblical Christianity* Viebahn claims that 'there is no profession which is so in agreement with Christianity as the profession of soldier'. This, he believed, was the clear teaching of Scripture; the commandment not to kill was neither applicable to war situations nor to the authorities' right to impose capital punishment.[78]

The testimony of Scripture and the testimonies of 'men of God' were employed to strengthen the resolve of Christians to fight. The country knew that all soldiers had taken a 'holy oath' and sworn 'by God' to obey Hitler as chief of the armed forces (an oath offerred by the military in gratitude for Hitler's crushing of Röhm). But victory could only be gained, Nagel wrote in July 1940, when people's characters and attitudes were right. A dissatisfied and impatient frame of mind would not contribute to what all hoped would be 'a splendid final victory'.[79] The 'magnificent spirit' of the supreme commander of the German armed forces had produced the wonderful victories to date. Evangelicals should patiently wait for the Führer's command to 'send our soldiers to fight England'. The troops marched in 'unshakeable faith in the man whom God sent to us in our time of greatest need and whom He had called to be the saviour of our floundering Reich'. God had elected this man to be 'the reorganiser of Europe'.[80] The war reports speak of the quasi-religious faith Nagel, and many like him, had in the man whom Providence had specially chosen to bring about, if not the millennium, then a state of peace on earth which would hold back the Antichrist in the East.

There seems to have been just one development in war-time which evangelicals had perhaps not expected. The *Allianzblatt* reported in February 1940 that the Catholic Bible Society in Stuttgart, whose purpose it was to acquaint Catholics with the Bible and persuade them to read it, had begun to send Bibles to Catholics who were serving in the Wehrmacht. Special *Bible Letters* addressed to soldiers at the front, to soldiers lying wounded in hospital and to the returning emigrants, had been made available. It was 'very remarkable' that more and more of 'our Catholic co-religionists' were wanting Bibles.[81] The war had led to 'no adverse effects' on the operations of the Society. On the contrary, its work had expanded. The official bulletin spoke of 25,000 copies of the New Testament being sent off to soldiers in one month alone.[82] This one side-effect of the war was noted with a great deal of satisfaction. It was no doubt seen as one of the hidden works of God in the midst of destruction.

The Bible was almost certainly a source of comfort for many soldiers facing death. The Catholic Archbishop Bertram wrote on 3 January 1943 that the religious literature of the Church was 'an indispensable factor in promoting a spirit of the utmost self-sacrifice and the most resolute endurance throughout the nation'.[83] No evangelical could question the practical use of such values in times of war or of peace. They were central to the Christian message, and to the message of unorthodox groups like the Jehovah's Witnesses. Those who refer to Hitler's alleged plans for the churches after the war could do well to bear in mind that another key Nazi leader, Heinrich Himmler, told the Reich security head Kaltenbrunner on 21 July 1944 that the character and behaviour of the Witnesses and evangelical groups like the Mennonites – sobriety, honesty, dilligence, industry, abstinence from alcohol and tobacco and a non-materialistic approach to life – made them ideal as pioneers of National Socialist ideology in the conquered territories of the East. Himmler told Kaltenbrunner that he hoped to end the persecution of the Witnesses after the war. This respect for the Witnesses and other 'fundamentalist' religious groups was, as Michael Kater (1969) has shown, not unique among those National Socialists who are perceived to have rejected orthodox Christianity. This might have led to rather different conclusions after any German victory, particularly if Hitler had died. Kater notes (1969,200) how Himmler had, on 21 March 1936, called upon all police units in the Reich to have consideration for the children of Witnesses who had been imprisoned. He ordered that police take care not to arrest both parents in families known to be associated with the Witnesses. There was certainly a recognition that the 'Protestant' work ethic at least, as well as strong Christian families, could be a boon to the National Socialist state, in peace-time and in war.

There is not a single doubt expressed in the pages of the *Allianzblatt* or the *Gärtner* or the *Wahrheitszeuge* that the war might not be just. The historian of the Brethren movement in Germany, Gerhard Jordy, has also noted that, as far as the foreign policy and military successes of the National Socialists is concerned, 'the language of Hitler and violence' had taken over the pages of *Die Tenne*. Elements of the Nazi *Blut und Boden* ideology, a greater respect for one's ancestors (*Ahnen*), and the resuscitation of 'national values' in the Third Reich were all particularly appealing to the Brethren. A latent fear that these periodicals might be prohibited can not explain the exuberance felt and expressed as a result of the foreign policy and military successes of Hitler's government. The Baptist *Wahrheitszeuge* claimed on 14-21 January 1940 that the 'restructuring' of Europe and, in particular, the 'liberation' of the regions in Eastern Europe, could lead to new opportunities to evangelise and reach areas which had once been closed to the gospel. On 2-9 June 1940 the same paper said that Baptist 'hearts are drawn to express thanks and admiration' for the 'breath-taking' lightning attacks on Holland, Belgium and Scandinavia. In August 1940 it noted how England had turned down 'Hitler's offer of peace (*Hitlers Friedenshand*)'. The consequences of war for religious practice did not even lead to a refusal to publish articles on the war. When, in one night, one million kilograms of bombs fell on English towns, the *Wahrheitszeuge*, described the bombings as 'the judgement which has fallen upon those [the English] who had wilfully provoked Providence'. British bombs on Berlin, however, are mentioned in connection with the destruction of houses of God. Even years of defeat did not dent the patriotism of evangelicals and their sense that God was on Hitler's side. Those who resisted Hitler's regime are frequently denigrated as being opposed to the counsels and rule of God. On 8 November 1939 the chairman of the newly created Bund freikirchlicher Christen (Federation of Independent Christians), a re-grouping of Plymouth Brethren following the banning of their Christliche Versammlungen on 13 April 1937, sent a telegram to Hitler expressing their relief and thanks that 'the Lord over life and death' had spared the life of the Führer. At the same time the Brethren newspaper *Gnade und Friede* printed a statement on its title page. It said the Brethren were 'full of grateful joy' that Hitler's life had been so 'miraculously' preserved from the 'loathsome assassination attempt' on the Chancellor on 8 November in Munich. He promised that the members of the Federation would double their efforts in prayer for the Führer and petition God that He would 'continue to protect him by His wondrous grace' against all attacks from the enemies of a 'just peace'. An equally astonishing record of this unfailing fidelity to the National Socialist cause is the telegram sent by two evangelical leaders, Paul Schmidt of the Baptist Church and Otto Melle of the Methodist Church, on 24 July 1944 to the Führer after the unsuccessful attemp on his life. The telegram reads as follows: 'In the name of the Association of Free Churches we wish to express our most heartfelt congratulations on your having been saved from such a heinous assassination attempt. With deep joy, thanks to God and the assurance of our continuing intercession for you, the Führer, Signed Otto Melle, Paul Schmidt'.[84] The sincerity of widespread evangelical faith in, and devotion to, Adolf Hitler can not be denied. The fact that the Alliance Prayer Week and evangelistic services could take place throughout the war no doubt made it even more difficult for patriotic Germans to express disloyalty to their government.

In the post-war period one can detect a stubborn resistance to facing up to historical truths and learning the correct moral lessons. This comes out clearly in the report given by Paul Schmidt, a future General Secretary of the German Evangelical Alliance, to the meeting of the Federal Council of the Baptist Federation in Velbert in May 1946. It sought to discuss the path taken by the Federation of Free Church Fellowships in the years 1941 to 1946.

Neither the Jews nor the Confessing Church nor support for the German war effort by the member churches are mentioned. The more well-known Stuttgart Declaration of Guilt by the Council of the *Evangelische Kirche in Deutschland* had, of course, also failed to name one concrete ecclesiastical sin for which confession was made. Equally disappointing was the report of the Conference of the Brethren Churches in West Germany, meeting in August 1945 in Wuppertal-Elberfeld. The representatives of the assemblies (they were reorganised after the government ban in 1937 as a Federation of Independent Christians) complained to the conference: 'Why do catastrophes always come upon our people? Why not, just once, upon England?'[85] Such tones set the stage for the continuation of that guilt-ridden course of action in the post-war period: non-confession of sin and a desire to forget quickly. In facing the horrors of their own past evangelicals proved to be no different from other members of their society.

Notes

1. Daniel 2,33 and 2,42. The reference here is to the 'fourth kingdom' (in German, *das vierte Reich*) which will be divided, partly strong and partly brittle ('its feet partly of iron and partly of clay', v.33). Dispensationalists have interpreted the ten toes as representing ten kingdoms which make up the resurrected Roman Empire – the Fourth World Empire. In Daniel Chapter 7 a similar vision of four beasts is retold; the fourth beast has ten horns, i.e. ten kings (Dan 7, 23-24). Among the ten appeared a 'little horn', possessing 'eyes like the eyes of a man, and a mouth uttering great boasts'(Dan 7,8). This is interpreted by Daniel as 'a king insolent and skilled in intrigue' (Dan 8,23) – a satanically inspired ruler over the European ten-state confederacy, the revived Roman Empire. This Empire will control Palestine, where, in the dispensationalist view, the Antichrist will have his seat (Dan 9,26-27). Expositors maintain that this person, an apostate Jew, will reign as king at Jerusalem but will also be a false prophet, a religious imposter (Dan 11,36-39). On evangelical interpretations of this Viertes Reich and the Antichrist, F.A. Tatford (1978, Chapter 15). See also EA 15.06.1936 (Nr 11), 174f; EA 15.05.1936 (Nr 9), 142.
2. 1 John 4,3.
3. EA 17.09.1933 (Nr 38), 621, 623-4.
4. EA 17.09.1933 (Nr 38), 622. Bernhard Peters explained the conquest of Abyssinia as being a natural result of Italy's lack of natural resources and its 'surplus' population. The Italians were a people, he said, 'longing for more living space (Lebensraum)', EA 15.06.1936 (Nr 11), 175.

5. EA 06.08.1933 (Nr 32), 511.
6. EA 15.01.1934 (Nr 1), 17.
7. EA 11.06.1933 (Nr 24), 383. Most of the first paragraph ('Indeed...an end') is not in reported speech. The opinions expressed must be those of the writer (Peters) unless the editor had simply not noticed the grammatical error, in which case Hitler's views are being communicated here.
8. EA 30.01.1935 (Nr 2), 30.
9. EA 15.06.1935 (Nr 11), 175-176.
10. EA 29.02.1936 (Nr 4).
11. EA 30.01.1935 (Nr 2), 31.
12. S.H. Steinberg (1944, 282).
13. EA 05.11.1933 (Nr 45), 735-736.
14. EA 12.11.1933 (Nr 46), 751. The *Allianzblatt* reported in detail on the political manoeuvering in Europe and on the foreign press reactions to political discussions.
15. EA 30.11.1936 (Nr 22), 358-359.
16. EA 05.11.1933 (Nr 45), 736. On the same day single list elections gave the National Socialists a 92% majority in the Reichstag in 1933. In the Reichstag election of 29 March 1936 98.8% voted for the list. A.Bullock (1973, 324, 346).
17. EA 05.11.1933 (Nr 45), 731.
18. EA 12.11.1933 (Nr 46), 752. The call to support the Reich Chancellor ended with the prayer:'May the eternal God be gracious to us, may He bless the Führer and make the German nation a blessing on earth'.
19. EA 03.12.1933 (Nr 49), 781-782.
20. EA 05.11.1933 (Nr 45), 736.
21. EA 12.11.1933 (Nr 46), 751.
22. EA 15.02.1935 (Nr 3), 46-48.
23. D. Thomson (1968, 623).
24. A. Bullock (1973, 332-333).
25. K.D. Bracher (1973, 369); K. Zilliacus (1945).
26. A speech praised in Britain by Deputy Prime Minister Baldwin in the House of Commons and by a number of Lords in the upper House (Baldwin called it a 'ray of light', a Lord claimed it was a 'turning point in the fortunes of Europe'), EA 15.06.1935 (Nr 11), 176.
27. EA 15.06.1935 (Nr 11), 176.
28. EA 15.12.1935 (Nr 23), 371.
29. EA 12.02.1933 (Nr 7), 109f.
30. EA 15.03.1936 (Nr 5), 79. The First World War, the *Allianzblatt* explained, was 'the work of a decades-old policy of encirclement organised by the mightiest of coalitions against Germany'.

31. EA 30.10.1936 (Nr 20), 327. The Franco-Soviet treaty of mutual assistance in case of an unprovoked attack was ratified by the French Chamber of Deputies on 27 February 1936, A. Bullock (1973, 342).
32. H.J. Laski (1941, 56).
33. EA 15.05.1936 (Nr 9), 143. One year prior to this, the *Allianzblatt* had reported that 'the Führer spoke of Germany's obligation to observe all the commitments voluntarily undertaken including the recognition of the demilitarised zone as long as the other states observe their duties resulting from these treaties', EA 17.06.1935 (Nr 11), 175. Hitler argued, of course, that France and Britain had not kept their part of the bargain and so – in spite of his great desire for peace – he was no longer bound to keep his part. Mr Atlee declared on 14 February 1937 that the British Government had 'connived at German rearmament because of its hatred of Russia. It has sown the wind and is reaping the whirlwind'. Sir Arthur Balfour, a leading figure in the business world, in a speech reported in the *Sheffield Daily Telegraph* on 24 October 1933, said that 'one of the greatest menaces to peace in Europe today is the totally unarmed condition of Germany'. Such a view was generally held in the Conservative Party, the City and the F.B.I. at the time. According to K. Zilliacus (1945, 36) the 'great bulk' of the supporters of the National Government in 1933/36 'positively *liked* the Nazi regime..because they looked upon it as a bulwark against Communism'. The British Government, to preserve the economic interests of the propertied classes abroad, actually helped Hitler to rearm and broke the provisions of the Versailles Treaty by granting licences so companies could export aeroplane engines and parts to Germany. The Anglo-German Naval Agreement gave Hitler permission to build a navy 35% of the size of the British Navy, this too being a violation of the Versailles Treaty.
34. EA 29.02.1936 (Nr 4).
35. EA 30.01.1935 (Nr 2), 32.
36. EA 30.10.1936 (Nr 20), 326-327. The privileged classes in France and Britain, and elsewhere, were 'loud in their enthusiasm for the rebels against the constitutional government' and the governments of these countries 'did not hesitate to refuse to the Republicans that right to purchase arms which was theirs by international law, and deliberately chose to close their eyes to the fact that the rebels' victory was being organised for them by Germany and Italy'. 'The great powers among the democracies were..at no point free from a very real sympathy for the dictators, not least because their privileged classes sympathised with some of the results of their rule', H.J. Laski (1941, 29). The People's Front in Spain was not standing on a Marxist platform. There were only 15 Communists in the Spanish Parliament in 1936, divided into two rival factions. There was one Communist Minister. In the whole country the Communist Party had 10,000 members. The idea spread by the government-controlled media in Germany that Bolshevism

controlled Republican Spain was very far from the truth, K. Deschner (1990, 36). The British *Evangelical Christendom* provided a completely different interpretation of events in Spain: it was a civil war 'provoked by the Roman Catholic Church, conducted by the Church and *protracted by the Church* (EC's emphasis), as can be proven by the conduct of the Bishop of Segovia'. The EC also offered 'convincing proof that the [Republican] Government is not opposed to religion in general'. *Evangelical Christendom*, 1936, 181-182.

37. EA 15.01.1938 (Nr 1), 15; EA 15.07.1938, 183.
38. D. Thomson (1968, 626-628).
39. S.H. Steinberg (1944, 274-275).
40. A. Bullock (1973, 43).
41. EA 11.12.1932 (Nr 50), 816.
42. EA 16.04.1933 (Nr 16), 256. The changes which had already taken place in 1933 were especially 'mysterious and astonishing' for those analysing them in the light of the 'end times described in the prophetic Word'. Bernhard Peters was wondering 'whether the time had come when, according to prophecy, the old Roman Empire was once again being formed'.
43. EA 23.04.1933 (Nr 17), 271.
44. EA 28.05.1933 (Nr 22), 350. Dollfuss, a Christian Social Party member, governed by emergency decrees before promulgating, in April 1934, a clerical-conservative dictatorship (a 'German Christian Austria'). In July 1934 he was murdered by Nazis. D. Thomson (1968, 691). See also EA 08.10.1933 (Nr 41), 670-671.
45. EA, 08.10.1933 (Nr 41), 670-671. Mussolini, at that time, was very much opposed to Austrian unification with Germany. In fact, he mobilised Italian troops along the Brenner Pass, ready to fight any German invasion of Austria. Mussolini's resolve, however, weakened as he became increasingly dependent on Germany. He approved of the agreement between Austria and Germany in July 1936 but was not told about the *Anschluß* before it actually took place (12/13 March 1938).
46. EA 11.06.1933 (Nr 24), 383.
47. Czechoslovakia, Yugoslavia and Rumania.
48. EA 06.08.1933 (Nr 32), 512.
49. K. Deschner (1990, 63-72).
50. EA 08.10.1933 (Nr 41), 671.
51. EA 15.01.1934 (Nr 1), 18.
52. EA 12.02.1935 (Nr 3), 48.
53. EA 15.06.1935 (Nr 11), 175.

54. H.J. Laski (1941, 56). Seyss-Inquart became Governor of the newly created province of the Ostmark (the Eastern March). Nazi putsch attempts in 1934, numerous provincial Nazi risings and another putsch in January 1938 had all failed.
55. K. Deschner (1990, 72-73); K. Denzler/ V. Fabricius Vol 1 (1988, 92-94).
56. EA 15-30.04.1938 (Nr 7/8), 101-102.
57. EA 30.05.1938 (Nr 10), 128-130.
58. EA 30.05.1938 (Nr 10), 128-130.
59. EA 30.12.1938 (Nr 24), 340.
60. K. Zehrer (1986, 98). On the role of the Free Churches in the Sudeten crisis, K. Zehrer (1986, 55-59).
61. EA 26.03.1933 (Nr 13), 207.
62. EA 11.06.1933 (Nr 24), 382.
63. EA 11.06.1933 (Nr 24), 383.
64. EA 30.01.1935 (Nr 2), 31. The Polish newspaper is not named. In explaining the German-Polish treaty in the Reichstag in May 1935, Hitler emphasised 'unmistakeably that Germany had nothing to gain from a European war'. Germany only wanted 'freedom and independence' and for this reason was willing to conclude non-agression pacts with all of her neighbours. 'He only ruled out a pact with Lithuania and spoke with legitimate indignation of the persecution of Germans in the Memel province', EA 15.06.1935 (Nr 11), 175. The Baltic port of Memel had been ceded to the Allies in 1919. In March 1939 German troops occupied the area, Hitler arriving by sea to make a speech in the city on 23 March.
65. EA 15.03.1936 (Nr 5), 80.
66. S.H. Steinberg (1944, 285).
67. EA 15-30.09.1939 (Nr 17/18), 244.
68. EA 15-30.09.1939 (Nr 17/18), 234.
69. EA 1-15.06.1940 (Nr 11/12), 92-93. 'The cancellation of our paper for a while surprised us all', Nagel wrote. In the same issue the 'Guidelines on Conducting the Work of the Gnadau Association During the War' were published (Nr 11/12, 93-94). Worship services were to continue as normal. If evening services could not take place because of a blackout, pastors were encouraged to hold meetings in the afternoons. Pastors should ensure, in case they were called up for military service, that regular meetings could continue to take place. 'In places where no brethren are available to preach the Word or to conduct Bible studies or prayer meetings, sisters suited for these tasks should be authorised to lead simple meetings'. Prayer was especially important. 'Apart from prayers for ourselves or our own fellowship, we should always pray too for our German nation and Fatherland, for the Führer and his advisers, for the troops fighting at the front and those who have been

wounded, for their loved ones back home, for our brethren in the Wehrmacht, for the Church and our fellowships and their leaders[...].'

70. EA 1-15.02.1940 (Nr 3/4), 30. The Polish population in these areas was expelled to make room for the ethnic Germans from the Baltic states and south-eastern Europe. The secret protocol appended to the German-Russian non-agression pact of 23 August 1939 divided up Europe into spheres of influence: Germany got Lithuania and western Poland, the Soviet Union was allowed to take Finland, Estonia, Latvia, eastern Poland and Bessarabia. On 27/28 September, however, Germany agreed to the Soviet demand to have Lithuania included in its sphere. In June 1940 Russian troops occupied all three Baltic states. The call that Bishop Pölschau mentions here was originally directed at Abram (Genesis 12) and also included the verse: 'I will bless those who bless you, and whoever curses you I will curse' and 'I will make you into a great nation'. That nation was the Jewish nation.
71. EA 01-15.06.1940 (Nr 11/12), 94-95.
72. EA 01-15.02.1940 (Nr 3/4), 30.
73. EA 01-15.05.1940 (Nr 9/10), 76-77; EA 01-15.07.1940 (Nr 13/14), 99.
74. EA 01-15.05.1940 (Nr 9/10), 99.
75. EA 15-30.12.1940 (Nr 23/24), 184. Billy Sunday, the flamboyant American preacher, comes to mind, who in 1918, while the war was still in progress, told God in a prayer before the House of Representatives that the Germans were 'a great horde of wolfish Huns whose fangs drip with blood and gore'. He said on another occasion during the war: 'If you turn hell upside down, you will find 'Made in Germany' stamped on the bottom', G.M. Marsden (1982, 142). In terms of popularity and fame, Billy Sunday was the Billy Graham of his generation.
76. EA 15-30.12.1940 (Nr 23/24), 184.
77. EA 15-28.02.1941 (Nr 3/4), 23; *Der Gärtner*, Nr 6, 6 February 1983, 87-88.
78. EA 01-15.06.1940 (Nr 11/12), 85-87. General von Viebahn was a member of a German Brethren Assembly which generally taught that a soldier who is converted should remain in that profession (1 Corinthians 7,20-24), but a Christian should not voluntarily enlist if there is no obligatory military service in his country. This view contradicted the stance taken by one of the founders of the Brethren movement in Britain, J.N. Darby, who taught that a Christian could not be a soldier although he was of course free to decide for himself. G. Jordy (1986, 25-26).
79. EA 01-15.07.1940 (Nr 13/14), 110. No Protestant or evangelical Protestant is known to have refused to swear the oath every soldier had to swear:'I swear by God this holy oath that I shall unconditionally obey the Führer of the German Reich and People, Adolf Hitler, the Commander-in-Chief of the German Armed Forces, and that I will always be ready, as a brave soldier, to lay down my life' (oath of 2 August 1934). On the contrary, the

Confessing Church called on its members to support the war (2 September 1939), in: H. Bergschicker (1982, 311).
80. EA 01-15.08.1940 (Nr 15/16), 117-118. Nagel is presumably referring to the 22 June armistice agreement dictated by Hitler to Marshal Pétain's representatives in the forest of Compiegne near Paris. The battle for France was thus ended. On 14 May the Netherlands had surrendered; on 28 May the Belgians capitulated.
81. EA 01-15.02.1940 (Nr 3/4), 30.
82. EA 15-30.04.1941 (Nr 7/8), 63. A report on the Church situation circulated at the Tenth Confessing Synod of the Old Prussian Union (November 1941) noted that 'since the spring of 1941 no Christian literature of any kind is being printed, permission for the use of paper for this purpose being withheld'. The report also noted that in the Protestant Church 'the sympathies for the Führer and for National Socialism have always been stronger [than in the Catholic Church] and even today this is still the case on the whole...Today this trust in the Führer contends desperately with a realisation of the truth. Even in the Confessing Church organisations in the Wuppertal a rumour was circulating recently that Hitler had experienced a conversion, that he now confesses the Christain faith and, like Bismarck before him, reads the daily lectionary of the Moravian Brethren'. P. Matheson (1981, 94, 96).
83. P. Matheson (1981, 98).
84. Bernd R. Densky (1983, 20,53); G. Jordy (1986, 65—67, 248-250); Amtsblatt des Bundes Evangelisch-Freikirchlicher Gemeinden in Deutschland, Nr 8, 10 August 1944; Friedhelm Menk (1986, 138).
85. G. Jordy (1986, 291); Paul Schmidt (1946).

Chapter Nine

Evangelical Christendom, the British Evangelical Alliance and National Socialism

The British evangelical paper *Evangelical Christendom* reported regularly on events in Europe, including the home of the Protestant Reformation, Germany. Surprisingly, very little mention is made of the German branch of the Evangelical Alliance in the paper[1] and the Executive Council of the British organisation at no time throughout the period 1933-1945 – if we are to follow the Agenda Book or the Minutes Books – discussed the position taken by the German branch on Hitler's regime at their meetings. This is not to say, however, that the British organisation was not informed or concerned about conditions inside Germany. It most certainly was, as the reports in *Evangelical Christendom* reveal. The sources of its information, its interpretation of that information as well as the subject matter of the reports clearly differed from those of the German branch. These differences had nothing to do with theological questions, but rather with political and national prejudices which, not surprisingly, help to shape Christian views on current events. The following lines will highlight some of these differences, but do not aim to provide an exhaustive treatment of the subject.

Evangelical Christianity painted a bleak picture of the religious situation in Germany at the beginning of 1933, prior to Hitler's appointment. 'Nowhere is the situation said to be more serious than in Germany', it claimed, 'where the Reformed Churches have to do battle with disconcerting economic conditions, advantage of which is taken by Roman Catholic and Communist propaganda'. Church income had fallen by one million marks over the year and many Church hospitals, homes for the aged, orphanages and other home mission institutions had had to close down. Of 7,000 parishes in the Old Prussian Union, 1,000 were said to be without ministers. There was no income to pay the stipends. Elsewhere, the police had closed many churches in Saxony because they were in such a state of disrepair that their condition had become a 'public danger'.[2] On top of the economic and personnel problems facing Protestantism, there was also spiritual division, caused by political differences. One correspondent noted that in the previous year or two there had been increasing confusion and uncertainty in German evangelical circles. Politics had had a very unhappy and even 'dangerous' influence in the congregations.

In recent elections sides had been taken so passionately that Christian brethren were sharply divided and the work of many churches was seriously threatened. Cases were known where families were so divided they would not even eat together in the same room. Hitler's appointment had clarified matters. Christians had acquiesced 'willingly or unwillingly' in the new order of things. The question that moved all hearts was whether the state would attempt to 'dictate to the Churches what they are to believe'.[3]

It was a time of crisis and challenge. A 'strong party in Hitler's movement' was demanding that the Old Testament, owing to its Jewish origin, should not be taught in the Church. This demand was getting support from a number of 'liberals' in the Church who claimed the Old Testament was not suitable for young people 'on moral and historical grounds'. A 'new paganism' was in the offing perhaps, although Hitler had 'solemnly promised to respect the freedom of the Churches'. The correspondent expressed his belief that Hitler had recognised that the 'steam-roller action', which had been so widely used in the political and industrial spheres, could hardly be practised on the Church.[4] There were 'undoubtedly difficult times ahead for the Church' but there was no need to despair. Church attendance had improved and many young people were 'wistfully looking for help' in their spiritual quest.[5]

On 27 July 1933 the Secretary of the Executive Council in Britain reported on his visit to Germany, and on the situation in regard to the Nazi regime and the Evangelical Churches. The danger of interference with religious liberty and personal liberty of conscience was referred to, and declared to be an unresolved issue.[6] In July 1933 *Evangelical Christendom* described the events of the summer of 1933 – the appointment of a State Commissioner for the Protestant Churches in Prussia, the dismissal of Church leaders, editors and staff of Church newspapers – as 'a virtual reign of terror'.[7] What many had feared would take place had happened in Germany – the German Protestant Churches had become 'the instrument of the State'. Religious freedom, for the time being, was 'dead' in Germany.[8]

Evangelical Christendom notes that some Christians in Germany did not accept this interpretation of events and complained the paper was 'too pessimistic' in its appraisal of personal liberty under the Hitler regime. In seeking to refute this opinion, the editor suggested that information available in Britain was unavailable in Germany. He expressed surprise at the 'strange reports' appearing in British newspapers concerning German Christians who supported Nazi dictatorship. He advised that final judgement on the sweeping changes taking place in Germany should be reserved for a later time. Similarly, James Gray, the editor of the *Moody Bible Institute Monthly*, told his readers in May 1933 to suspend their judgement on Germany's dealings with the Jews until 'both sides have an opportunity to be heard'.9

The Council of the World Evangelical Alliance forwarded on 23 December 1933 a New Year's Message to the German Protestant Churches, copies being sent to Reich Bishop Müller and Dr von Bodelschwingh, in which this ambiguity was also expressed:

> The Council of the World's Evangelical Alliance (British Organisation) has watched with gratification the steps taken by the central Government to encourage the unity of German Protestants, and, by its recent action against extremists, to maintain the purity of the Faith, the liberty which is inseparable from the Gospel of Christ, and freedom for the unhindered preaching of the Word of God in the Churches.10

The Council noted that the Message had been printed in German evangelical newspapers and had 'generally' been favourably received.11

Evangelical Christendom also used reports taken from *The Times*, whose Berlin correspondent noted that the pastors leading the struggle for the purity of the *Evangelische Kirche* 'have one great weakness – that they are profoundly afraid of offending the State' and being 'manoeuvred into a position of antagonism to the State'. The opposition, moreover, 'fully' sympathised with the German Christian demand for the unification of the Protestant Church. This was seen to be the trump in the Primate's hand. The very same pastors who arraigned the Reich Primate Müller from their pulpits rose with their congregations and 'greeted with the Hitler salute the banners of National Socialism as they are borne into the church before divine service begins'.12

The claims of the German Christians 'undoubtedly expressed the feelings of many churchgoers', the corresondent of *Evangelical Christendom* believed. The political mood was shared not only by the laity but also by a leadership which had always been 'mainly in the hands of Conservative, Nationalist and Monarchist elements'. This no doubt predisposed the Christians to the 'patriotic revival'.13 The paper wondered why Christian parents allowed their children to enter the Hitler Youth organisation and found the answer in the widespread fear that any boy or girl refusing to join would be considered unpatriotic, and 'might even be suspected of being an enemy of National Socialism'. The fact was that German youth was patriotic 'as it has never been before', and was more than anxious to 'show loyalty to Adolf Hitler'. With patriotism the Church had no argument.14

Apart from the innate conservatism and patriotism of German Protestantism, a strict censorship of the press in Germany was blamed for the political loyalty of Christians. *Evangelical Christendom* used the rather incredible argument that people in Germany knew little of what was happening before their very eyes.15 Strict censorship, it was mused, left Christians in Germany and the people as a whole informed only as far as the state considered it desirable.16 'Is it possible', the editor wondered, 'that the Führer himself is ignorant of the indignation which is felt in all Christian circles outside Germany at the restrictions on religious liberty' as revealed by the suspension of Dr Karl Barth?17 The notion that Christians knew the policies of National Socialism and agreed with them was only unwillingly recognised by the staff at *Evangelical Christendom*.

In 1934 the Executive Council of the British Evangelical Alliance considered the religious situation in Germany at its meetings on 24 May, 5 July and 25 October. The General Secretary, H. Martyn Gooch, visited Austria and Germany in the summer and at the 5 July meeting presented a written report on the subject. He also 'made verbal references to some matters associated with his visits to Christian leaders in Germany on which he had not been able to comment in writing'.18 Mr Gooch, in a letter to *The Times* on 13 July, described the conflict within the Protestant Churches as being 'directed against heresies, and not against Herr Hitler or the German Government'.19 The issues at stake, he said, 'ought not to be politically regarded'.20 This was the line taken by *Evangelical Christendom* too. The Protestant '*opposition*' (EC's italics) was 'not anti-Nazi in any political sense'.21 Pastors and others 'otherwise loyal to the State' were in concentration camps.22 The editor did not believe that the Catholic resistance to the Nazi Party was motivated by love of freedom for its own sake. In fact, *Evangelical Christendom* argued, the Pope had 'greatly strengthened the power of the first and principal dictatorship' in Europe by concluding a treaty with the Italian state in 1929. 'Can there be any doubt that this greatly helped the idea of dictatorship throughout Europe, and this tended to help produce the German one?' Moreover, was not the dictatorship in Austria 'definitely supported by the Papacy?' The Church of Rome was itself 'autocratic and intolerant' and therefore could not genuinely appeal to the principles of civil and religious liberty.23 This was, of course, a long-lasting and deeply held view within

British evangelicalism. Anti-Catholicism had been one of the prime motivating forces leading to the creation of the Evangelical Alliance in Britain and Ireland.

What of Protestant support for Nazi dictatorship? The weakness of Lutheranism was seen to lie in its experience of civil and religious liberty. This had led Protestantism to reject those principles in favour of autocratic, 'Christian' government. This was one reason why, as Niemöller said, the Protestant Churches had remained silent when the Gestapo came for the Communists, the socialists, trade unionists and then the Jews. The Council of the World's Evangelical Alliance (British Organisation), as it was officially titled, prepared and adopted a 'Resolution on Religious Liberty' at its 25 October 1934 meeting and forwarded copies through the German Embassy in London to Adolf Hitler, Reichsbishop Müller and also to Dr von Bodelschwingh, Dr Koch and Pastor Niemöller as representatives of the new German Confessional Churches.[24] The Council assured the Confessional Churches of its prayerful sympathy and wholehearted support in their opposition to 'a return to the religion of ancient German tribal life'.

> While the Alliance regards with appreciation efforts being made by the Third Reich for the moral good and unification of the German people, it shares the opinion of some that internal ecclesiastical divisions have militated against an adequate response by the German Evangelical Churches to the appeal for their moral support; nevertheless, the Alliance cannot but regard with regret and alarm the measures taken and now being enforced to replace liberty of conscience by Erastian oppression. While appreciating the need for a more simple and efficient organisation of the German Evangelical Churches, the Alliance deplores the high-handed action which has already deprived many German pastors of their office and means of livelihood, and is the cause of widespread international indignation. The Alliance earnestly petitions the Führer of the German Reich to uphold that liberty of conscience in faith and worship which has for centuries prevailed in Germany, and urges upon the central ecclesiastical administration a more patient and unifying policy in keeping with the principles of the Gospel of Christ.[25]

A second 'Message on Religious Liberty in Germany' from the World's Evangelical Alliance was adopted at the 26 September 1935 meeting of the Council, signed by the General Secretary, H. Martyn Gooch, the Chairman, R.C. Hart Dyke, and the Honorable Secretaries, W. Talbot Rice and J. Chalmers Lyon.[26] The situation was, however, perceived to be ever-changing and confused. Towards the end of 1934, *Evangelical Christendom* announced that religious freedom had become recognised by the authorities and said 'the present hopeful situation is due in large measure to the personal action of the Führer'.[27] In 1935 a correspondent told *Evangelical Christendom* there were 'good reasons for saying that the new minister for Church affairs, Kerrl, is sincerely working for the bringing about of peace in the Lutheran and Reformed Churches'. Kerrl, he added, 'appears to have made a favourable impression on those whose sympathies are with the Confessional Churches' and 'his decrees have had, on the whole, a favourable reception'.[28] In 1936, however, *Evangelical Christendom*, relying on the authority of an article written by Karl Barth for the *Manchester Guardian*, admitted it had been 'too optimistic' concerning Kerrl's role.[29] In 1937 the paper quoted from a speech made before the members of the Edinburgh Rotary Club by Baron von der Ropp of the Christian Brotherhood Movement and the Christian Storm Troops[30], a man described as a 'distinguished representative of German Christianity'.[31] Ropp claimed that Germany under Hitler, after years of decline, was now experiencing a 'revival' of national life. The nation was turning from atheism and towards God.[32] The editors seem to have been made uncertain by such glowing reports from men they judged to be above reproach. 'It must be understood that the situation changes rapidly', *Evangelical Christendom* explained, 'and what may be printed as correct for one week may require some modification later'.[33]

The paper's special correspondent in Berlin sent in 'an accurate and up-to-date account' of the religious situation in 1936, in which it was stated that the Nazi Party hoped to overcome the division between the two main Christian confessions (Protestant and Catholic), regarding it to be a 'cause of weakness' in the country. The Army, the Navy, the Reichsbank (Dr Schacht), Big Finance, and a proportion of officialdom especially the Foreign Office, in short the conservative powers in the country, were eager to preserve 'Christian civilisation' such as they had been used to, and were, therefore, supporting the attempt to reunite the Evangelical Church with the help of the Church Committees. The moderate men in the Evangelical Church, above all in the Lutheran Churches of Bavaria, Württemberg and Hanover, believed, the reporter said, that the political establishment would be able to tame radical elements within the Party, while the 'extremists of the Niemöller type' were pessimistic and expected the worst. The 'extremists' were in favour of breaking off all relations with the state as soon as possible, so as to have a 'freer hand' in the future, and consolidate their forces before conditions got much worse. It was also surmised that the 'extremists' did not have quite so much to lose, for on the whole 'in the areas where they are strong the glebe system is in force'. A couple of farms belonged to the Church in each village, and the income was given over for the use of the pastor and the Church School. In the other areas, however, in Bavaria and Württemberg for example, the clergy were said to be much more dependent on Church taxes, and these, of course, were levied by the state on their behalf. If Church and State were separated, the report continued, the Church taxation system 'will fall to the ground, and those dependent on it will be in a desperate position'. The truth was (and still is) that without state involvement in the collection of taxes, the whole ecclesiastical appartus would grind very quickly to a halt. For these basic economic reasons the 'moderates' were disposed to support the Church Committees set up by the Church Minister Kerrl, believing that the danger of the Church being dominated by a pagan state was very remote indeed and being impressed by the 'observable growth of peace in the Church'. The Church Committees had had an 'undoubtedly moderating influence' on the Church leaders who were left over from the Reichbishop's regime. In fact, the correspondent expressed his view that the 'German Christian' leaders were gradually disappearing:'they go on leave and don't come back again'. The 'undoubted' progress made in ameliorating the situation would continue so as long as the Committees 'can keep the hands of the Party off the Church'.[34]

During the first months of 1936 a number of distinguished Christians from Germany were welcomed at the Alliance House in London. No doubt there was an open exchange of views, but, as *Evangelical Christendom* noted, 'there is much which transpires at the Alliance House which cannot be reported on under this heading [Religious Liberty in Germany] or elsewhere'. Dr Otto Melle, President of the German Free Church Federation and also President of the Blankenburg Evangelical Alliance Conference, also paid a visit and reported on the 'unhappy Church dispute which has brought so much misunderstanding into the religious life of Germany'. Melle said he would like Free Churchmen in Britain to realise the struggle was 'an inevitable development in the relationship between Church and State'. That link had, in the past, led to repeated difficulties, he said. The Free Churches, for their part, were fortunately 'keeping aloof' from the contest, and their ministers and members strove to be 'perfectly neutral'. It was a matter for the 'National Church' to settle, whereas the Free Churches in Germany had a 'task of special magnitude' and had 'full liberty to preach the Gospel of Jesus Christ and to uphold the work of our own congregations'.[35]

Otto Melle is the only leading figure in the German Evangelical Alliance who is given the opportunity to discuss the situation in the Third Reich in the pages of *Evangelical Christendom*. Other German Free Church leaders are not interviewed; indeed, in 1934, the paper expressed criticism of the leaders of the Baptist World Alliance following its World Congress held in Berlin in August of that year. The 'credulity' of its leaders had been traded upon, the paper said, and the Congress as a whole had been 'bluffed', especially when calm consideration is given to the facts. Three 'facts' were listed. Firstly, the official Baptist organ was supressed in Germany. Secondly, only censored reports were permitted in the German newspapers. Thirdly, what Reichbishop Müller said to the Baptist leaders at the Congress was not borne out by subsequent events in their relation to liberty of conscience. The present government of the German Church had, to sum up, betrayed Christianity to 'the powers of this world'.[36]

This particular report had very little to do with the facts of the matter. The *Wahrheitszeuge* had not been suppressed. The report of the Congress was published in Germany and freely circulated. The non-German representatives of the Baptist Alliance were treated very generously by the German authorities and the Congress used the occasion to call for resistance to every form of racial discrimination and persecution and publicly expressed sympathy for the Confessing Church. The hosts, the German Baptists, were even openly criticised at the conference by their English brethren for making compromises. This was rejected with the argument that they 'thanked God that He had used the NSDAP to free Germany from capitalism, from injustice and from immorality'.[37] This politically loyal feature of the German Baptist Church was not mentioned; political emotions, as Karl Barth said during a visit to England in 1936, were already dominating the debate.

Evangelical Christendom was far more interested in the views and activities of Karl Barth and Martin Niemöller than those of Free Churchmen or Alliance figures. In 1935 the Council invited Karl Barth to visit London, which he was unable to accept.[38] The Executive Council also discussed the forthcoming trial of Niemöller at its 27 January 1938 meeting and considered what action could be taken on his behalf through *The Times* or other press agencies. This was left to the discretion of the General Secretary.[39] At the Council meeting on 24 March 1938 the General Secretary reported that a telegram had been sent to the Foreign Secretary, Lord Halifax, asking if he would consult with the German Foreign Secretary at their meeting in London concerning the position of Dr Niemöller, who, subsequent to his trial, had been confined in a concentration camp.[40] Between 1935 and 1939 nine articles appeared which discussed Barth's importance or printed long quotes from his articles or speeches; between 1934 and 1939 ten articles appeared which discussed Niemöller's role. Neither of these figures had any known links with evangelicalism; indeed, Barth in particular was known, in Germany, to be a theological enemy of evangelicalism. Barth knew, of course, that many English Churchmen were only interested in the struggle of the Confessional Church because they erroneously believed it was a struggle against Hitler and against National Socialism'.[41] In fact, it was not that, and Niemoeller himself had 'never pursued political ends, and had not used the pulpit for political designs'[42] but it could be instrumentalised in the Western press to create feelings of hostility which German evangelicals did not feel. One German pastor described the 'persecuted clergy'– not only 'the extremists of the Confessional Church, but the moderates too' – as the 'eager supporters' of Adolf Hitler. The majority certainly was, the pastor said. Nothing could be further from the truth than to portray these Confessing pastors as 'political opponents' of National Socialism. That was the true 'tragedy' of the situation. 'If it were not for the ideology', he quotes them as saying, 'we should be perfectly happy under the present regime'.[43] There were, however, only certain aspects of that ideology which some pastors found offensive.

Readers' letters made it clear that the line taken by *Evangelical Christendom* was not always accepted. Letters from Germany made it clear to the editor that there was a good deal of criticism of Christians in England who spoke of 'oppression and religious persecution' in Germany. This was not the perception of many individuals in Germany. 'How it is possible for our friends in Germany', the paper questioned, 'to contend that religious freedom prevails under Hitler's Government we do not understand'. This did not, however, lead Christians in England to do other than 'use any and every diplomatic and friendly influence to change the order of things in Germany'.[44] Such meddling was not always appreciated and led to more undiplomatic exchanges.

The unequivocal support given to the Confessing Church by *Evangelical Christendom*, which included criticism of religious figures in Britain like the Bishop of Gloucester, who 'had launched a regrettable attack on fellow Christians in Germany' and had 'made charges against Pastor Niemöller' in the pages of *The Times*[45], was mixed with incomprehension at the support Hitler and his Party enjoyed in the country. For example, its headlines constructed an enmity between *cross* and *swastika*[46] while correspondents reported 'surprisingly little, if any, dissent appears to be manifest in the use of this strange and heathen object on the part of the new order in Germany'.[47] Evangelicals in Germany, as we have seen, accepted the new emblems of the state just as they accepted the new state. Scripture taught them no other attitude to authority.

Surprisingly, perhaps, it was the issue of anti-Semitism that was the focus of *Evangelical Christendom*'s rejection of National Socialism and the area where the editors realised it took up a position differing from that of their German brethren. Already on 27 April 1933 the Executive Council considered the persecution of Jews in Germany and adopted a resolution unanimously, which was sent to the German Ambassador in London, with the request that a copy be forwarded to the President and Chancellor of the German Republic, to the Chief Rabbi in Britain and others.[48]

> The Council of the World's Evangelical Alliance (British Organisation) representing Christians of all Protestant Churches in this and other countries, deplores the persecution and wrongs which Jewish people in Germany are suffering at the hands of those who profess and represent the Christian faith, and who are guilty of acts utterly alien to all Christian spirit and teaching. The Council, further, earnestly petitions the President and the Chancellor of the German nation to take steps to ensure to all law-abiding Jews in Germany freedom from persecution, full liberty of conscience, and religious freedom.[49]

The Chief Rabbi, J.H. Hertz, wrote to the General Secretary, saying he was 'deeply touched' by the unanimous resolution and said it was his 'earnest prayer that your action will strengthen the forces of justice and brotherhood that are struggling to stem this terrible outbreak of racial hatred'.[50] On 27 June 1933 a huge meeting of representatives of all religions and opinions was held in the Queen's Hall, London, presided over by Lord Buckmaster, to protest against the racial discrimination being exercised against the Jews. This may be seen as a fruit of the Council's work, though not of its work alone. At the same time, however, protests reached the Alliance from Evangelical representatives in Germany who 'think that the World's Evangelical Alliance ought not, through the Resolution of its Council, to have condemned the persecution'.[51] It has already been pointed out that German evangelicals felt the actions taken by their government in the spring of 1933 were perfectly justifiable. There was 'surprisingly little dissent'.[52]

Persecution – at least of Jews – remained a matter on the agenda of the Council. On 28 November 1935 it discussed the steps being taken in Britain to express united sympathy and to afford practical help where necessary and possible. The General Secretary suggested the desirability of arranging a public united meeting which should be a gesture of sympathy with the Jewish people as a whole, and especially in Germany. This proposal was 'generally' approved.[53] At the meeting on 23 January 1936 the Council discussed the relief being given to 'outstanding cases of Jewish Non-Aryans in this country and others who had been obliged to leave Germany and were finding it difficult to obtain a livelihood or even to stay in this country'.[54] A second resolution was unanimously accepted on 24 November 1938 following the anti-Semitic pogrom:[55]

> The Council of the World's Evangelical Alliance shares the widespread concern and sorrow with which the whole British nation, in common with peoples of other civilised countries, have learned of the barbarous violence and cruel legislation inflicted upon the Jews in Germany. They desire to assure the Jewish people as a whole, through the Chief Rabbi in London, of the deep and heart-felt sympathy with them in their travail and sorrows at this time, and themselves remembering all Jewry in prayer before Jehovah, their God and ours, call upon Christians everywhere to pray unceasingly at this time for God's ancient people. The Council further pledge themselves to do anything possible through the World's Evangelical Alliance to relieve the shocking plight of the Jewish refugees, and express the hope that His Majesty's Government will offer the widest possible asylum to these refugees in parts of the British Empire, and thus help to alleviate the sorrows of these persecuted people suffering for no other reason than their race.[56]

Once again, the Chief Rabbi conveyed the 'deep-felt thanks of my community' for the resolution: 'In the agony through which hundreds of thousands of my co-religionists are now passing, it is fortifying to read your strong repudiation of all persecution and your deep sympathy with the heart-rending plight of the refugees'.[57]

Letters were sent to heads of Churches appealing for a public protest.[58] Faced with the spectacle of German Jewish refugees in 1939 and massacres of Jews in Poland and elsewhere in 1943 the Council tried to alert politicians including the Prime Minister, to mobilise the Anglican Church (telegrams were sent to the Archbishop of Canterbury and the Bishop of Chichester) and to help organise a meeting in Central Hall on 3 March 1943.[59] The World's Evangelical Alliance was clearly moved by compassion 'to be of assistance and to plead for those who cannot plead for themselves'.[60] It said that Christians in England were deeply concerned about German anti-semitism and the 'tyranny' of the existing Nazi regime, against which there 'has so far been surprisingly little dissent expressed by German Protestants'.[61] German Protestant silence was declared to be most 'distressing' for it appeared to evangelical leaders in Britain that no distinction was even being drawn drawn between those Jews who had become Christians and those who still remained in the Jewish faith. They had heard reports that the anti-Semitism in Germany was 'sometimes more bitter against baptised than unbaptised Jews'. These leaders could only wish that there was, somewhere in Germany, an 'inarticulate' protest before God against the 'prevailing persecution' of the Jews.62 For, it was believed, and here they followed a Confessing Church line of thinking, that 'nothing less than the Evangelical Christian faith itself' was at stake. They were appalled that no opposition had been mobilised on behalf of the two score Jewish-Christian pastors among the 16,000 Evangelical clergy. 'German congregations do not want the Gospel preached to them by these men', they lamented.63 Moreover, the Protestant Church leaders in Germany had declared that they regarded it as 'inexpedient' under present circumstances to baptise any Jews. On the surface this seemed like cowardice. In reality, *Evangelical Christendom* explained, it was 'probably the result of the predominant Nazi sympathies' of most of the Protestant Church leaders. The paper called on British Christians not to judge them too harshly, but rather attempt to put themselves in their place and imagine what they would do in similar circumstances. It was, the editor felt, 'regrettable' that this was in fact the case, not least because, in the eyes of many of the Jews and 'non-Aryans', the politics of Protestant church leaders had led to 'bitter disillusionment' inside the Church and an aversion to Christianity itself. The paper regretted, in addition, that few countries in the world were prepared to welcome Jewish refugees, with the result that many had to remain in Germany, where all means of existence were being slowly but surely taken from them.64

The Archbishop of Canterbury, Dr William Temple, in a sermon preached on Dr Niemöller's birthday at the German Lutheran Church in London in 1943, also felt it was his 'duty to point out the limitations' to which the witness of German Christians had been subject. There had been, he noted, a protest from the Bishop of Münster and other Roman Catholic Bishops against the treatment of Christian institutions, such as the closing of religious establishments throughout Germany. There had also been a protest from the Protestant Bishop of Württemberg against the suppression of Christian literature and the veiled threat to abolish the religious rite of confirmation. There had, however, been no protest so far as he knew against such crimes as the attempt to exterminate the Poles or the horror of the massacre of the Jews. It had been protest in self-defence rather than protest on behalf of outraged justice and of brotherly love. This, of course, was Barth's main criticism of the Confessing Church. Fortunately, not all Christians were as blind as the leaders of the Confessing Church to the growing tragedy. The Christians of Holland and of France for example, Dr Temple said, at great risk to themselves and their Churches, had condemned the treatment of the Jews. This could not be said of the Christians of Germany. 'We are are obliged', Temple said, 'to express our sorrow that the Christians of Germany have failed in this respect. For what is at stake is not merely the survival of an ecclesiastical institution, but the capacity of the Christian fellowship to give fearless testimony to Christian truth'.[65]

German evangelicals, most of whom were wary of even contact with the Confessing Church groups, were even less concerned about raising their voices for the helpless. In Britain, however, there was such a mood. In an address given at the 90th Anniversary of the World's Evangelical Alliance on 11 May 1936, Dr Conrad Hoffman emphasised the danger that the Jews could be exterminated and talked of the 'great tragedy' that whereas Germany 'does not want these people, no other country in the world wants them either'.[66] In trying to deal with anti-Semitic prejudices, however, *Evangelical Christendom* revealed a few of its own. There was, however, a much greater willingness to make distinctions and avoid generalisations compared to their German counterpart. There was a difference, the paper stated, between Christian regard for the Jews 'in the light of Scripture promise and precept' and dislike of their social customs and business methods, which were 'often bywords among those of other races'. 'Are there Jewish Communists?' the paper asked. 'Of course there are, but there are Gentile Communists too. The only difference is that when a Jew joins an organisation he generally attains dominance and the Jewish Communist is at once distinguished'.[67]

Nor were British Christians necessarily more willing than their German brethren to offer practical help. The Christian Church had not accepted responsibility for Jewish Christians in Germany, *Evangelical Christendom* lamented. For example, the Archbishop of Canterbury's appeal for a 'moderate sum' for their relief was closed owing to the inadequate response.[68]

As the massacres of Jews in concentration camps 'by machine gun and poison chamber, by torture and famine'(Chief Rabbi J.H. Hertz)[69] became common knowledge in Britain in 1942, the Council of the World's Evangelical Alliance welcomed the statement made by the Secretary of State for Foreign Affairs in the House of Commons on 17 December 1942 condemning the 'bestial policy of cold-blooded extermination' and expressing the resolution of the British Government to bring those responsible for these crimes to justice.[70] A resolution was adopted, urging the government 'to press on with all practical measures for affording help and relief to the victims of these atrocities' and to grant asylum to refugees from the occupied countries of Europe in parts of the British Empire. The Council further expressed its hope that the British Government would give assurances of financial assistance and food supplies to neutral countries in which refugees had already found or may find asylum.[71]

Copies of the resolution were sent to the Prime Minister, the Foreign Secretary, Members of Parliament, the Lord Mayor of London and the Chief Rabbi (who once again expressed his deep gratitude). Mr H. M. Gooch was active rallying those concerned about the suffering of the Jews in Europe. He read from Scripture and read out letters of support sent to him by the Lord Mayor of London and the Chief Rabbi to a meeting on 3 March 1943, which was supported by representatives from ten Embassies or Legations. It was presided over by Archbishop Lord Lang, who noted that 'in Germany itself there seemed to have been no audible voice of protest raised'.[72]

Though evangelicals, and others, tried to activate the decision-makers in the country, the official response of the government remained largely symbolic, not substantial. After discussing the 'de-Christianising of their English Sunday', Dr Temple talked of the horror Members of the Commons felt after listening to the stories of persecution and how the they 'all stood, and in a moment of silence they mourned the awful suffering of the Jews'.[73] Throughout the 1930s, however, only a very small number of Jewish refugees from Germany – about six or seven thousand were in the country in 1938 – managed to pass the rigid immigration controls in force in Britain. Their presence in Britain unleashed, moreover, storms of protest, encouraged by the yellow press. Many became victims of the activities of Sir Oswald Mosley's British Union of Fascists, the National Socialist League of William Joyce and John Becket, and the Imperial Fascist League, whose organ *The Fascist* rivalled any Nazi publication published in Germany.[74] 'By a particularly mean trick', wrote Louis Golding in 1938, the 'political menace of Germany and the possibilities of German espionage are being manipulated to prejudice the position here of German Jews who are victims of the German terror'. England had become 'Jew-conscious' to an extent that she had never, perhaps, been since the Expulsion of 1290.[75]

The numbers remained inconsiderable, in Britain and its Dominions. Just a few weeks after the Christian meeting of 3 March, Anthony Eden, the British Foreign Minister, had talks with the Presidents of the American Jewish Committee and explained it was 'absolutely impossible' to enable Jews to emigrate from the occupied countries; nor was he in favour of supplying food shipments, to Turkey for example, where the 60,000 to 70,000 Bulgarian Jews might have found admittance if Britain had shown a willingness to help to evacuate them. The British Government was not willing, for fear that the Germans really would release large numbers of Jewish refugees. In December 1943 Britain opposed a plan to evacuate Jews from France and Romania and in May 1944 the British War Cabinet's committee dealing with refugee questions rejected the idea to work towards an agreement enabling Jews to leave the Nazi sphere of influence as this might lead to more Jews being 'dumped' in Britain.[76] 'In the present state of sentiment', Louis Golding wrote, 'it is out of the question to imagine that England is likely to behave magnanimously'.[77]

Nor was Britain's attitude to Palestine conducive to helping the Jewish refugees in Europe, in spite of the Balfour Declaration of November 1917. Throughout the 1930s the government tried to whittle Jewish rights away and the 1937 Royal Commission proposed to partition Palestine, granting to the Jews a small proportion of the land which did not include Jerusalem. In May 1939 the government decided to limit the number of Jewish immigrants into Palestine to a total of 75,000 over the next five years. This was to ensure that the Jewish part of the population (which totalled about 430,000 in 1938) did not exceed one third of the total population, so as to pacify Arab fears that a Jewish state might arise in the area. The war did nothing but harden the British resolve to limit Jewish immigration into Palestine. The quotas allowed by the May 1939 policy decision were never filled and, in 1942 and 1943, the numbers of non-Jews equalled the numbers of Jews being admitted. In 1944 between 9,000 and 12,000 Greeks were settled in the region. Jewish refugees on board the *Struma* were even turned away in 1942, which led to their tragic deaths at sea.[78] Britain also refused to consider a proposal of granting temporary asylum to Jews in Libya in 1943/1944[79] and the strong British presence on the Intergovernmental Committee on Refugees, as well as the anti-Zionist stance taken by Sir Herbert Emerson (who directed the Committee), did nothing to ease the plight of Jews in Europe.[80]

It is not surprising that *Evangelical Christendom* took a diametrically opposite view of the war from the one expressed in *Evangelisches Allianzblatt*. 'With feelings of respect and sympathy we regard our fellow-Christians in Germany', the British Alliance stated in 1941. 'To them, difficult as it is, it is in our hearts to send brotherly greetings'. Yet they warned their brethren that the day would come when German Christians would 'deeply regret how far their country has departed from the Faith, and from the path of righteousness'. The paper wondered whether German iniquity, their 'insensate lust for war' against all the principles of freedom and righteousness, was the direct result of more than a century of German Biblical criticism and of 'undermining of the authority of the Word of God'. 'Germany has taken the lead in this and is now suffering, and will yet suffer, the consequences'.[81]

German Christians did not see the war quite in this way. Indeed, as *Evangelical Christendom* noted later in 1941, the Lutheran Church sent 'an effusive telegram' to Hitler after the attack on Russia, assuring their Leader of 'the unchangeable faithfulness and devotion of all Evangelical Christians in the Reich'. The telegram was reprinted for the benefit of British evangelicals.

> You, our Leader, have banished the Bolshevist danger in our own country and now call our nation and the nations of Europe to the decisive onslaught against the deadly enemy of all order and all Western Christian civilisation. The German nation, and with it all its Christian members, thank you for this deed. The fact that British policy is now openly using Bolshevism as an auxiliary against the Reich makes it finally clear that it is concerned not with Christianity but only with the destruction of the German nation. May Almighty God assist you and our nation to carry off against the double enemy the victory to which all our decisions and actions must be devoted.[82]

Evangelical Christendom criticised what it felt was 'a good deal of pacifism, or semi-pacifism, among both clergy and ministers' in Britain as well as the lack of 'all-out enthusiasm and co-operation in such movements for united national Prayer for Victory as those finding expression at the Central Hall, Westminster'.[83] In 1942 the evangelical weekly could tell readers Britain was fighting not simply for 'the future of civilisation and the human race', but more importantly for the 'survival of Christianity, in its very essence'. British Christians should pray for victory.[84]

Referring to Lord Halifax, who had spoken in 1940 of Hitler as Antichrist, *Evangelical Christendom* expressed its view that 'Hitler is not *the* Antichrist, although he may be a forerunner'.[85] Others in the British establishment, such as Sir Robert Vansittart, also publicly stated there was 'no doubt or argument as to the anti-Christian nature of the Nazi regime'.[86] God expected every Englishman to do his duty; once again, God had chosen Englishmen to do His work on earth.

The World's Evangelical Alliance was pressed during 1944 to express its position on the treatment of Germany after the conclusion of hostilities. It felt unable to give a final answer at the time.[87] The Archbishop of Canterbury reminded his diocese that 'there must be, and are, good German Christians', who will, 'if they belong to Christ, be brought to a sense of guilt before God and man which will enable them to receive from fellow Christians in this and other countries a spirit other than one breathing blind hatred, condemnation and retaliation'.[88] The relation of 'mutual confidence and acknowledgement of the Unity in Christ' had through the war become 'diffuse and interrupted'.[89] The World's Evangelical Alliance deplored the deaths of many brethren from the Continent who 'were united with us in the same faith', making specific mention of the death of the editor of the *Evangelisches Allianzblatt*, Gustav F. Nagel,[90] and noted that in the circles of the Evangelical Alliance in Germany there was a 'deep acknowledgement of the guilt' of which some groups of Christians were not free. The German brethren had confessed 'that they have not always been true witnesses of our Saviour' during the past few years and that they had been influenced by the 'spirit of worldliness, or injustice and cowardliness'. They had asked, in their prayers during the Week of Prayer, for forgiveness, a greater experience of the glory of Jesus Christ, a better understanding of His plan and a greater willingness to follow Him and to suffer with Him.[91]

The Centenary of the World's Evangelical Alliance was celebrated in Germany too with the publication of a leaflet *Hundert Jahre Evangelische Allianz* but the Week of Prayer included no specific confession of guilt towards the Jews and other groups who had been persecuted by a government the *Allianzblatt* had applauded. Instead, one returned to evangelistic business as usual. The missionary responsibility of the Christians towards 'the Jews in their midst' [sic] was once again acknowledged by German evangelicals, and it was seen to be of 'great importance' and 'a sign of the growing sense for service', that the renewal of the Jewish Mission in Germany was restarted on the basis of the Evangelical Alliance.[92]

The new Chairman of the German Branch of the World's Evangelical Alliance, Pastor Zilz, as well as the Vice Chairman, Bishop Sommer, visited Britain in June 1947 and were offered the right hand of fellowship by the General Secretary, H.M. Gooch, and the two Honorary Secretaries, Rev. H. R. Gough and Rev. C. Lyon. In a message carried back by Pastor Zilz to the Blankenburg Committee and all those attending the Blankenburg Conference at Marburg (2-5 July 1947), H. Martyn Gooch prayed that 'God may use the

Evangelical Alliance in these days of His judgement over Germany, and the whole world, to show the German people a new vision that these days of darkness over Germany 'fall out rather unto the furtherance of the Gospel' (Phil. 1,12)'.[93]

Notes

1. *Evangelical Christendom* [hereafter EC], 1936, 195.
2. EC, 1933, 32.
3. EC, 1933, 115.
4. EC, 1933, 116.
5. Ibid.
6. Minutes of the Committee of Council of the Evangelical Alliance, Volume VII, 472.
7. EC, 1933, 151.
8. EC, 1933, 188.
9. EC, 1933, 228; T.P. Weber (1987, 198).
10. EC, 1934, 4.
11. Ibid, 5.
12. EC, 1934, 24.
13. Ibid, 125.
14. EC, 1934, 64.
15. EC, 1934, 30.
16. EC, 1934, 181.
17. EC, 1935, 29.
18. Minutes, Volume VII, 511f.
19. EC, 1934, 117.
20. Ibid.
21. EC, 1935, 67.
22. EC, 1935, 107.
23. EC, 1935, 204.
24. Minutes, Volume VII, 519; EC, 1934, 194-195.
25. EC, 1934, 194f.
26. Minutes, Volume VII, 564-565; EC, 1935, 218.
27. EC, 1934, 218.
28. EC, 1935, 235.
29. EC, 1936, 23.
30. EC, 1935, 135.

31. EC, 1936, 108.
32. EC, 1937, 43.
33. EC, 1936, 50.
34. EC, 1936, 51-52.
35. EC, 1936, 108.
36. EC, 1934, 181.
37. K. Zehrer (1986, 32).
38. Minutes, Volume VII, 573-574.
39. Minutes, Volume VIII, 54.
40. Ibid, 60.
41. EC, 1936, 24.
42. EC, 1938, 142.
43. EC, 1938, 95.
44. EC, 1938, 95.
45. EC, 1937, 139; EC, 1938, 159f.
46. EC, 1935, 109; EC, 1941, 24; EC, 1942, 83-84.
47. EC, 1933, 228.
48. Minutes, Volume VII, 464.
49. EC, 1933, 97-98.
50. EC, 1933, 98.
51. EC, 1933, 150.
52. EC, 1933, 188.
53. Minutes, Volume VII, 563.
54. Ibid, 573-4.
55. Minutes, Volume VIII, 93-94.
56. EC, 1939, 4.
57. Ibid.
58. Agenda Book, 1938, 18.
59. Ibid, 28, 33, 83-4, 86.
60. EC, 1934, 116.
61. EC, 1933, 188.
62. EC, 1933, 192f.
63. EC, 1934, 24.
64. EC, 1938, 208.
65. EC, 1943, 56.
66. EC, 1936, 231.
67. EC, 1933, 193.
68. EC, 1938, 161.

69. Chief Rabbi J.H. Hertz, EC, 1943, 33.
70. EC, 1943, 33.
71. EC, 1943, 34.
72. EC, 1943, 33.
73. EC, 1943, 32.
74. Louis Golding (1938, 152f).
75. Ibid, 153.
76. David Wyman (1986, 142-145, 391, 465).
77. Louis Golding (1938, 173).
78. David Wyman (1986, 229f); Louis Golding (1938, 188).
79. David Wyman (1986, 359).
80. Ibid, 203-5.
81. EC, 1941, 22.
82. EC, 1941, 134.
83. EC, 1942, 56.
84. EC, 1942, 56.
85. EC, 1940, 139.
86. Robert Vansittart (1941, 10).
87. EC, 1944, 92.
88. EC, 1945, 62.
89. EC, 1946, 79.
90. EC, 1946, 80.
91. EC, 1947, 23.
92. EC, 1947, 23.
93. EC, 1947, 69-73.

Chapter Ten

Post-War Trends

The attempt has been made in the chapters above to explain why there was widespread support among evangelicals for the spirit, policies and goals of National Socialism. There seems to have been some realization of this in 1945. Erich Beyreuther interprets a section of the two-page leaflet produced to commemorate the centenary of the World Evangelical Alliance in 1946, *Hundert Jahre Evangelische Allianz*, as a confession of guilt.[1] Without specifically mentioning Adolf Hitler or National Socialism or the period of the Third Reich or the persecution of Jews, Communists, homosexuals or gypsies, German evangelicals confessed they had 'not always immediately recognised the prevailing errors in the years that lie behind us and given a clear, courageous testimony against them'. In future, the Church of Christ 'must involve itself much more decisively, more solidly and more responsibly in the serious and great tasks of the present'. As Beyreuther points out, moreover, this section was not to be found on the front page of the leaflet, but tucked away on the second. It was not given prime importance by the Evangelical Alliance in Germany.

Friedrich Heitmüller, in his memoirs, named two major sins committed by the Evangelical Alliance between 1933 and 1945. The leadership had gradually but decisively withdrawn and disassociated itself from the Confessing Church and even avoided those who had had problems, as a result of their preaching, with the Gestapo. They too seemed to see 'enemies of the state' as their enemies. Secondly, the Alliance had disassociated itself from the Jewish people by removing the traditional prayers for Jews and missionary activities among the Jews from their Prayer Programme; public prayer for Jews, the leadership had argued, would only endanger the work of Christian fellowships. Heitmüller claims he, as a leading member of the Alliance movement in Germany, repeatedly objected, unsuccessfully, to this change and sees the drop in attendance at Alliance Conferences during the period as an expression of the loss of confidence of ordinary believers in the line taken by their leaders. This division extended even into the ranks of the Blankenburg Committee where, after 1935, hardly a meeting took place without criticism being expressed of the pragmatic opportunism practised by leaders. In public, especially at the Blankenburg Conferences, some brethren clearly spoke the

Word of God 'into the situation at that time'. Heitmüller locates the roots of this behaviour in their understanding of the Biblical concept of governmental authority in general and and its application to the Third Reich in particular. Evangelicals also felt, he says, that it was only fair to give the political experiment of National Socialism a chance to change Germany for the better.2

The leaflet celebrating the centenary of the Evangelical Alliance refers to the 'blessed ministry' and 'important service' that the *Allianzblatt* had performed over the previous decades. At the time, one year after the end of the war, there was still no conviction that the paper had perhaps led people astray. We have outlined above, using material from the *Evangelisches Allianzblatt* some areas where evangelicals felt attracted to this experiment:a strong patriotism; the enforcement of law and order; an authoritarian leadership style; opposition to democracy in principle and the democratic constitution of Weimar in particular; a dislike of party politics; the introduction of school prayer; censorship of the media, particularly the removal of sexual content; the official emphasis on clean and healthy living; the fight against promiscuity and prostitution; the emphasis on the traditional roles of men and women; the tightening up of the blasphemy law; the job creation programmes; anti-Communism; an aggressive and nationalistic foreign policy. Support for National Socialism was given not in spite of, but *because of* evangelicals' study of *Mein Kampf* and the NSDAP Party Programme. This movement, which was understood to be an expression of divine intervention in German history, was loyally supported right up to the end of the war in 1945.

The problem of resistance and submission to authority in the Third Reich has not been thought through by evangelicals in the period after the war. Evangelicals were no different from other Germans in quickly making their peace with the Nazis in their midst and not attemting to make restitution to those groups who suffered most under the Hitler regime. They too bear responsibility for what Ralph Giordano called 'the second sin'.3 The centenary conference held in the City Mission church on the Gardepionierplatz between 31 August and 3 September 1946 did not begin to consider the impact of National Socialism on the evangelical community. The only criticism expressed of evangelical spirituality during the meetings was an oblique reference by a university professor to the 'most despicable' abuse of the Book of Revelation by believers in the past and present to interpret the signs of the times. Indeed, conservative theologians such as Helmut Thielicke seemed, at least in the initial post-war period, far more concerned about the dismissal of 'good' Nazis from their jobs and other forms of denazification than with the *victims* of National Socialism. Certainly, the words he found to criticise the conditions in American and British internment camps in 1947 were words he failed to apply to German camps prior to 1945; his description of *denazification* – 'the murder of souls and the murder of religious faith' – had not been used after 1933 to describe *nazification*.[4] The presence of 53 former NSDAP members in the first German Bundestag of 1949 disturbed nobody.[5]

German evangelicalism has remained solidly conservative in the political and theological sense.[6] Evangelicals have, since 1945, waged a struggle against the main theological streams of thought in Germany, setting up alternative structures (media, Church Festivals, education, overseas aid organisation) without, however, as yet breaking with the Lutheran, Reformed and United Churches. On 6 March 1966 20,000 evangelicals founded the so-called *Bekenntnisbewegung 'Kein anderes Evangelium'* (the Confessing Movement 'No Other Gospel') in Düsseldorf, which claimed, and claims, to be continuing the *Kirchenkampf* of the period 1933-1945. One of the founders of the *Bekenntnisbewegung* in 1966 was Professor Künneth, a respected theologian whose books *Die Nation vor Gott* (1933) and *Antwort auf den Mythos* (1935) explicitly agreed with Alfred Rosenberg's views on the 'poisoning of the German character by the Jewish spirit' and the 'destructive influence of World Jewry'.[7] One critic says a knowledge of Künneth's past works helps to understand why evangelical groups in Germany were among the most vocal supporters of South Africa during the post-war period.[8]

This grouping combined with other evangelical movements on 7 October 1970 to form the *Konferenz Bekennender Gemeinschaften* (Conference of Confessing Fellowships).[9] The roots of this movement can be traced back to 1950 when attacks were made on the theology of Rudolf Bultmann and has continued unabated with more recent attacks on the theology of Karl Barth.[10] At the same time the *Nationalpietisten,* or nationalistic pietists, sought to restore the traditional, radically conservative values of German Protestantism.[11] Though there are evangelical groups in Germany – the Baptist 'Initiative Schalom' or the Free Church 'Aktion Hoffnung gewinnen' were examples in the 1980s[12] – which have been involved in activities to preserve peace, justice and creation itself, it is widely accepted that at least 90 per cent of German evangelicals are strongly conservative in their political outlook.[13]

At the time this *second* Confessing Church movement was founded, well-known evangelicals compared their situation with that in the Third Reich. Gerhard Bergmann said the 'theological error of the so-called German Christians [is] child's play compared with what is at stake today' and Pastor

Wilhelm Busch considered the 'false doctrines' of today 'even worse' than those of the German Christians.[14] Then, as today, evangelicals were not concerned with criticising their *political* environment, but the *theological* context of their lives, in particular the mixing of what they would see as left-wing politics with Christianity. Thus, the press service catering to the constituency of the German Evangelical Alliance *idea spektrum* quoted Professor Bodenstein (Kiel) in 1987 as saying German Protestantism had 'replaced its religious message with a political one' and had 'landed precisely where the German Christians could be found during the *Kirchenkampf*'. The Church had become a 'mouth-piece representing the political demands of Eastern Europe'. His evidence: the joint *Word on Peace* of the Protestant Churches in West and East Germany, the rejection of President Reagan's SDI programme and the support for Gorbatschow's disarmament proposals.[15]

Others claim that evangelicals and the Christian Democratic Union (one of the two main conservative parties in Germany[16]) are the real 'German Christians' in post-war Germany. The so-called Christian parties, CDU and CSU, the 'pseudo-Christian reasons' given in support of German democracy, evangelical journalists working for security services, Christian support of rearmament and defence against Communism, the American electronic church preaching the virtues of capitalism – all these were symptoms, according to Pastor Dr Ulrich Duchrow (Heidelberg) in a lecture to the Critical Barmen Conference, of a new 'German Christianity'. There were unmistakeable parallels between 1934 and 1984, he said.[17]

As a term to denote compromise with the world's values and ideologies or even subservience to a non-Christian or anti-Christian system, the term *German Christian*, in contrast to the movement of that name, has survived – if only as a term of abuse.

In contrast to the German Christians in the Third Reich it is true to say that evangelicals in post-war Germany have grown to accept democracy in the political realm as an acceptable form of government. Since the mid-1980s, however, there have been a number of signals that a sizeable proportion is not happy with the state of affairs in the Federal Republic of Germany. Christain Starke, editor of *idea spektrum*, which is the evangelical weekly with the highest circulation in Germany[18], has expressed his 'basically positive' opinion about the Federal Republic of Germany. He was thankful for the freedoms and rights guaranteed to him, as a citizen and a Christian, by the German constitution. Democracy was the best of all the bad systems man had designed. Christians too had to abide by the rules of the democratic game and should not break the law as a means of expressing their convictions. The thirteenth chapter of the Letter to the Romans had to be obeyed.[19] The environmental and peace movements in Germany, as well as their political embodiment the Green Party, have come in for particularly critical treatment in the pages of *idea spektrum* for this very reason. Church groups blockading nuclear power plants and military bases can not expect the support of evangelical organisations, though individual evangelicals are involved in protest groups.

Starke also expressed criticism of certain traits inherent in twentieth-century German evangelicalism. The ability to criticise, to question and to be discriminating in one's thought were qualities which were often seen as negative features. Many evangelicals had also become consciously unpolitical; politics was considered to be an inherently 'dirty business', something Christians shouldn't even be interested in. Political abstinence, in contrast to the convictions of evangelicals in the seventeenth and eighteenth centuries, was now considered to be the done thing. At the same time, the primary socio-political concern of evangelicals – the 200,000 abortions each year in Germany – was drawing some evangelicals into the camp of the extreme right-wing party in the country, the Republicans, the party which, perhaps more than the others, was opposed to the freedom to abort in a hospital at the taxpayer's expense. This worried Starke and he asks whether an anti-abortion stance could ever justify 'voting for a party which, in other fields, propounds policies which express hatred of people'.[20]

In fact, evangelicals are not only voting for the Republicans, some are members and one, Markus Motschmann, was a District Councillor for the party in Berlin-Schöneberg in 1989.[21] In the anti-abortion movement there are numerous links between evangelicals and ex-Nazis, members of Opus Dei, and extreme right-wing groups.[22] Here too the German past is ever present. Anti-abortionists often compare what they term the 'embryocaust' with the holocaust, abortion hospitals with Auschwitz – without, however, calling for new Nuremberg Trials for those they call mass murderers.

The Republicans benefited in the 1980s and early 1990s from the difficult economic situation and widespread disillusionment not only with politics generally, but with the CDU and CSU in particular, which have appeared unable or unwilling to stop abortions taking place and which did not, as they had promised and evangelicals had hoped, bring about a 'spiritual and moral change' in the atmosphere of the Federal Republic.[23] Evangelical leaders held talks with members of the German Cabinet and Secretaries of State in

January 1983 and expressed 'basic agreement' with their views on the theological basis of politics and norms of social ethics.24 Within three years hopes of major changes had evaporated and conservative Christians, Protestants and Catholics, joined ranks with Conservative politicians to form a 'Christian Forum' in 1986 which aimed to deal with the 'massive moral neglect' afflicting Germany.25 'No sanctions against adultery, sexual promiscuity, homosexuality and lesbianism being tolerated in public, AIDS, pornography, drug addiction and crime are spreading like epidemics', stated the Fulda Declaration of the Forum. The German government, moreover, blinded by 'a Marxist and materialist ideology' of equality, was 'forcing men and women into an egoistic, competitive struggle' for jobs. The Forum called on the government to put an end to the public financing of abortions. One of its spokespersons, the psychotherapist Christa Meves, warned that 'a state which commits murder should not be surprised when Christians withdraw their support from it. The murder of about 280,000 children every year could lead to God judging the Federal Republic'.26

Apart from this conservative ecumenical movement, there arose strongly evangelical political parties. The oldest is the 'Deutsche Zentrumspartei'. In 1985 the 'Christliche Liga' (Christian League) was founded. In the same decade the 'Christliche Mitte' (Christian Centre) and the 'Partei Bibeltreuer Christen' (PBC) (Party of Bible-believing Christians), were also formed to express evangelical grievances, particularly with the abortion laws.27 The General Secretary of the Christliche Mitte, Adelgunde Mertensacker, has said that 'the politics of the Christliche Mitte should be understood as *practical Christianity*' (my italics). The party wanted, she said, to 're-Christianise the German people; to protect human life from conception to its natural death; to restore and preserve the environment and farming communities; to preserve the rights of women and mothers, of the family and parents, to educate their children; tough and drastic measures to stop crime and corruption; the protection of young people from health and moral dangers'.28 Its youth group, Junge Mitte, claims it wants 'no drugs, no pornography, no bad films which contain violence' in Germany; it calls for 'Christian schools, more religious information in the media, good religion lessons in school'.29

The Programme of the Christliche Liga contains perhaps the most extreme statements made by these new parties, though it calls for similar measures as the others. It calls for a healthy national pride to fill the vacuum in Germany which had been exploited by 'nationalists, internationalists, communists, terrorists, and all kinds of hooligans'. These groups, along with 'international socialism as well as the right-wing and capitalist empires', were being controlled by Freemasonry. Their goal was to destroy liberal democracy and set up a 'dictatorial world system with an undogmatic and unchristian world religion'. The sovereignty of the German state should no longer be limited by Articles 53 and 107 of the UN Charta, the special rights granted to the victor nations should be abolished and a peace treaty, long overdue, should be signed.[30]

These parties have rarely received more than 0.1% to 0.2% of votes cast in elections. The 9% of the vote won by the PBC in Frankenbach near Giessen in the state election of January 1991 was an exception to the rule.[31] Most evangelicals have stayed loyal, if they have voted at all, to the (predominantly Catholic) CDU and CSU. Given the low level of support these explicitly Christian parties have gained, there has been much talk of fusion.[32] Political unity has, however, remained unattainable. Talks about a possible fusion of energies took place in 1993 between the Christliche Liga and the Partei Bibeltreuer Christen, but the PBC Party Conference in November 1993 rejected the proposal. The press service of the Alliance *idea spektrum* reported on 13 June 1994 that, together, the three main 'Christian' parties had won 0.6% of the vote in the European elections on 12 June: the PBC gained 93,021 votes (0.3%), the Christliche Mitte 67,084 votes (0.2%) and the Christliche Liga 40,433 votes (0.1%). In the local elections in Hessen on 2 March 1997 the PBC managed to treble the number of votes it received in some towns compared to 1993. In some places in the Lahn-Dill district, for example, the party succeeded in getting over 6.0% of the total vote. The General Secretary of the PBC, Norbert Höhl, the only party official to hold a seat in local government in Hesse, won 10.3% of the vote in Marbach. Such results point to the beginnings perhaps of an embryonic Christian-fundamentalist religio-political movement in Germany, positioned clearly to the right of the Christian Democratic Union/Christian Social Union, though, as yet, its growing political self-confidence has not proved to be of any great social relevance.[33]

A further sign that evangelicals still have problems accepting liberal, pluralistic democracy came to light in 1988 when the head of the Gnadau Association, Kurt Heimbucher, refused to accept the *Bundesverdienstkreuz*, the Distinguished Service Cross, one of the highest honours awarded by the German republic. In a letter to the German President, Richard von Weizsäcker, Heimbucher, who was for a number of years Deputy General Secretary of the Evangelical Alliance and a member of its ruling body for twenty years, said that he, and many other people had, as Christians, become 'very alienated' from the Bundesrepublik. He gave a number of reasons. The state granted women the right to choose whether to have an abortion or not (some evangelicals called this the *Fristenendlösung*) and no longer protected the unborn. At the same time the state was abandoning its duty to protect citizens from crime:there were too few policemen and women were afraid to go out at night for fear of being attacked. Certain groups of people – he doesn't name them, though he is perhaps thinking of environmental protesters and the squatters in empty houses particularly in the Hamburg Hafenstraße – enjoyed freedom from prosecution, while decent, law-abiding citizens were prosecuted for the most minor of offences. Whenever the police took strong action to put an end to 'chaotic activities' they soon became the nation's whipping-boy. The state, he said, was too 'lax and helpless' to deal with scandal and corruption. Heimbucher, a Bavarian pastor, was 'very upset' when the German government signed treaties in the 1970s to 'give away the German territories in the East'. For him, a man who loved his fatherland, Breslau and Königsberg were just as much a part of Germany as Weimar and Dresden.

It is not difficult to see that Heimbucher, one of the top representatives of German evangelicalism, had not made his peace with parliamentary democracy and the post-war settlement. As the historian of the Gnadau movement pointed out in a commentary on Heimbucher's decision, his choice of words awakened associations which reminded one of the arguments used by evangelicals in 1933 to justify the rule of Hitler.[34] In an interview with the *Frankfurter Rundschau* in February 1988, Heimbucher said he supported the state's policy of 'strengthening marriage and the family and its peace and environmental policies'. Interestingly, he expressed his fear that 'pietism could become reactionary'. His own hope, however, was that it might once again become a 'progressive, conservative' movement.

His autobiography quite candidly reveals unresolved questions relating to evangelicals' reactions to the National Socialist regime. He explains that his enthusiasm for the *Jungvolk*, an organisation preparing youngsters for the Hitler Youth, had much to do with the values he had learnt in his parental home: loyalty to a cause, honour, truthfulness, love of one's country and above all the emphasis on fulfilling one's duties. These duties were not always related, however, to actually helping those in need. He describes how he and his family had stood and watched as Jews in his home town of Nuremberg, some of whom were neighbours, were put on to lorries and taken away. Nor had he forgotten his mother's comment on watching the synagogue opposite the Church of the Holy Spirit burn to the ground in 1938: 'Hopefully', she had said, 'our whole town and country won't be going up in flames one day like this synagogue here'. In Heimbucher's opinion hardly anyone knew of the murderous acts being committed by his father's generation. The 'death machine' operated in secrecy, 'screened off' from the German population. Nor can he stomach the self-righteousness of the victor nations and the lack of repentence on the part of the Roman Catholic Church. Nowhere in fact can he talk of German guilt without pointing the finger at others. 'Couldn't the English and French have prevented the war? Why did they allow Hitler so much space and let him seize one territory after the other? Why did they sign treaties with Hitler on the Obersalzberg in 1938? Why did the Roman Catholic Church or the Pope not intervene once the Reichskristallnacht had taken place? Why did the bishops still turn up at the receptions given by Hitler?' In particular, they had allowed very few, if any Jewish refugees into their countries. These powers had 'acted culpably'; it would be wrong, he wrote, not to point this out.

On the other hand he emphasised that German history was much more than those twelve years of a barbaric National Socialist tyranny. Particularly in the aftermath of the war many had 'succumbed to the temptation' of forgetting the centuries of German achievement by focussing on the Third Reich. Yet the victor nations had committed 'equally heinous crimes' against the German population. 'You did not hear of the victor countries beating their breasts and confessing their guilt', he said. Yet these very same nations had insisted on conducting a 'biased' trial against leading Nazis in the 'heavily fortified' Palace of Justice in Nuremberg. The wave of 'degrading' denazification trials conducted by 'dubious' characters sitting on 'arbitrary' juries and passing 'questionable and unjust' sentences on people who 'had only done their duty in the Third Reich', men and women who 'did not refuse their cooperation, who were motivated by idealism, who had done much good and had never committed a crime'. He blames the early death of his father on the 'dishonouring' and degrading treatment the latter had received from such a denazification court.[35]

The future will clearly depend in part on how such views and public pronouncements of the leaders of evangelicalism in Germany are received by evangelicals. A 'flood of letters' to Heimbucher following his rejection of the award suggested to him that there was widespread alienation from the political system of the Federal Republic. Pluralism is accepted, but only within limits. No doubt, Heimbucher notes in the interview with the *Frankfurter Rundschau*, there were also Christians who voted for non-Conservative parties, 'even for the Greens'. Much will depend on them too. The evangelical weekly *idea spektrum* will help shape opinion in the new millennium just as its forerunner *Evangelisches Allianzblatt* did in the 1930s.

Kurt Heimbucher did not live to see the Berlin Wall opening in November 1989. History once again cast long shadows over the unrest in East Germany and an influential evangelical journalist, Helmut Matthies, called on the churches to speak out. They had made 'remarkable' speeches on the Nazi dictatorship that had come to an end fifty years ago, he said, but seemed tongue-tied in the face of 'the unbelievable injustice of today, just 150 kilometres to the east'.[36]

His comments found an echo among readers who felt German Protestantism had become politically biased, with more faith in Marxism than Christianity.[37] Dr Siegfried Schauer (Fulda) also drew a parallel with 1933: 'Just as in 1933 the official Church is silent. It takes your breath away!'[38] Others reminded Matthies that everything that needed to be said about East Germany had already been said at the Eisenach Synod of the East German Protestant Church Federation in September 1989. Dr Joachim Schmidt, a member of the High Consistory in Hesse and Nassau wondered whether Matthies just wanted to hear 'a stirring appeal' for reunification. The commentary 'shows that Mr Matthies wanted to remind the churches of their duties to the nation, or rather what he feels to be their duties'. He asks: 'Didn't we go through all this before in 1914 and then in 1933?' An evangelical news agency 'should be too good for the catchy phrases of crackerbarrel politics'.[39]

Heimbucher would have enjoyed the headlines in *idea spektrum*: 'The miracle in Germany is a miracle worked by God: Great and Almighty God, We praise You', 'It's Time to Thank God in East and West', 'The Prayers of Many Were Not in Vain', 'We all thank God', 'Prayers have been answered' (16.11.1989). Shortly before the currency union on 1 July 1990 the headlines read: 'We are Looking Forward to July 1st: God has Done Great Things', 'God brought about the Change in East Germany: Prayer for the Economic and Currency Union', 'The Churches and the People', 'The Evangelical Alliance in East Germany: Economic Recovery is Just Around the Corner' (28.06.1990). Not for the first time in its history, the Alliance was swept away by the swell of patriotic feeling in Germany, interpreting political events as gracious acts of God. The 'divine' idea of a currency union, however, contributed to the economic downturn in East Germany from which the whole country including the churches are still suffering.

The years following reunification have been a time of regrouping for evangelicals. The Alliance organisations in the two Germanies amalgamated. Superintendent Jürgen Stabe from Annaberg-Buchholz in East Germany and Pastor Dr Fritz Laubach from West Germany became joint chairmen of the new organisation. Hartmut Steeb (Stuttgart) remained General Secretary of the organisation. The Executive Committee of the Alliance had thirty-eight members in 1994. In 1993 the Deputy General Secretary of the Evangelical Alliance, Pastor Manfred Kern, an East German, expressed criticism of the media for singling out pastors for their contacts with the East German security services prior to 1989. He reminded Germans that the Free Churches and Gnadau Fellowship groups had been among those relatively few ecclesiastical groups who had thanked God for bringing about German unification. While playing down past treachery and stressing the loyalty of East German Christians to the new political elites, Kern noted the serious problems facing the Alliance in the new Germany. In the east of the country there was a dearth of religion teachers. Re-trained civics teachers were still clinging to their 'old athestic convictions' while the churches were preoccupied with bureaucratic matters. Evangelism was being neglected as a result, he said. The Evangelical Alliance sought in this situation to provide guidance and direction for those disoriented by the collapse of Communist ideology and the Soviet Union. For example, it made and cemented contacts with similar groups in Moscow, Omsk and Karandar.[40]

The annual conference of the Evangelical Alliance in Bad Blankenburg has gone through a few changes too. The numbers of West Germans attending doubled between 1990 and 1993 but they remained a small minority of not more than ten per cent of the total number of guests. In 1993 the number of visitors was still a very significant 3,500. There is a general feeling among the East Germans that the depth of fellowship is no longer what it was prior to 1989. The food had once been cooked by volunteers; now it was prepared by a catering company. The queues for meals had disappeared, but there were also fewer conversations which those queues had occasioned. The conference was nevertheless still fulfilling its function as a 'spiritual maternity ward', to quote the retired secretary of the Gnadau Association in the German Democratic Republic, Johannes Dressler (Woltersdorf).[41]

The issues concerning evangelicals have remained much the same. The psychotherapist Reinhold Ruthe led a seminar on the dangers of occultism at the Blankenburg Conference in 1993. There had been an explosion of interest in the esoteric during the past decade, he noted, which had produced all kinds of neuroses and psychotic illnesses. 56% of Germans dabbled in astrology and 28% read their daily horoscope, he told the audience.[42] Other Christians wrote of their concern that Germany was disappearing in a multicultural, multi-ethnic unitary state subject to the authorities in Brussels. Such a Europe was the anti-Christian confederation prophesied in the Bible for the end-times, said one concerned reader.[43] The General Secretary expressed in 1993 his dismay at the 'limitless pluralism' prevailing in the provincial churches, particularly the fact that millions of marks were being spent every year by these churches on events and projects which had no basis in the creeds of those churches. The *Kirchentage* and feminist study centres were singled out for his opprobium. Pastor Fritz Laubach, one of the Alliance's chairmen, interpreted the 1992 abortion law passed by the Bundestag as a 'rejection of the Christian view of the person', a reflection of a widespread 'atheistic materialism' among the population. Profit was the all-consuming goal of modern Germans. There was widespread dissatisfaction and ungratefulness which hung 'like a judgement of God' over the German nation. 'Is this because Germany has become more atheistic as a result of reunification?', he wondered.[44] Germany had indeed become more 'Protestant' and *ipso facto* more 'atheistic' after 1990. The figures are telling. Whereas 67% of West Germans in 1996 had some kind of religious faith, the corresponding figure for East Germans was only 31%. 76.9% of the population of Saxony-Anhalt, with 2.9 million inhabitants, had no connection with either of the two main denominations in 1996. In Mecklenburg the figure was 75.6%, in Berlin 57.8%, in Brandenburg 71.3%, in Saxony 69.7% and in Thuringia 59.5%. In contrast, 93% of the population of Bavaria were members of those denominations. On top of this, the numbers leaving the *Evangelische Kirche* and *Katholische Kirche* in Germany have been increasing continually since 1963 and reunification has not slowed this process down. In 1993 285,000 Protestants and 153,753 Catholics left their respective churches; in 1994 the figures were 290,000 and 155,797 respectively.[45] The de-Christianisation of German society, though still veiled by the official numbers of church members, presents evangelicalism with new worries and challenges.

Secularism and humanism at home, and Islam abroad, have replaced social democracy and Soviet Communism as the evangelical bogeymen. The church-sanctioned marriage of gay and lesbian couples as well as the blessing and ordination of practising homosexuals are issues likely to unsettle and perhaps split Protestant churches in the future. Wolfram Kopfermann's spectacular separation from the *Volkskirche* in September 1988 – and the subsequent founding of the Freie Evangelisch-lutherische Anskar-Kirche in Hamburg – suggested that charismatic believers (Kopfermann was head of the inner-church renewal movement, the so-called *Geistliche Gemeinde-Erneuerung*, between 1978 and 1988) would find it very difficult in the long run to tolerate the extreme pluralism within German Protestantism.[46] Generally, however, most pietists still reject the idea of setting up a new, truly evangelical *Evangelische Kirche*. The trend in the late 1990s is to encourage the founding of independent evangelical fellowships within the prevailing congregations. Burghard Affeld (Osnabrück), chairman of the *Konferenz Bekennender Gemeinschaften*, sees the future in such loose groupings being open to disaffected evangelical Catholics as well as those Christians who had for conscience's sake left the *Evangelische Kirche* but had not found a spiritual home in a Free Church. One such grouping is the Alternativgemeinde 'Friedenshof' which has experienced a 140 per cent growth in members between 1991 and 1996.[47]

More worrying for mainstream churchman was the founding on 31 October 1996 (Reformation Day in Germany) of the first *Bekennende Evangelische Gemeinde* in Neuwied. This was not a new independent church, nor a church separated from the *Evangelische Kirche*. The new body saw itself as the 'rightful heir' of the Reformational inheritance and of the 'ecclesiastical resistance during the National Socialist and Communist dictatorships in Germany'. Heinz Jürgen Fischbach (Montabaur), chairman of the *Evangelischer Aufbruch Mittelrhein* which initiated the project and one of the seven elders of the church, expressed his hope that the fellowship would become the nucleus of 'the second Reformation' in Germany. Ecumenical links were activated and deputations from the American Presbyterian Church and the Independent Reformed Church of the Netherlands were sent to attend the founding conference. A local aristocrat, the mother of the Prince of Wied, became patron of the church.

Two dozen evengelicals had responded to what they saw as dangerous and unscriptural trends in the church of the Rhineland. In 1993 the Kreissynode of the district of Wied voted to adopt a policy of granting homosexual couples the Church's blessing. Evangelicals believed that 'sexual perversion' was being further countenanced by a document produced in 1996 (Sexuality and Lifestyles) by the ordained clergymen of the province. Such clerical toleration of perversion, the critics said, 'did not even take place at the time of the Nazi dictatorship'. The Bible was being 'dragged into the dirt in a most diabolical manner'. Moreover, pastors who criticised or rejected such new practices were being disciplined, suspended and sent into early retirement. Over fifty cases of such discrimination (the critics talk of outright 'persecution of Christians') have been documented. Secondly, apostasy from the truth as expressed in the Word of God was seen in the public denials of Christ's physical resurrection by the Göttingen theologian Professor Lüdemann. It seemed intolerable that such teaching was not stopped at once. Thirdly, the elders had become convinced that socialists and communists had successfully infiltrated the Rhenish Church and 'seized the key positions' in the edifice. Michael Inacker, writing in the *Welt am Sonntag* on 3 November 1996, agreed that this 'social democratisation of many church councils' as exhibited in the Rhineland was tantamount to apostasy from God's truth. The political bent of many church statements was clearly not to the liking of the dissidents. Equally, mainstream clerics were appalled at the intolerance of the self-styled resistance fighters. In the *Rhein-Zeitung* of 11 November 1996 Pastor Wilfried Neusel speculated on the links between the Neuwied group and fascists. It was 'unforgiveable', said Pastor Martin Seidler, that they had equated their position with that of Dietrich Bonhoeffer. Yet that was precisely what the *Kirchenkampf* had taught them: no tolerance should be shown to those who had left the credal and biblical basis of the *Evangelische Kirche*. The Rhenish Church had, in evangelical eyes, become nor merely influenced by the sociopolitical *zeitgeist* of the 1960s and 1970s; it had, in Professor Thomas Schirrmacher's opinion, actually become an embodiment of that rebellious *zeitgeist*. It had ceased to be a Christian church. 'We are declaring a state of emergency', said Fischbach in the *Wetzlaer Neue Zeitung* on 2 November 1996. Nobody should later have any opportunity or justification, he said, for reproaching Protestant Christians a second time in the twentieth century with having been silent or failing to raise a protest. In the spring of 1997 pietists like Bernhard Kaiser, a lecturer at the Freie Theologische Akademie in Giessen who wished to reform the church rather than leave it, began to discuss the need for a *Notsynode* and a *Notkirchenleitungsamt* to avert the ideological dangers threatening the very existence of German Protestantism. The opportunity provided in 1966 to re-form the *Evangelische Kirche* before evangelicals leave *en masse* should not be allowed to pass by a second time.[48]

Active church members are already a tiny minority in Germany; evangelicals are probably a majority of that minority. One of the prime goals of the Evangelical Alliance is to reverse that trend by gathering evangelicals from all traditions for the purposes of prayer, Bible study, evangelism, nursing and educational projects, on the basis of the theological legacy of the

Reformation, pietism and revivalism. On 10 March 1990 Billy Graham spoke in the pouring rain to 15,000 people assembled in Berlin. One fruit of this evangelistic meeting was the setting up of an organisational network called Pro Christ '93, which, in March 1993, started a series of campaigns to turn each believer into an evangelist.[49] That campaign was still continuing in the late 1990s.

Nearly fifty years of experience within what is essentially an Anglo-American form of democracy have not obliterated the memory of the Third Reich from the evangelical consciousness. The concerns evoked by the secularisation of society and its growing non-Christian minority have no doubt helped to focus minds on the *raison d'etre* of the Evangelical Alliance and the wider movement of which it is itself an expression. There are symptoms of unease and disaffection in that movement, but generally it is forward-looking rather than backward-looking. Mainstream evangelicalism is unlikely to take on a reactionary character. Most noticeably, it has become strongly philo-Semitic and a major supporter of the state of Israel. Politically, if not religiously, most evangelicals have moved far from the positions of their forefathers. Admittedly, evangelical groups such as the *Evangelische Notgemeinschaft in Deutschland* continue to express extreme anti-socialist and anti-libertarian views and its press organ *Erneuerung und Abwehr* reaches thousands of Christians. Its call for the *Evangelische Kirche* to repent of its accomodation to the East German dictatorship and its toleration of socialists in its midst has to date fallen on deaf ears. In the view of the *Notgemeinschaft* – its name reminds one of Niemöller's *Pfarrernotbund* – only a confession of guilt can stop the spiritual rot at the heart of the Church.[50] The political sympathies of this group, once ubiquitous, are now certainly not representative of the evangelical community. Evangelicals have changed their political spots. This has not been due, however, to any thoughtful analysis of their own past. The portrayal and analysis of National Socialism in the *Evangelisches Allianzblatt*, as in other evangelical weeklies, are still largely unknown in Germany. It is hoped that this study has shed some light on that inglorious past and will help to keep the memory of the Third Reich alive.

Notes

1. 100 Jahre Evangelische Allianz (Nuremberg 1946); Erich Beyreuther (1969, 113-114). It deserves mentioning again that the only German who rescued more than 1,000 Jews from

concentration camps was not an evangelical, but a *bon viveur*, a drinker, a womaniser and a spiv, Oskar Schindler.
2. E. Beyreuther (1969, 97-98, 107); Friedrich Heitmüller (1950, 128-130).
3. Ralph Giordano (1987).
4. R. Wielandt, Bericht über die Hundertjahrfeier der Evangelischen Allianz in Berlin vom 31.08.-3.9.1946 in der Statdtmissionskirche am Gardepionierplatz (n.d, n.p.); Die Schuld der Anderen. Ein Briefwechsel zwischen Helmut Thielicke und Hermann Diem (Göttingen 1948). Helmut Thielicke's interpretations of the holocaust and National Socialism were discussed in *Christianity Today*, 27 January 1978, 8-17.
5. *konkret*, Nr.3/1985.
6. *Salz der Erde. Ökumenische Zeitung für Nordelbien*, Nr.2/1987; Reinhard Frieling (1984); Was Evangelikale glauben, *idea Dokumentation*, Nr.1/1989.
7. Hans Prolingheuer's article on 'The Stuttgart Confession of Guilt' in *Junge Kirche*, Nr.10/1985, 531ff, criticises Künneth's post-war attempts to explain his writings as 'support for the Jewish people' (footnote 41). The *Allgemeine Jüdische Wochenzeitung* (Nr.XXXIV/38), a Jewish weekly, criticised Künneth's memoirs as an attempt to whitewash his own past and claimed this final book was tantamount to 'walking past those who had fallen into the hands of murderers, like the priest and Levite in Jesus' parable, for a second time'. H.-J. Barkenings, the reviewer, questioned whether Künneth was, as the title of his memoirs suggested, 'committed to the truth'.
8. Hans Prolingheuer (1985).
9. *Salz der Erde*, op.cit., 5-7; *Evangelische Kommentare*, 1968, 368-374.
10. Georg Huntemann (1985).
11. H. Albertz/ H. Böll/ H. Gollwitzer (1975, 94-119).
12. *Salz der Erde*, op.cit., pp.14-15; Fundamentalismus in der Protestantischen Kirche, in:*Die neue Gesellschaft/Frankfurter Hefte*, March/1989, 210-214.
13. Materialdienst der Evangelischen Zentralstelle für Weltanschauungsfragen, Nr.8, 01.08.1988; *Frankfurter Rundschau*, 05.08.1988. An evangelical reply to this criticism is in *idea spektrum*, Nr.32/1988.
14. *Evangelische Kommentare*, 1968, 369.
15. *idea spektrum*, Nr.5/1987.
16. The other being the Bavarian Christian Social Union of which W. Künneth was a founder member, H. Albertz/ H. Böll/ H. Gollwitzer (1975, 113).
17. Evangelicals and the CDU – the 'German Christians' of Today? *idea spektrum*, Nr.10/1984 and readers letters in Nr.13/1984. Pastor Klaus Overath, in a letter to *idea spektrum*, said the influential evangelical weekly served not only Jesus, but 'again and again the CDU as well'. *idea spektrum* Nr.7/1983.
18. Its circulation was 20,000 per week in 1990, *idea spektrum*, Nr.7/1990. The word *idea*

stands for *informations dienst der evangelischen allianz* – Information Service of the Evangelical Alliance.
19. Grundsätzlich positiv, *Punkt* , Nr.11/1989.
20. *Punkt*, Nr 11/1989.
21. Christ und Republikaner – geht das?, *Punkt*, Nr.7-8/1989, 16-19.
22. Lebens- und LustfeindInnen, *Neues Deutschland*, 27.12.1991.
23. Die Evangelikale Wende-Religion, *Salz der Erde*, op.cit., 12-13.
24. *idea spektrum*, Nr.3/1983.
25. *idea spektrum*, Nr.37/1987; *idea spektrum*, Nr.22/1988.
26. *idea spektrum*, Nr.37/1987.
27. The programme of the Christliche Liga deals with the right to life of the unborn in the very first section, the PBC in the second section of its programme – after dealing first with 'Israel in God's Plan' and the 'Battle against Anti-Semitism'. Grundsatzprogramm der Christlichen Liga. Die Partei für das Leben (Schwäbisch Gmünd 07.01.1989); Die Neue Kraft in Deutschland! Grundsatzprogramm der Partei Bibeltreuer Christen (Karlsruhe 22.11.1989).
28. *Kurier der Christlichen Mitte* (n.d., n.p.). This leaflet is sent to enquirers. These policy goals can be found in the monthly paper of the same name produced by the party.
29. Ibid.
30. Grundsatzprogramm (07.01.89), 24.
31. *Salz und Licht.*, Informationen der Partei Bibeltreuer Christen, Nr.1/1991, 2.
32. *idea spektrum*, Nr.31/1989.
33. Jürgen Wüst, Renaissance des Christlichen in der Politik? Kleine christliche Parteien in Deutschland, in: Materialdienst der Evangelische Zentralstelle für Weltanschauungsfragen, Nr 8/1994, 232-240; *idea spektrum* Nr 10/1997, 10.
34. Evangelikale Staatskritik, *Evangelische Kommentare*, Nr.3/1988; *CODE*, August/1988; Kurt Heimbucher (1989, 191-4). Heimbucher headed the Gnadau organisation for 17 years and joined the Executive Committee of the Evangelical Alliance in 1967. Heimbucher had made news in 1984 for criticising the World Council of Churches, *idea spektrum*, Nr.6/1984. Heimbucher died just a few months after this award affair, at the age of 59, *Frankfurter Rundschau*, 27.07.1988. In an article which appeared 5 years after his death he was called 'one of the great evangelical personalities of the post-war period'. He saw Gnadau as the 'spiritual opposition' within the Protestant Church. *idea spektrum*, Nr.32/1993.
35. *Frankfurter Rundschau*, 10.02.1988; Kurt Heimbucher (1989, 180-7).
36. *idea spektrum*, Nr.41/1989.
37. Helmut Matthies/Jens Motschmann (1976).
38. *idea spektrum*, Nr.46/1989, 36.

39. *idea spektrum*, Nr.42/1989.
40. *idea spektrum*, Nr 19/1993.
41. *idea spektrum*, Nr 32/1993, 5-7.
42. *idea spektrum*, Nr 39/1993, 5.
43. *idea spektrum*, Nr 24/1993.
44. Evangelische Allianz intern, Nr 1/1993.
45. FOCUS, Nr 15, 6 April 1996; *Süddeutsche Zeitung*, 26 March 1996.
46. W. Kopfermann (1990).
47. idea Dokumentaion, 4/1997.
48. idea Dokumentation, 21/1996.
49. Evangelische Allianz intern, Nr 1/1993.
50. *idea spektrum*, Nr 19/1993.

List of Works Cited

Albertz, Heinrich/Böll, Heinrich/ Gollwitzer, Helmut, Pfarrer, die dem Terror dienen? (Hamburg: Rowohlt 1975)

Balders, Günter, Ein Herr, ein Glaube, eine Taufe. 150 Jahre Baptistengemeinden in Deutschland 1834-1884 (Wuppertal-Kassel 1984).

Baumgärtel, Friedrich, Wider die Kirchenkampf-Legenden (Neuendettelsau: Freimund 1976)

Bergschicker, H., Deutsche Chronik 1933-1945 (Berlin 1982)

Bethge, Eberhard, Dietrich Bonhoeffer (London: Collins 1985)

Beyreuther, Erich, Kirche in Bewegung. Geschichte der Evangelisation und Volksmission (Berlin: Christlicher Zeitschriftenverlag 1968)

Beyreuther, Erich, Der Weg der Evangelischen Allianz in Deutschland (Wuppertal: R.Brockhaus 1969)

Bonhoeffer, Dietrich, The Way to Freedom (Glasgow: Collins 1977)

Bonhoeffer, Dietrich, Letters and Papers From Prison (London: Camelot 1953)

Bracher, Karl-Dietrich, The German Dictatorship. The Origins, Structure and Consequences of National Socialism (Bungay: Penguin 1973)

Bracher, Karl-Dietrich/ Funke, M./ Jacobsen, H.-A., Deutschland 1933-1945. Neue Studien zur nationalsozialistischen Herrschaft (Studien zur Geschichte und Politik Band 314, Bonn: Bundeszentrale für Politische Bildung 1993)

Bullock, Alan, Adolf Hitler. A Study in Tyranny (London: Book Club Associates 1973)

Catherwood, Frederick, A Better Way. The Case For A Christian Social Order (Leicester: Intervarsity Press 1976)

Conway, John S., The Nazi Persecution of the Churches 1933-1945 (London 1968)

Czichon, Eberhard, Wer verhalf Hitler zur Macht? (Cologne: Pahl-Rugenstein 1989)

Dahm, K.-W., Pfarrer und Politik. Soziale Position und politische Mentalität des deutschen Pfarrerstandes zwischen 1918 und 1933 (Cologne: Dortmunder Schriften zur Sozialforschung 1965)

Densky, Bernd Reiner, Die Zeit des Dritten Reiches in der baptistischen Wochenzeitschrift Der Wahrheitszeuge von 1933-1945 (Magisterarbeit, Universität Marburg, 1983).

Denzler, Georg/Fabricius, Volker, Die Kirchen im Dritten Reich, Volumes 1 and 2 (Frankfurt a.M.: Fischer 1988)

Deschner, Karlheinz, Kirche und Faschismus (Rastatt: Moewig 1990)

Deschner, Karlheinz, Das Kreuz mit dem Christentum. Eine Sexualgeschichte des Christentums (Munich: W. Heyne 1989)

Dibelius, Otto, In The Service of The Lord (New York: Holt, Rinehart & Winston 1964)

Duncan-Jones, A.S., The Crooked Cross (London: Macmillan 1940)

Ebenstein, W., The German Record. A Political Portrait (New York: Farrar/Rinehart 1945)

Engelmann, Bernt, Vorwärts und nicht vergessen. Vom verfolgten Geheimbund zur Kanzlerpartei (Munich: Bertelsmann 1988)
Etymologisches Wörterbuch (Berlin: Akademie Verlag 1989)
Fischer, Gerhard, Antifaschistisches Erbe – Mythos oder Auftrag? Lehren aus dem Widerstand von Christen in Deutschland (Berlin: Union Verlag 1986)
Frieling, Reinhard (ed), Die Kirchen und ihre Konservativen. 'Traditionalismus' und 'Evangelikalismus' in den Konfessionen (Göttingen: Vandenhoeck und Ruprecht 1984)
Geldbach, Erich, Evangelikalismus. Versuch einer historischen Typologie, in: Frieling, Reinhard (ed), Die Kirchen und ihre Konservativen.
Gerlach, Wolfgang, Als die Zeugen schwiegen. Bekennende Kirche und die Juden (Berlin: Institut Kirche und Judentum 1987)
Gerlach, Wolfgang, Zwischen Kreuz und Davidstern. Bekennende Kirche in ihrer Stellung zum Judentum im Dritten Reich (PhD Dissertation, Universität Hamburg 1972)
Giordano, Ralph, Die zweite Schuld, oder von der Last, Deutscher zu sein (Hamburg: Rasch und Röhring 1987)
Glaser, Hermann, Spiesser-Ideologie (Frankfurt am Main: Fischer 1986)
Gnadauer Gemeinschaftswerk (ed), Du, Herr, hast uns gerufen. 100 Jahre Gnadauer Gemeinschaftswerk (Berlin: Evangelische Verlagsanstalt 1988)
Golding, Louis, The Jewish Problem (Harmondsworth: Penguin 1938)
Gutachten des Instituts für Zeitgeschichte (Munich 1958)
Hampel, J., Der Nationalsozialismus, Band 1 (Munich: Bayerische Landeszentrale für Politische Bildung 1985), Der Nationalsozialismus, Band 2 (Munich: Bayerische Landeszentrale für Politische Bildung 1989)
Harrison, Archibald, The Evangelical Revival and Christian Reunion (London: Epworth 1942)
Hastings, J., Articles on 'Evangelical Alliance' and 'Evangelicalism' in: Encyclopaedia of Religion and Ethics (Edinburgh: T. & T. Clark 1912)
Heimbucher, Kurt, gez. Kurt Heimbucher. Notizen aus meinem Leben (Wuppertal and Zurich: R. Brockhaus 1989)
Heitmüller, Friedrich, Aus vierzig Jahren Dienst am Evangelium (Witten: 1950)
Heitmüller, Friedrich, Sieben Reden eines Christen und Nationalsozialisten (Hamburg: Fr. Heitmüller 1934)
Helmreich, Ernst C., The German Churches under Hitler. Background, Struggle, and Epilogue (Detroit 1979)
Helmreich, Ernst C., The Nature and Structure of the Confessing Church in Germany under Hitler, in: *Journal of Church and State*, 12, 1970.
Hickel, Helmut, Sammlung und Sendung. Die Brüdergemeine gestern und heute (Berlin: Evangelische Verlagsanstalt 1967)

Hirsch, Rudolf/Schuder, Rosemarie, Der Gelbe Fleck. Wurzeln und Wirkungen des Judenhasses in der deutschen Geschichte (Berlin: Rütten & Loening 1987)
Hitler, Adolf, Mein Kampf (English Translation by James Murphy 1939)
Hollenweger, Walter J., The Pentecostals (London: SCM 1972)
Holtorf, Jürgen, Die verschwiegene Bruderschaft (Munich: W. Heyne 1986)
Huntemenn, Georg, Ideologische Unterwanderung in Gemeinde, Theologie und Bekenntnis (Bad Liebenzell: Verlag der Liebenzeller Mission 1985)
Hütt, Wolfgang, Hintergrund (Berlin: Henschelverlag 1990)
Jordy, Gerhard, Die Brüderbewegung in Deutschland, Vol. 3 (Wuppertal: R. Brockhaus 1986)
Jung, Friedhelm, Die deutsche Evangelikale Bewegung – Grundlinien ihrer Geschichte und Theologie (Frankfurt a.M./Bern: Peter Lang 1992)
Junghans, Helmar (ed), Leben und Werk Martin Luthers von 1526 bis 1546 (Berlin: Evangelische Verlagsanstalt 1985)
Kaiser, Jochen-Christoph/ Greschat, Martin, Der Holocaust und die Protestanten. Analysen einer Verstrickung (Frankfurt a.M.: Athenäum 1988)
Kahl, Joachim, Das Elend des Christentums oder Plädoyer für eine Humanität ohne Gott (Hamburg: Rowohlt 1968)
Kater, Michael H., Die Ernsten Bibelforscher im Dritten Reich, in: *Vierteljahreshefte für Zeitgeschichte*, Jahrgang 17, 1969, Heft 2, April, 181-218
Klemperer, Viktor, LTI (Leipzig: Reclam 1982)
Klinksiek, Dorothee, Die Frau im NS-Staat (Stuttgart 1982)
Kogon, Eugen, Der SS-Staat. Das System der deutschen Konzentrationslager (Munich: W. Heyne 1979)
Kopfermann, Wolfram, Abschied von einer Illusion. Volkskirche ohne Zukunft (Hamburg and Mainz: C.& P. Verlag 1990)
Kreck, Walter, Friedliche Koexistenz statt Konfrontation (Cologne: Pahl-Rugenstein 1988)
Lambert, Lance, Battle for Israel (Eastbourne: Kingsway 1988)
Lange, Dieter, Aufbruch und Weg der Bewegung (1888-1933), in: Gnadauer Gemeinschaftswerk (ed), Du, Herr, hast uns gerufen (1988, 9-20).
Laski, Harold J., Where Do We Go From Here? (Harmondsworth: Penguin 1941)
Lüdecke, K., I Knew Hitler (London: Jarrolds 1938)
Marquardt, Manfred, Strukturen Evangelikal-Fundamentalistischer und Traditionalistischer Theorie und Frömmigkeit, in: Frieling, Reinhard (ed), Die Kirchen und ihre Konservativen
Marsden, George M., Fundamentalism and American Culture. The Shaping of Twentieth-Century Evangelicalism 1870-1925 (Oxford-New York: Oxford University Press 1982)
Massie, J.W., The Evangelical Alliance, its Origin and Development (London: Snow 1847)

Matheson, Peter (Ed.), The Third Reich and the Christian Churches (Edinburgh: T. & T. Clark 1981)
Matthies, Helmut/Motschmann, Jens, Rotbuch Kirche (Stuttgart: Seewald 1976)
Meiners, Peter, Zwischen Anpassung und Widerstand. Der CVJM-Westbund im Dritten Reich (Asslar: Schulte & Gerth 1985)
Menk, Friedhelm, Die Brüderbewegung im Dritten Reich (Bielefeld: Christliche Literatur-Verbreitung 1986)
Nagel, Gustav F., Das biblische Urteil über die sozial-revolutionären Bewegungen der Gegenwart (Giessen:Brunnen 1920)
Nagel, Gustav F., Karl Barth und der heilsgewisse Glaube (Neukirchen: Missions-buchhandlung Stursberg 1929)
Nagel, Gustav F., Der Staatsgedanke, biblisch und geschichtlich beleuchtet (Neumünster: Ihloff 1934)
Nagel, Gustav F., Deutschland vor der Christusfrage (Neumünster: Ihloff 1935)
Nitsch, Wilhelm, 75 Jahre Westdeutsche Evangelische Allianz 1880-1955 (Witten 1955)
van Norden, Günther, Der Deutsche Protestantismus im Jahr der national-sozialistischen Machtergreifung (Gütersloh 1979)
Nowak, Kurt, Evangelische Kirche und Weimarer Republik (Weimar: H. Böhlau 1988)
Nowak, Kurt, Geschichte des Christentums in Deutschland. Religion, Politik und Gesellschaft vom Ende der Aufklärung bis zur Mitte des 20. Jahrhunderts (Munich: 1995)
Oberman, Heiko A., Luthers Beziehungen zu den Juden: Ahnen und Geahndete, in: Junghans, Helmar (ed), Leben und Werk Martin Luthers von 1526 bis 1546, Festgabe zu seinem 500. Geburtstag, Band 1
Oehme, W., Märtyrer der evangelischen Christenheit 1933-1945 (Berlin: Evangelische Verlagsanstalt 1980)
Opitz Günter, Der Christlich-Sozialer Volksdienst (Düsseldorf 1969)
Orwell, George, 1984 (Bungay: Penguin 1991)
The Persecution of the Catholic Church in the Third Reich (London: Burns, Oates & Washbourne 1942)
Peters, Bernhard, Im Umbruch der Zeit. Ein Blick in die Völkerwelt (Karlsruhe: Bäuerle 1934)
Peters, Bernhard, Deutschlandwende! Europawende! Weltwende! Durchblick durch die Völkerwelt der Gegenwart (Worms: Missionsbuchhandlung 1933)
Peters, Bernhard, Arier und Jude. Ein Beitrag zur Judenfrage und ihrer Lösung (Worms: Missionsbuchhandlung 1934)
Pförtner, Hans, Das deutsche Volk als Retter und Ritter des Kreuzes (Flugschrift der Christlichen Wehrkraft, Nr 10, Munich 1934)

Pierard, Richard V., Protestant Support for the Political Right in Weimar Germany and Post-Watergate America: Some Comparative Observations, in: *Journal of Church and State*, Vol. 34 (1982), 239-262

Pinson, Koppel S., Pietism as a Factor in The Rise of German Nationalism (New York: Studies in History, Economics and Public Law, Columbia University, 193)

Prolingheuer, Hans, The Stuttgart Confession of Guilt, *Junge Kirche*, Nr 10, 1985, 531ff.

Rauschning, Hermann, Make and Break With the Nazis. Letters on a Conservative Revolution (London: Secker and Warburg 1941)

Reich, Wilhelm, The Mass Psychology of Fascism (Bungay: Penguin 1978)

Reichelt, Werner, Das Braune Evangelium. Hitler und die NS-Liturgie (Wuppertal: Peter Hammer 1990)

Rennstich, K., Der Deutsche Glaube. Jakob Wilhelm Hauer (1881-1962): Ein Ideologe des Nationalsozialismus (Information Nr 121, XII, 1992, EZW-Texte, Evangelische Zentralstelle für Weltanschauungsfragen Stuttgart)

Rouse, Ruth/Neill, Stephen C. (eds), A History of the Ecumenical Movement 1517-1948 (London: SPCK 1967)

Ruhbach, Gerhard, Der Weg der Gemeinschaftsbewegung im Dritten Reich (1933-1945), in: Heimbucher, Kurt, Dem Auftrag verpflichtet. Die Gnadauer Gemeinschaftsbewegung (Giessen 1988)

Rüppel, Erich G., Die Gemeinschaftsbewegung im Dritten Reich (Göttingen: Vandenhoeck und Ruprecht 1969)

Rüther, Günther, Geschichte der christlich-demokratischen und christlich-sozialen Bewegungen in Deutschland (Bonn: Zentrale für Politische Bildung 1987)

Sauberzweig, Hans von, Er der Meister – wir die Brüder (Offenbach a.M. 1959)

Scharrer, M., Kampflose Kapitulation. Arbeiterbewegung 1933 (Hamburg: Rowohlt 1984)

Schmidt, Paul, Unser Weg als Bund Evangelisch-Freikirchlicher Gemeinden in den Jahren 1941-1946 (Bericht an den Bundesrat vom 24.-26. Mai 1946 in Velbert)

Schreiber, Matthias, Martin Niemöller (Hamburg: Rowohlt 1997)

Spotts, Frederick, The Churches and Politics in Germany (Middletown, Conn.: Wesleyan University Press 1973)

Stammen, T., Die Weimarer Republik, Two Volumes (Munich: Bayerische Landeszentrale für Politische Bildung 1987)

Steinberg, S.H., A Short History of Germany (Cambridge: University Press 1944)

Stern, J.P., Hitler. The Führer and the People (Glasgow: Collins 1979)

Strahm, Herbert, Die bischöfliche Methodistenkirche im Dritten Reich (Stuttgart/Berlin: Münchener Kirchenhistorische Studien, Vol. 3, 1989)

Strübind, Andrea, Die unfreie Freikirche. Der Bund der Baptistengemeinden im Dritten Reich (Wuppertal-Zürich: R. Brockhaus 1995)

Stupperich, Robert, Otto Dibelius. Ein Evangelischer Bischof im Umbruch der Zeiten (Göttingen: Vandenhoeck und Ruprecht 1989)

Tatford, Frederick A., Prophecy's Last Word. An Exposition of the Revelation (London: Pickering and Inglis 1978)

Thomson, David, Europe Since Napoleon (Aylesbury: Penguin 1968)

Vansittart, Robert, Black Record. Germans Past and Present (London: Hamilton 1941)

Vollnhals, Clemens, Evangelische Kirche und Entnazifizierung 1945-1949 (Munich 1989)

Ward, W.R., The Protestant Evangelical Awakening (Cambridge: University Press 1992)

Weber, Timothy P., Living in the Shadow of The Second Coming. American Pre-Millennialism, 1875-1982 (Chicago 1987)

Wendelborn, Gert, Gottes Wort und die Gesellschaft. Zum Verhältnis von Frömmigkeit und sozialer Verantwortung bei den Evangelikalen (Berlin: Union Verlag 1979)

Winkler, H.-J., Legenden um Hitler (Berlin: Landeszentrale für Politische Bildung 1961)

Wolffe, John, The Evangelical Alliance in the 1840s: An Attempt to Institutionalise Christian Unity, in: Sheils, W.J., Wood, Diana (eds), Voluntary Religion (Oxford: Blackwell 1986)

Wulff, W., Zodiac and Swastica. Astrologer to Himmler's Court (London: Barker 1968)

Wyman, David, Das unerwünschte Volk. Amerika und die Vernichtung der europäischen Juden (Munich: M. Hueber 1986)

Zehrer, Karl, Evangelische Freikirchen und das 'Dritte Reich' (Berlin: Evangelische Verlagsanstalt 1986)

Zilliacus, K., Can The Tories Win The Peace? And How They Lost The Last One (London: Victor Gollancz 1945)

Index of Names

Affeld, Burghard 251
Arnold, Gottfried 13

Barth, Christian 15
Barth, Karl 30, 81f, 86, 226f, 230, 241
Bell, George 34
Bengel, J.A. 8
Bergmann, Gerhard 241
Bernstorff, Andreas von 17
Bismarck, Otto von 19, 38, 40, 42, 44, 46, 62, 200
Bodelschwingh, Friedrich von 93, 98f, 221
Bodenstein, Professor 242
Bonhoeffer, Dietrich 7, 79, 82, 95, 124, 184
Bonnet, Jean 15
Bonus, Arthur 87
Bräunlich, Ernst 33
Brockhaus, Ernst 73, 126
Brockhaus, Wilhelm 73
Bruns, Pastor 56
Burkhardt, Paul 67

Carlyle, Thomas 48, 63
Catherwood, Frederick 8
Chamberlain, Houston S. 41

Dibelius, Otto 90, 100, 179, 181
Dreibholz, Otto 17, 18, 35, 38
Dressler, Johannes 249
Duchrow, Ulrich 242

Eicken, E. von 17
Engler, Karl 178, 182

Fabri, Friedrich 16
Fischbach, Heinz Jürgen 251
Francke, August 8, 13
Frick, Wilhelm 146

Gauger, Joseph 18, 19, 21, 26
Globke, Hans-Maria 182
Göbel, Wilhelm 19, 22, 184f
Gooch, Martyn 222, 223, 232, 235
Graham, Billy 253
Gray, James 120
Großgebauer, Theophil 13
Grosz, George 122
Grünweller, August 57

Hammer, Herr 86
Harling, Otto von 171, 174
Hauer, Professor 93
Haugg, Werner 109
Heckel, Bishop 95
Heimbucher, Kurt 245f
Heitmüller, Friedrich 22, 36, 38, 85f, 90, 239
Hertz, Rabbi J.H. 228, 231
Hess, Rudolf 48, 91, 126
Hindenburg, President 59f, 99, 100, 101, 157
Hitler, Adolf 11, 22, 27, 37, 39, 45f, 47f, 56f, 60, 75, 83f, 94, 101f, 109, 119f, 129, 143f, 161, 191ff, 219
Höhl, Norbert 245
Hofacker, Ludwig 15
Hoffman, Conrad 231
Hoffmann, Wilhelm 15
Hossenfelder, Joachim 87, 88, 92
Hüfner, Pastor 207
Hugenberg, Alfred 22, 162

Jäger, August 99
Jakubski, Pastor 88, 89, 104f

Kaiser, Bernhard 252
Kaiser, Gustav 17
Kern, Manfred 249
Kerrl, Hanns 35, 105, 108, 110, 224, 225
Kießling, Johann 14
Kietzell, Fritz von 82

263

Kniewel, Theodor 15
Köberle, Adolf 95
König, Johann 15
Koch, Karl 78
Kopfermann, Wolfram 250
Kottwitz, Hand Ernst 14
Krause, Dr Reinhold 28, 92
Krawielitzki, Theophil 18, 36
Kröker 35, 124
Krummbacher, Gottfried 154
Krummacher, Gottfried Daniel 14
Kühn, Bernhard 17
Künneth, Walter 27, 91, 101, 241
Kuntze, Eduard 15, 16

Laubach, Fritz 250
Lehmann, Gottfried 16
Liebchen, Pastor 29
Löhe, Wilhelm 14
Lörzer, Provost 92
Lüdecke, Kurt 77
Lüdecke, Pastor 58, 173
Luther, Martin 13, 20, 42, 46, 84, 103, 184, 186

Matthies, Helmut 248
Melle, Otto 18, 22, 25, 31-37, 86f, 89, 109, 124, 134f, 179, 205, 211, 225
Mencken, Gottfried 15
Menge, Hermann 120
Mertensacker, Adelgunde 244
Meßner, H. 16
Meves, Christa 244
Michaelis, Walter 18, 25, 26-31, 95, 109, 123, 174
Möbius, Karl 18, 26,
Modersohn, Ernst 18, 29, 180
Monsky, Pastor 203
Motschmann, Markus 243
Müller, Friedrich 79
Müller, Karl 56
Müller, Bishop Ludwig 87, 89, 90, 91, 92, 94, 96, 97, 100, 103f, 134, 221, 226

Müller, Professor 84
Mussolini, Benito 63, 120, 145

Nagel, Gustav 17, 18, 25, 35, 37-49, 53f, 64, 88, 90, 121, 125, 145f, 163, 164, 207, 208, 235
Neufville, Carl de 17, 35
Neusel, Wilfried 252
Niemöller, Martin 29, 78, 79, 82, 95, 101, 124, 223, 224, 226f, 230, 253
Nuelsen, Bishop 32f, 134, 179

Ohnesorg, Otto 36
Oncken, Johann 15

Peters, Bernhard 19, 38, 53f, 59, 62, 93, 141, 142, 160, 172, 175, 193, 201
Pförtner, Hans 19, 22
Putz, Eduard 78

Raumer, Karl von 14
Rauschning, Hermann 77
Reich, Wilhelm 143
Reinthaler, Karl 15
Richter, Dr 126
Röhm, Ernst 29, 154, 157f
Rosenberg, Alfred 47f, 62, 89, 108, 141, 146, 241
Röttgen, Pastor 89
Rückert, August 204
Rust, Dr 99

Sasse, Martin 184
Saul, Dr 153
Schauer, Siegfried 248
Schirach, Baldur von 150
Schmidt, Albert 54
Schmidt, Joachim 248
Schmidt, Paul 22, 34, 185, 211
Schürmann, Karl 105
Siebel, Tillmann 14
Simoleit, F.W. 131
Smith, Culling Eardley 15

Sommer, Ernst 37
Spener, P.J. 13
Stabe, Jürgen 249
Stark, Professor J. 57, 93
Steinkopf, Karl 14
Stempfle, Bernhard 157
Stoecker, Adolf 21, 175, 177, 181
Strasser, Gregor 66
Streicher, Julius 154
Strathmann, Professor 55

Temple, William 230, 231, 232
Thadden, Adolf von 14
Thielicke, Helmut 240
Tholuck, August 15
Tolzien, Gerhard 130
Trillhaas, Dr 100

Urlsperger, Johann 14

Veidt, Pastor 56
Viebahn, Georg von 208
Vietheer, Heinrich 181

Wehrenpfennig, Erich 203
Weißgerber, Heinrich 14
Wichern, Johann 15f
Wöhrle, Wilhelm 208
Wurm, Theophil 80, 110

Zilz 35, 235
Zinzendorf, Nikolaus 9, 13f, 124

German Linguistic and Cultural Studies

Edited by Peter Rolf Lutzeier

At a time when German Studies faces a serious challenge to its identity and position in the European and international context, this new series aims to reflect the increasing importance of both culture (in the widest sense) and linguistics to the study of German in Britain and Ireland.
GLCS will publish monographs and collections of essays of a high scholarly standard which deal with German in its socio-cultural context, in multilingual and multicultural settings, in its European and international context and with its use in the media. The series will also explore the impact on German society of particular ideas, movements and economic trends and will discuss curriculum provision and development in universities in the United Kingdom and the Republic of Ireland. Contributions in English or German will be welcome.

Volume 1 Peter Rolf Lutzeier (ed.): German Studies: Old and New Challenges
Undergraduate Programmes in the United Kingdom
and the Republic of Ireland
249 pp. 1998. ISBN 3-906757-59-5 / US-ISBN 0-8204-3411-6

Volume 2 Nicholas Railton: German Evangelical Alliance and the Third Reich
An Analysis of the «Evangelisches Allianzblatt»
265 pp. 1998. ISBN 3-906757-67-6 / US-ISBN 0-8204-3412-4

Volume 3 Felicity Rash: The German Language in Switzerland
Multilingualism, Diglossia and Variation
321 pp. 1998. ISBN 3-906757-68-4 / US-ISBN 0-8204-3413-2